1001

Ways to
Introduce
Your Child
to God

1001

Ways to Introduce Your Child to God

Kathie Reimer

Illustrations by Ben Mahan

TYNDALE HOUSE PUBLISHERS, INC.
Wheaton, Illinois

Book development by March Media, Inc.
Book design by Harriette Bateman

Library of Congress Cataloging-in-Publication Data

Reimer, Kathie, date
  1001 ways to introduce your child to God / Kathie Reimer;
illustrations by Ben Mahan.
    p. cm.
  ISBN 0-8423-4757-7
  1. God—Study and teaching.   2. Christian education of children.
3. Christian education—Teaching methods.   I. Title.   II. Title:
One thousand one ways to introduce your child to God.   III. Title:
One thousand and one ways to introduce your child to God.
BT108.R45   1992
248.8′45—dc20   92-9730

Printed in Mexico

98 97 96 95 94 93
 8   7   6   5   4   3

To Lisa, *whose little song was the spark*

To Jim, *my strength*

To Mark, *my encourager*

To Mother, *my example*

and

To Jenifer, *a Gift of God to us all.*

Contents

Introduction

You and Your Child   *9*

    Basic Supply List   *14*

Part One: Introducing Your Child to Godly Attitudes

1. Introducing Your Child to Trust   *17*
2. Introducing Your Child to Self-confidence   *35*
3. Introducing Your Child to Happiness   *73*

Part Two: Introducing Your Child to Godly Relationships

4. Introducing Your Child to Kindness   *103*
5. Introducing Your Child to Obedience   *143*
6. Introducing Your Child to Honesty and Purity   *173*
7. Introducing Your Child to Witnessing   *203*

Part Three: Introducing Your Child to God Himself

8. Introducing Your Child to God through Creation   *225*
9. Introducing Your Child to God through the Church   *257*
10. Introducing Your Child to God through Prayer and Praise   *283*

Introduction

You and Your Child

Sons are a heritage from the Lord,
children a reward from him.
—Psalm 127:3

A child is born! The delivery room doctor, a hospital nurse, or a social worker in an adoption agency places a newborn infant in our relatively or totally inexperienced arms. What an awesome time of life! The vast majority of new parents sense the wonder and the magnitude of this emergence into parenthood.

Yet, beyond the awareness that something amazing has happened in the birth of a child is the sense of true worship often experienced by those who enjoy a personal relationship with the Creator God through his Son, Jesus Christ. Genuine worship is always an internal expression of the heart, whether in a cushioned pew amid a crowd of worshipers or in a wooden rocker with a tiny baby in one's arms.

We observe our delicate little baby as he kicks his wrinkled legs with new-found freedom and ease. We watch her open her little eyes to observe what she can about this amazing world of sight and sound that is no longer obscured and muffled. We see him cuddle contentedly in our loving arms. In the process of these delightful observations, we sense the lifting up of our own spirits to the Father of all power and creation, who has brought into being this brand-new life.

Not coincidentally, God has chosen the description of a contented baby, cradled in serenity at her mother's breast, to illustrate his relationship with us, his adopted and born-from-above children. In the meaning of the Old Testament name "El Shaddai," we glimpse the tender God who is our source of daily life sustenance, comfort, and security.

At the time of this marvelous event—the coming of a child into our home—it is most appropriate that we ask ourselves four questions:

- Why should I teach my child about God?
- When should I start teaching my child about God?
- What time of day should I teach my child about God?
- How should I teach my child about God?

Why Should I Teach My Child About God?

As we teach our child about God, we must first ask ourselves *why?* First and foremost, a child is designed and entrusted to us by God. Our children do not actually belong to us but are loaned to us to be directed, trained, and shaped into the useful, godly people that our Creator intends for them to be.

In addition, we know our child has needs that only a relationship with God can satisfy. A child needs a sense of security (and don't we all!). Proverbs 14:26 says to us, "He who fears the Lord has a secure fortress, and for his children it will be a refuge." Another reassuring Scripture passage can be found in Isaiah 54:13: "All your sons will be taught by the Lord, and great will be your children's peace."

As our children grow up in an unstable world of constantly changing global events and social values, they need a strong, personal sense of confidence and peace during the crucial childhood years. A true knowledge of the Lord God and his unchanging Word can provide a vital sense of security for our child and for us.

Closely linked to this overall sense of confidence and security is a young child's need for a refuge from fear. Every child experiences the negative feelings of fear. The world of a child is a big, perplexing environment, full of unknown, confusing, and frightening signals. Even in the home where Jesus is central in importance, every little child will occasionally feel afraid! At those times, she needs to know that, in addition to the loving protection her parents provide, the all-powerful God will be her closest companion. She can learn at a very young age verses such as "When I am afraid, I will trust in you" (Ps. 56:3).

When Jennifer was a tiny child of two, she was awakened by a sudden predawn thunderstorm. Responding quickly to her cries for "Mommy! Mommy! Mommy!", the little girl's mother rushed into her room. In the glow from the lightning's flash, she saw Jennifer standing in her crib, tightly gripping the side rail, with a wide-eyed look of terror on her face. "Mommy, Mommy," she cried, "is Jesus afraid?"

Touched by her child's unexpected

question, the mother replied, "No, honey, Jesus is not afraid at all." Her tiny child, considered by some too young to have any concept of spiritual truth, immediately began to relax and soon went back to sleep. Although many spiritual principles were still beyond her ability to comprehend, Jennifer recognized that Jesus is real and in him lies security and protection!

In addition to their need for security and freedom from fear, small children have a special need for order in their lives. Preschool children, especially, thrive in an atmosphere of order. (Remember that order differs from orderliness, and a child seems to get along quite well when his toy box has been completely emptied onto the playroom floor!) Children find security in the routine of doing things at the usual time and with familiar people in charge. Variety can be interesting at times, but order is of great value to a young child. Fortunate is the child who experiences the orderly control of Christian parents, who in turn order their own lives under the authority of the heavenly Father.

A tiny child also needs answers to many questions. It has been said that no adult scientist was ever half as curious as a young child! Children learn by asking questions from the time they are very small, and many of their queries are profound in their implications. At the age of three, Mark asked his mother, "Who makes hurricanes?" He recognized that God was the maker of the world and its weather, but that God is good and hurricanes are bad—and he questioned how to reconcile the two! At such an opportune moment, a parent needs an instant dose of God's wisdom. He will enable us to give satisfactory answers to our child's questions as we rely upon his wisdom and his Word. "They called on the Lord and he answered them" (Ps. 99:6) is God's truth for today and all through the lifetime of your child.

When Should I Start Teaching My Child About God?

We may be willing to teach our child about God and his truth but not know how early in our child's life to begin. When should we begin to teach our child about God?

The apostle Paul wrote these words concerning when or at what age Timothy was first taught the holy Scriptures: "Continue in what you have learned and have become convinced of, because you know those from whom you learned it, and how *from infancy* you have known the holy Scriptures, which are able to make you wise for salvation through faith in Christ Jesus" (2 Tim. 3:14–15, emphasis added).

We simply do not know at what point a very young child becomes spiritually aware. Studies reveal that a young child may not be able to comprehend abstractions as a preschooler. But many truths from the Bible can be understood by a tiny child, and those which are not perfectly clear to him will be understood as he naturally matures. A little child, bent over as he studies a tiny bug on a blade of grass, excitedly exclaims, "Oh, Mommy, 'sook' at dat bug! God made him! I love God!" The young mother senses that within the spirit of her child is an awareness that goes beyond the mere parroting of words and truths that he has been taught.

We can begin teaching our child about God as soon as she arrives in our home as a newborn baby. The lessons will be very basic and vitally linked to our expressions of love and physical care for our child, but teaching none-theless. Then a child has five or six golden years of exceptional receptivity and retention. No subsequent period in childhood can compare with these pre-school years for learning. As many par-ents can attest, the tiny child will absolutely amaze us with her capacity to learn television advertising jingles or to memorize verbatim whole story-books frequently read to her.

When shall I teach my child about God? From the moment of birth with a concentrated and loving effort during the first five years.

What Time of Day Should I Teach My Child About God?

The Old Testament also addresses what time of day we should teach our child about God and his Word. Deuteronomy 6:7 instructs parents, "Impress (these commandments) on your children. Talk about them when you sit at home and when you walk along the road, when you lie down and when you get up."

This command to parents is a literal one. We are to teach when we are sit-ting together with our children, per-haps at the dinner table where physical hunger is satisfied, on the living room sofa, our child snuggled on our lap, or on the playroom floor. *Any* time of com-fort, closeness, and natural, unstrained conversation is a good one to present God's truth to our children.

We are to teach "when we lie down and rise up," at the close of a tiring day and as the new day begins, often with a burst of fresh preschooler energy. In the morning most children are eager to spend a little undivided time with Mommy or Daddy. As bedtime nears, your child may want to snuggle up to hear a Bible story. The soothing sound of the loving parent's voice and our un-divided attention appeals to our child. He may not sit for long, if at all, but the tiny child hears and absorbs much, even as he plays.

These activities are ones we perform daily or weekly, year after year. The ele-ment of habit is present, but the em-phasis is more on a life-style of natual conversation about the Lord. Like the New Testament admonition to "pray without ceasing" (see 1 Thess. 5:17), the Deuteronomy passage presents our re-lationship with God as one of constant closeness and instant communication.

When to teach your child each day will depend upon your family sched-ules, obligations, needs, and activities, but especially upon the receptivity of your child. It is less important to teach at the same time each day than to in-struct the child at a time when he is most receptive. The length of a "daily Bible lesson" with our child, whether a game, craft, story, puzzle, or other activity, needs to be sufficient to teach him, but brief enough to leave him eager for more. Methods will change and our teaching may primarily become instruction by example rather than spoken admonition as our child nears adulthood. A lifelong commitment will be required, but what joy in life could possibly compare with seeing our grown child actively loving and serving God?

How Should I Teach My Child About God?

That is where the following activities and lesson plans start. In these games, crafts, and ideas, adult and child are interacting and learning as they have fun together. Obviously, an adult must be involved, and parents are the natural and logical teachers. However, these ideas may be used by other relatives, friends, teachers, and professionals who have the responsibility for the care of young children.

The activities and ideas that follow are presented cafeteria-style so you can select those which best fit your own child. They are listed by the child's chronological age, by the types of activities involved, and in some cases by special needs your child may have. Many games are simply playful, back-and-forth exchanges between adult and child. Almost all ideas can be carried out in ten minutes a day or less. Some involve only three or four minutes of your time, leaving your child and you eager for the next day's spiritual lesson. Certainly, when it is appropriate and the child's interest continues, spend additional time instructing him in God's truth. Nothing you do is more important.

In addition, be very sensitive to those priceless captured moments each day that allow your child to see God's reality applied to natural situations. The important thing is that God be very real to you as a parent. It is also advantageous to adopt your child's own attitude that playing is the best way to learn.

Age-level activity groupings are somewhat arbitrary. Few children are "average" under any type of classification; some younger children may enjoy activities listed for those who are older. Older children occasionally have fun with baby toys and may delight in a game designed for a baby or toddler. Many times a child will prefer to repeat a familiar activity rather than perform a new one. A majority of the ideas may be carried out with more than one child at a time, and some are ideal group activities. Games and crafts may be selected or adapted for the handicapped, the developmentally delayed, and the exceptionally gifted.

Introductions are only beginnings; they presuppose that more knowledge and intimacy will follow. After making the vital introduction of God to our child, we must not let the acquaintance end there. We must continue to make our child's contact with the living God so frequent and so personal that our child will grow to know him as his most intimate companion.

Each time you teach your child about God through moments spent together, breathe a prayer for the Holy Spirit to empower you and to reveal himself through you, "so the next generation would know [the praiseworthy deeds of the Lord], even the children yet to be born, and they in turn would tell their children" (Ps. 78:6).

Basic Supply List

Many activities in this book call for using common household items like the ones below. You probably have most of them. Keep them in a special closet or box where they are easily accessible.

white paper
roll of butcher paper or shelf paper
construction paper
paper bags
newspapers
old magazines
glue or paste
transparent tape
crayons
felt-tip markers
string or yarn
cotton balls

cotton swabs
blunt scissors
paper cups
food coloring
flour
salt
gelatin
elbow macaroni
liquid starch
liquid detergent
tempera paints or watercolors
paintbrush

PART ONE

Introducing Your Child to Godly Attitudes

Chapter 1

Introducing Your Child to Trust

Blessed is the man who trusts in the Lord, whose confidence is in him.
—Jeremiah 17:7

The goal of all activities in this chapter is to teach trust in God as we demonstrate trust in one or two important persons who take care of the baby or child's personal needs. We can communicate our dependability by the way we respond to our child, and we enable him to trust and love in later relationships. Even more important, we can better enable him in future years to trust and love the living God.

Beginning now, weigh your words carefully before you say them to your child. When you tell him you will do something, be very sure that you do it. When you threaten punishment for unacceptable behavior, follow through as you have promised. Parenting will be immeasurably easier if your child understands that you can be trusted to mean what you say.

From the moment we receive a precious child, we have been given both a great sign of God's trust in us and the opportunity to show His trustworthiness to another human being in day-to-day living. We are doubly blessed!

The Baby

Trust is nurtured in our baby by the way we pick her up, hold her, and talk to her. When we meet her needs as quickly as possible, we let her know we will be there to make her secure and comfortable. A small baby's cry is not a demanding form of manipulation. It is her only means of oral communication. Our quick response will help eliminate her need to cry to get us to act on her behalf.

Fresh diapers, warm milk, tender touches, and secure handling communicate to the baby, "You are very important to me. You can trust me to take good care of you."

Whisper

As you daily care for your baby's needs, whisper in his ear, at close, tender moments, the name of Jesus. Say "Jesus loves you, darling," or simply, "Jesus." Be the instrument of spiritual as well as physical bonding for your child.

Or you may whisper a simple phrase like one of these:

"God loves you, Sarah. Mommy loves you, too."

"God made you, Chris. Daddy is so glad he did."

"Trust Jesus. He's right here with you. So is Mommy."

"Jesus loves you, my beautiful baby."

"God made Mommy, Daddy, Suzie, even Skippy."

God and Jesus are thus introduced, and the baby will begin to connect a pleasant feeling with a comforting sound and, eventually, with a loving Savior.

Wind Chimes

Hang wind chimes that have a quiet, pleasing sound in your baby's room. Each time you enter to pick her up from her bed, gently set the chimes in motion and then say, cheerfully, "Mommy's here." You may want to add, "Jesus loves you, Kristy. Mommy loves you, too."

Music to Rattle by

Use a baby rattle or similar toy such as a bell. Rattle or ring the toy gently on one side of the baby where he can barely see it as he lies on his back. Remember to keep the toy in the same place where it made the sound. Later, place the rattle even farther away and out of view completely. Then do the same on the opposite side of the baby.

You may also stand behind the baby's head and shake the rattle over him, moving it slowly back toward you. Baby's neck and back will get some mild exercise as his eyes follow the rattle.

After a brief time of playing this game, use the rattle to keep time as you happily sing "Jesus Loves Me" or some other gospel song.

Sway with Me

Teach your baby that you can be trusted by showing her frequent affection even before she cries for it. As convenient as it is to leave baby alone when she is content, that is sometimes a good time to pick her up and cuddle her. She will then learn that expressions of love come often, not just when she demands it.

There are, obviously, exceptions to this practice. A nursery worker or parent with twins or several small children must leave well enough alone much of the time. However, even they can find frequent times to show affection to their quiet baby. Parents sometimes later voice the sincere regret that their "best" baby, who would quietly lie or play by herself for long periods of time, received less attention than any other of their children.

As you are holding your baby, play music for her on a music box, tape, or record player, or simply hum or sing a tune as you gently sway to the music. As she grows older, the music may become a little more upbeat and fun, but baby's early months are a good time for gentle, close-to-parent handling. Many lovely Christian praise and lullaby tapes are available at Christian bookstores. The messages the words convey, too, will become important vehicles of simple truths to your child.

Early Outdoor Fun

Lie down outside with your baby on a blanket under a tree. Even a new baby will enjoy watching and listening to the leaves rustle above him. Hang a rattle, a bell, or a beach ball from a low-hanging branch where your baby can hear and see it. Stay close to him, cuddling, stroking, and talking to him. He will learn that Mommy and Daddy can be counted on to be nearby and that outside is a delightful, secure place to be.

Talk to him about the wonders of God long before he can understand your words. He will enjoy your voice and closeness, and in a short time, your words will begin to have meaning to him.

I'm Back Here

When your small baby is on her tummy and cannot see you, frequently place your cheek next to hers, pat or rub her back, and talk tenderly to her.

She will be learning that even when she cannot see you, you are there to love, protect, and care for her. How much like a picture of our loving heavenly Father!

It's in the Right Place

As much as possible, when your baby is small, keep crib toys visible in the same places each day. The baby will begin to look for them in time, and as she becomes tired of them, new toys may be substituted but placed in the same spots. Your baby enjoys the familiar and is learning through repeated sights and routines that her world is a dependable place to be. In time, she may be better able to transfer that concept to the secure spiritual realm in which we prosper as God's children, in spite of an insecure world around us.

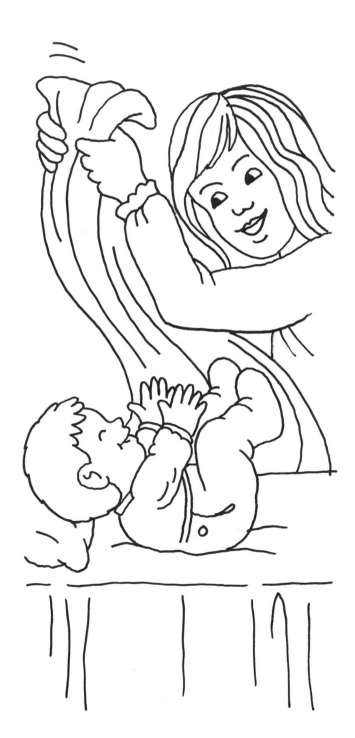

Peek-a-Boo Baby

Who does not use this game with his small child, even from early baby days! It is an ideal way to show baby that the familiar face that disappears behind hands or objects can be trusted to come back again . . . right away!

A parent's face represents to the baby all that the mother and daddy do for him. It means care, food, comfort, rocking, safety, love, and warmth. Peek-a-boo means that that familiar person disappeared for a moment, but came back where she belongs!

Nursing Talk

At your baby's most pleasureful moments, especially while she is nursing or contentedly lying on your shoulder, say, "Suzie, Jesus loves you." Let that matchless name be one of the first she ever hears, and it will probably be one she early learns to say . . . and very soon learns to love.

New Toy

When introducing a new toy, or while entertaining baby with a rattle or mobile, say, "God is so good, Jimmy. He helps us have fun!"

Comfort for Our Baby

When baby is distressed, pray the name of Jesus within her hearing. You may wish to say, "Jesus, please comfort our baby," or "Lord Jesus, help Jennifer to sleep peacefully."

The Vacuum Is My Friend

If your baby develops a fear of the vacuum cleaner, you may need to introduce the vacuum to him. Carry him in your arm or in a snuggly pouch near you as you vacuum. When he is able, let him help push the vacuum or turn it on and off.

If he still remains afraid, try to vacuum in rooms farther away from him, moving him from room to room. When he is concerned about loud noises that you can do nothing about (wind, sirens, thunder, trains, planes overhead), use those moments to play with him, sing or talk reassuringly to him, or sway with him to music.

The Toddler

The toddler is beginning to develop some fears other than the natural ones of falling or of being left on a table undressed and uncovered. (These fears are actually better described as unpleasant feelings that leave him with a sense of insecurity.) The toddler, however, has had enough bumps and falls and has heard enough warnings that he is at times actually fearful.

We caution him about the big car in the street that will "get him" and the hairy dog that is sure to bite his fingers. He catches glimpses of tense adult television dramas. We sometimes overdo necessary warnings or allow him to overhear adult conversations where fears or scary stories are dramatically told.

Even a toddler can begin to learn about God's power to protect, guide, and guard him. In addition, a child of this age still needs the constant reinforcement of the truth that his parents, too, are trustworthy.

May these activities, prayerfully, help to teach those truths.

Bible Heroes

Show pictures or flannelgraph figures of Bible characters, one at a time.

Say, "This is David from the Bible. God made David *strong!*" (Show muscles to dramatize the meaning and encourage your child to do so for fun.) It is not necessary yet to tell about David's killing the bear, the lion, or the giant Goliath. A toddler may be more frightened than reassured by those details.

Or you may say, "This is Jacob. God took care of Jacob as he slept at night!"

Or, "This is Daniel. God kept Daniel so safe!"

Put up your child's own picture. Say, "This is Davey. God keeps Davey safe!" Or say, "God makes Davey strong! Thank you, dear God."

Calm and Cool Bible Animals

Show pictures from books or magazines of a bear, a lion, a sheep, a goat, or a dove. (To make the pictures less likely to tear, glue them on poster board cut the same size or protect them by covering front and back with clear adhesive paper.)

Place them in the pages of a Bible and let the child remove them one by one. As she does, briefly comment about each, giving its name, such as "The Bible tells about a bear." If the child is interested, give her a few positive facts about each animal. She probably will be more interested in simply removing the pictures from the Bible and giving each a quick glance. But by doing so, the child is being taught that the Bible contains interesting things to know.

Where's the Toy?

Hide a small ball, toy, or treat in your fist. Let the child see you do it; then place it behind your back, and bring both fists forward. Tell him if he can find the ball, he can have it. When he does, be trustworthy to give it to him. Do not tease him; that will undermine the concept of trust you are trying to teach.

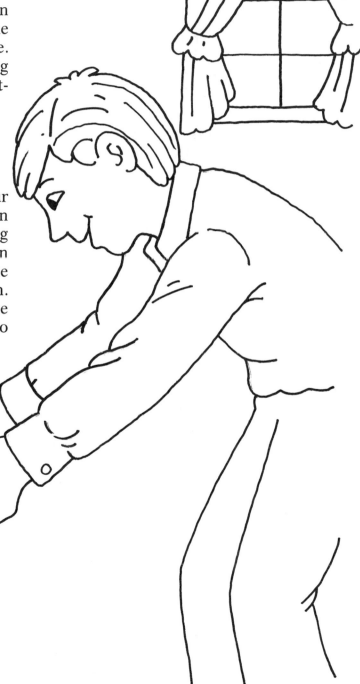

Jump to Me

Put your child up on a low table, stable cabinet, or other slightly elevated place in your home. Let her jump into your waiting arms. Give her a big hug as you let her feel secure in the fact that you will catch her. This familiar game is always a child's favorite, and she wants to do it again and again.

(If you feel she may repeat this activity without you there or she will be encouraged to climb where she should not, wait until she can better understand the rules of the game.)

I'll Be There

Before playing this game, you may wish to carry your child on a house tour of his own home, naming the rooms as you do. Then have him sit down in a central location and say, "Daddy's going to hide in the kitchen" (or a nearby spot). Go quickly and hide there, making sure you will be visible to the child when he comes to find you. Then call to your child, "Bobby, come and find me." When he does, say a friendly "Hi! You found me!"

This simplified version of Hide and Seek helps the toddler to trust his parents' words as well as to enhance his developing mental vocabulary. In addition, it is good obedience training.

Where Did I Put It?

A similar game is played with a toy or other familiar object. Hide the object somewhere in the room or a nearby area of the house. Then say, "Find the kitty, Erin . . . it's in the chair!" (or bedroom, under the stool, etc.). Make the object easy to find but not so visible that she can see it from where she stands. She will be learning in a very natural manner that your words can be trusted.

Try Something New

Cut a tasty fruit or snack into small bites or use a kitchen tool to shape watermelon into balls. Make sure your child is hungry, and say, "It's good!" as you set the food before him. As he tries it, he will realize your words can be trusted. Do not use any food that he won't enjoy.

Bible Story Books

Purchase from a Christian bookstore one or two inexpensive books that have a reassuring topic such as "God takes care of me." You may wish, too, to use simple Bible stories that you can tell in a couple of sentences. Jesus and the children, Mary and Joseph watching over baby Jesus, Moses as a baby, and Jesus as the Good Shepherd would be good choices. A picture to look at will help the toddler begin to understand.

Fun with Chants and Rhymes

A simple chant does not have to be a perfect example of metrical arrangement in order to convey a message and provide enjoyment for a preschooler. Use some of the following chants or create your own for a lighthearted means of teaching a biblical truth.

Noah built a big, big boat.
Made it strong and sure to float!

Daniel in the lions' den
Mean ol' king had put him in.
God made sure those lions didn't bite;
Angels kept Daniel safe all night.

Fisherman, fisherman
What do I see?
You caught a big fish.
How can that be?
Jesus told me how!
Now watch and see!
Whee! [*act like you are casting out and reeling in a fishing rod*]

Jesus, Jesus . . . He is strong.
Loves me, keeps me all day [*night*] long!

Jesus takes good care of me.
Jesus loves and comforts me.
Jesus, you're so kind and just.
Jesus, you're the one I *trust!*

Thank you, God, for all my toys
'Specially made for girls and boys.
Thank you, God, that you're the one
Who makes me able to have Fun!

Who sees me having Fun?
God does!
Who sees me share my toys?
God does!
Who sees me with my friends?
God does!
Who likes to see me play?
God does!

Ages Two to Three

What's Dangerous?

Begin this activity by saying, "What's dangerous, Jeremy?" (Make the word *dangerous* sound a little foreboding to better communicate its meaning, but don't make it too scary!) Then ask other questions like, "Is a cookie dangerous?" Smilingly say, "No," with him and shake your head. Ask more questions, sometimes silly ones: "Is a sock dangerous?"

Intersperse questions that involve truly dangerous experiences or objects: "Is a sharp knife dangerous?" "Is the big street dangerous?"

As a conclusion, ask, "Who watches over Jeremy?" Say, "Mommy does . . . and (excitedly) *Jesus!*" (A hug is in order!)

Whenever I Am Afraid

As soon as the child can talk, or even before, since she already understands many of our words, teach: "When I am afraid, I will trust in you [God]" (Ps. 56:3). You do not need to teach the Scripture reference to this age child.

When she is frightened, ask caringly, "Are you afraid, Kristy? Remember, 'When I am afraid, I will trust in you [God].' He's right here with us!"

As the child gets older and daytime thunder troubles her, let that be a time to practice her homemade band—beating on a lid or a can, ringing a bell, and marching around a room.

As an alternative, you may play a marching record that will help to drown out the thunder and give the child something to do.

See if she can complete a simple game like jumping across the room or rolling a ball to the chair before the next clap of thunder. Counting or singing a short song also serves the purpose of making the child better able to cope with her fear.

My Pet Trusts Me

Let your little child help take care of your family pet. He can help pour water in the dish, or carry food to the feeding place.

Say, "We take care of Muffy. God takes care of Johnny and Mommy and Daddy. God wants us to be happy like Muffy is." (Talk about his tail wagging if he is a dog or his purring if he is a cat.)

Emphasize, "Muffy trusts in us to take good care of him and give him food, water, and a warm place to sleep. We can trust in God to take good care of us. He gives us food, water, and a nice place to live."

Blindfolded Tasting

This activity may be liked better by a three-year-old child, or by a two-year-old who plays it with an older sibling who has first turn. Then the younger child will better understand what is taking place and that the game is fun.

Seat your child in front of you on the floor and place the blindfold on her. If she does not like to be blindfolded, use sunglasses with black paper taped over the lenses or simply let the child close her eyes.

Say, "I'm going to put something in your hand. It will be fun. Trust me." Then place a small object in her hand and let her guess what it is or simply remove her blindfold so she can see it.

Blindfold her again and say, "I'm going to make a pretty sound for you. It will sound pretty. Trust me." Ring a pleasant-sounding bell, play a music box, or quietly sing or hum a tune.

For the third time, blindfold the child. This time say, "Here's something to eat. It will taste good. Trust me." Then place the tasty food in her mouth.

Night Brings Light

Take your little child on a short night walk with flashlight in hand or out in his own backyard. Comment on the night sights and sounds, and then say in a pleasant voice: "Do you know what we can trust God to give us after the night? Morning! Thank you, God, that we can trust you to give us night and then morning again!"

We Can Trust the Shepherd

Briefly tell the Bible story of the little lamb that wandered from the flock and was found by Jesus, who brought him safely back to the fold. Explain that the lambs trust the shepherd to take care of them and to protect them.

Let the child be the little lost sheep who baas; you be Jesus calling him, finding him, and carrying him back to the sheepfold. To make a sheepfold, arrange sofa cushions in a square or two chairs with backs facing and a sofa cushion standing upright between them for the "back wall." The space under the kitchen table also makes a good sheepfold.

Carry the child on your shoulders, if you are strong enough! As you do, say, "Jesus said, 'I am the good shepherd.' You can trust Jesus to take good care of you."

Elijah

Tell this story from Elijah's life: "A man named Elijah was out in the hot, sandy desert. There wasn't any food in the desert, but Elijah didn't worry. He trusted God. He knew God would take care of him. And sure enough, God did! He sent big birds called ravens to Elijah, and in their claws they carried food! 'Thank you, God!' said Elijah."

Then say, "God gives us food when we need it" (see Ps. 145:15).

To emphasize this story, you may act it out with the child, letting her sit or lie on the floor while you "fly" to her with pretend food in your "claws."

May I Trust You, Please?

To familiarize your child with the concept of trust and to help instill in him dependability, use the word *trust* in your conversation often. For example, say, "I need the baby's diaper. May I trust you to bring it to me, please?"

Or ask him to take his unbreakable plate from the table to the sink counter and say, "May I trust you to carry your plate to the sink, please?" If he accidentally drops the plate, tell him kindly that you know he was trying his best and that it was only an accident. See if he would like to try it again.

 # Ages Four to Five

Numerous Bible stories teach the concept of trusting our dependable God. As you are telling these stories to your child, emphasize the element of trust involved.

It's even better to act out the story with or without props. A costume trunk or box is an excellent source to keep available for this age child.

T-R-UST

This little activity may seem a bit silly to you, but it is sure to please your little child and teach her an important phrase, too. When she is in a happy, active mood, teach her this cheer, and do it with her. After all, the fact that we can trust Jesus is something to cheer about!

T-R-UST!
T-R-UST!
T-R-UST!
TRUST . . . [*drag the word out as you roll your forearms around each other in front of you and bend forward*]
JESUS ! ! ! [*throw your arms up and out to the sides*]

The I-Can-Trust-You Day

Select a rather special unbreakable object belonging to you, a note with something important written on it, or a letter to mail. Ask your child if you can *trust* him to take care of it all day for you. Ask him to put it in a safe place that he will remember. (Help him find one, if necessary.) At the end of the day, ask if you may have it back. Tell him and show him with a hug how thankful you are that you can trust him to take care of something important to you.

Is It True?

Children who are four and five years old have extremely active imaginations and sometimes have difficulty telling the difference between a make-believe story and one that is an actual lie. This little question and answer game may help.

Tell her statements like the following and ask her to say if they are true or not true.

"I am a daddy."

"I have green hair."

"The couch has three pillows on it."

"Snakes are furry."

Then let the child have a turn to make statements, and you label them true or not true. End the game with, "Whose words are *always* true? God's!"

Trust Like Elijah

Let your child color a simple picture of a bird you make. Let him draw food in the bird's claws. Or cut a picture of a bird from a magazine and let him paste it on a paper, adding the food to the picture with crayons or markers.

Let the child paste feathers on a picture of a bird that you have drawn. (You do not have to be particularly artistic to draw a bird, as long as you can make a simple head, body, tail, wings, and feet!) Use feathers that you have found on a nature hunt in your own neighborhood or purchase a package of them at a craft or discount store.

Let the child color the blue sky on a piece of paper. Cut out for him a small bird and let him glue it on the sky. If you wish, you may let him also glue on some pieces of cotton for clouds and a small piece of cracker for the food in his claws.

Patiently help him as he learns to use glue or paste; almost all little children have difficulty regulating the amount of glue that arrives on the paper! To make it easier for your child to spread glue without excess, pour some into an empty deodorant bottle and let him roll it onto the paper where he wants it to go. Glue sticks also work well, or pour a small amount of white glue on a disposable plate or lid, and let the child "paint" it on with a brush.

Trust Verses

Each week, teach your child one of the following verses dealing with trust in God.

"Trust in the Lord and do good" (Ps. 37:3).

"I will fear no evil, for you are with me" (Ps. 23:4).

"Trust in the Lord with all your heart" (Prov. 3:5).

"When I am afraid, I will trust in you" (Ps. 56:3).

"O Lord my God, I take refuge in you" (Ps. 7:1).

"See that the Lord is good; blessed is the man who takes refuge in him" (Ps. 34:8).

Little reward and motivation will probably be needed with this age child. He usually finds it enjoyable and easy to learn Bible verses in order to please you. Do not insist that he do so, however. If you sense resistance to memorizing, ask him to try it only once more, and then cheerfully stop. Your saying the verse several times to him will help him learn it. Eventually, of course, you want him to try.

Here is a tip that may help. Let the child be the Bible verse king or queen at supper or lunch. Make a decorative paper crown and crown the child as he sits down to eat, if he has learned a Bible verse. You may even wish to decorate his throne with streamers or a pretty cloth draped over it.

Word for the Week

Let *trust* be one of several Bible words you select to emphasize for one week at a time. Write the word on a piece of construction paper or poster board that has been cut around the edges in zigzags or scallops. Do not make it too large. Attach it to a visible place with a small piece of plastic-tacking putty or some other adhesive that will not damage walls.

Decide upon a definition for each word that the child will understand, and help her to understand the meaning. Let the word appear first in a central place each week, and then in other places in the house. The child may move it and surprise you, or you may surprise her.

When it is discovered, the finder says, "I found the special word!" Ask her what it is and, perhaps, what it means. She then secretively proceeds to move it somewhere else. The parent does not immediately go to search for it but waits to find it as he goes about his routine tasks.

Treasure

Place cutout footprints in a line in the house, leading to a treasure. The treasure may be a small chest or box containing anything the child likes: a treat, a piece of bubble gum, some stickers, or a small toy. It would be appropriate one time to place a small new Bible at the end of the footprint trail. You would then have a wonderful opportunity to stress to your child the great treasure the Bible really is!

Before the hunt begins, explain to the child that you have hidden a treasure somewhere in the house, but he must trust the footprints to lead him to it. Will he? "OK . . . Go!"

Or, you may tape stickers or picture-clues throughout the house and say, "You must trust the pictures to tell you where to go next." Emphasize the concept of trust. You may accompany him on this treasure hunt and "read" the pictures to him.

This activity is especially helpful when leaving a fearful or hesitant child with a baby-sitter. Save the activity for them to begin as soon as you leave for the evening. The child will usually send you off with his blessing—the sooner, the better!

Lean on Me

This game has been a favorite for many generations but serves well to help the child begin to understand the concept of trust.

Stand behind your child, about one and a half feet away from her back. Tell her to make her legs very stiff and to fall backward into your arms. Say, "You can trust me. I will always catch you when we play this game."

Tell her that Jesus wants us to trust him. He is strong enough and is always there to help us. We can lean on him. Let the little child know that when she feels afraid or small, she can imagine herself leaning on Jesus for help.

Trust Stories

The story of the hiding of baby Moses by his mother in the Nile River is a good example of trust and of the guidance of God. When you tell the story, emphasize that God could be trusted to watch over baby Moses even when his parents were not present, and he does the same for us.

The Scripture "I will be with you" (Exod. 3:12) is a good one to teach or quote to your child. Hebrews 13:5 is another Scripture that gives wonderful comfort to people of all ages: "Never will I leave you; never will I forsake you."

The thrilling stories of Daniel in the lions' den and Shadrach, Meshach, and Abednego in the fiery furnace are vivid examples of trusting in God's power.

After these stories have become familiar to your child, play "Who Am I?" Describe the character's experience and let the child guess who it is; or say the name and encourage him to tell the story.

Ask, in conclusion, "Who did they all trust?" The child will happily answer, "God!"

Chapter 2

Introducing Your Child to Self-confidence

I can do everything through him
who gives me strength.
—Philippians 4:13

Godly confidence is a biblical concept. It is not the prideful self-confidence exalted by the secular world; rather, it is the can't-lose combination of a human being plus God, functioning in the power, strength, wisdom, and sufficiency of the Almighty. The I-can-do-all-things-through-Christ attitude enables one to dream, to attempt, to succeed, and to enjoy a dynamic, productive, rewarding life.

Loving parents do not want their children to be crippled by self-effacement, weakness, fear, or low self-esteem. A lack of self-confidence can haunt an individual throughout his life. It can make him miserable, preoccupied with himself, and unable to attempt what he could otherwise accomplish.

God's plan for each individual is a balanced life—a personal confidence that frees us to make a here-am-I-send-me commitment to all that God asks of us, without degenerating into the sinful pride that leads to disaster. The Bible emphasizes over and over that we are valuable to God, that he loves us, that he is always available to meet our needs, and that he delights in fellowship with us.

Jesus himself instructed us, "Love your neighbor as [you love] yourself" (Matt. 19:19)—not *instead of* or *more than* yourself, but as much as you love yourself. The implication is evident in Jesus' words: the right kind of self-love will express itself in selfless love for others. The apostle Paul also emphasized that each believer is important in the body of Christ, just as each part of the human body is important (see 1 Cor. 12:27).

Instilling godly self-confidence within our child is a task that must begin very early. She will begin to formulate her own sense of worth, or lack of it, by the way we handle her, speak to her, and relate to her childish imperfections. She will look to us to mirror back to her what she is really like. In unspoken words, she will question, *Is Mommy glad I'm here? Does Daddy think I'm fun to hold and play with? Are they happy when I can do new things?* A child reared by wise parents who emphasize her personal worth from day to day will be more likely to believe the liberating truth that the almighty God considers her life to be of infinite value.

Many good parents make the mistake of putting down their child through casual, little comments made in his presence. They may be unaware that their words and innuendos make an impression upon their little child. However, they are giving him clues about who he is and what he is like.

A parent is the authority in a child's life; and if she says that this child is a "handful," "a brat," or a "big-mouth," then the child assumes that he really is—and will probably live up to his parent's casual assessment of him! Conversely, if a child overhears compliments about his behavior and disposition, he will try awfully hard to be the kind of child his parent has said he is!

A tiny child has no innate understanding of confidence, nor does he comprehend the concept of humility; but we can help him develop these and set him on a course toward a productive life. What a priceless gift to give our child—a future of dependent independence, a belief that he can truly do everything through Christ and, therefore, be willing to try his best at each opportunity.

How *can* we help our child develop proper self-love and self-confidence without causing her to become unduly selfish and prideful? There are no easy answers, but the following six guidelines may help.

1. *Teach her about her worth and potential in God's sight.* Tell her that God knew her and loved her before the world even began. Emphasize that God will take care of her and lead her all through her life, if she will let him. Use "love" names for her such as "God's precious little girl" and "the Lord's beautiful little jewel," even though her behavior may not always sparkle!

2. *Let him know often how precious he is to you*—not because of how he looks or performs, but because he is God's *gift* to you. Emphasize his positive qualities and behavior as much as possible. No one feels very confident when he is constantly in the doghouse.

3. *Do not be afraid to discipline her.* We guard and protect what we value, and are obligated to protect our child from improper and ungodly behavioral patterns that will damage her life and potential. When we use discipline, however, we should convey to our child by our words and actions that we love her and are confident that she will display improved behavior in the future.

4. *Avoid using descriptions of him that tend to undermine self-esteem* such as: "You're impossible!" "You're a mess!" "You drive me crazy!" "You'll never learn!" Instead, sincerely tell him that he is wonderful, a "good boy."

5. *Direct her thoughts frequently toward the needs and feelings of others.* Help her to care and share and to avoid a preoccupation with herself and what she wants.

6. *Teach him to depend daily upon his heavenly Father for help with small tasks.* Emphasize by your words and example that our accomplishments and victories come because God graciously gives us our senses, our strength, and our healthy minds.

 # The Baby

Talk Confidence

When your baby is very young, hold her facing you, about six to eight inches from your face. Talk to her quietly. As she is able to make sounds, repeat them to her.

Tell your baby how pleased you are that she is beginning to talk. (Every sound a baby makes is an elementary building block in her speech development. The sounds will become combinations of sounds and eventually, words and sentences.) Explain to your baby that she will soon be able to say sounds like Da-da and Ma-ma and that you are so pleased with the wonderful way she is learning to talk! She will be gaining confidence from your tender touch, your facial expressions, and your pleasant voice.

Reaching and Pulling!

Tie a colorful scarf or bandana around your neck. Lean over your baby with a big smile on your face, and move close enough that he can see you and reach the scarf. He will begin to kick and wave his tiny arms at first, but very soon he will find himself accidentally grasping the scarf and later, very deliberately catching hold of it!

The presence of your happy face and warm closeness to your baby greatly enhances his enjoyment of this game. Subconsciously, he will be learning that his hands and eyes work together and that he can always enjoy being close to God.

Learning about Me

Lay your baby across a soft pillow with her arms in front of it. This position makes it easier for her to hold her head up and look around. Put an interesting object in front of her that she can observe for a while and then replace it with a propped-up mirror for her to watch the "other" precious baby!

Talk with her about how special she is to you and to God. Be very specific as you talk about and her wonderful little eyes, ears, mouth, and hair. When she seems tired, turn her on her back for a while or pick her up for some loving moments.

Your baby's confidence in what she can do and wants to do is increasing with her freedom to move and look around her. As she begins to gain strength in her neck and back, try positioning her in a cardboard box with pillows or thick blankets rolled up behind and in front of her. Scoot the box into the room where you are working so that she can enjoy your company.

Moving a Shape

Make a flat, colorful felt cutout of a heart, circle, or shape of your choice (about six inches in size). For variety, you may wish to glue a different color of the same size and shape on the back of the first with cardboard in between for support.

Attach one end of a soft, thick piece of yarn (approximately eighteen inches long) to the shape and the other to baby's wrist as he lies on his back in bed. Pass the shape *out* between the crib bars and then *in* over the top rail on the side closest to baby. As he moves his arm, the action will cause the shape to also move. Baby will look to see what is happening, and the action will be repeated again and again. (You may need to make adjustments in the placement of the shape and the length of the string to allow baby to better observe the cause and effect of his actions.)

Stand near his crib the first few times he tries the game. Pat his tummy gently and say, "Good boy! You made the shape move! Do it again! Good boy!" Let your baby continue on his own, but remain in his room any time you have something attached to the baby.

Later, you may wish to tie a small bell or rattle on the string to encourage your baby's developing auditory skills as well as his visual abilities. Remove the string as soon as your baby loses interest in the game. Tell him you are so glad God gave him strong arms so he can move the shape all by himself! Talk about how good God is to us.

You will find it interesting to see if his general kicking and waving motions become more specifically directed to the arm that moves the shape as his marvelous brain begins to make the connection between cause and effect.

Confidence-Building Mobiles!

Tie a cord across the width of your baby's crib. From it, hang objects that she can see and touch. When she is able to pull the objects close enough to put in her mouth, substitute an elastic strip for the ribbon to make pulling easier.

Colorful large beads or empty spools make ideal I-can-reach-it-myself toys, and they make an interesting clacking noise if more than one is used. Other suggestions are a small, safe mirror, rattles low enough to grasp, or rubber squeeze toys that make a sound.

Observe your baby frequently to insure her safety and to talk to her about what she is able to do. Sing to her a song about Jesus' love or make up your own tune about God's giving us hands and eyes and ears! If you purchase a manufactured mobile, try to find one she can touch as an active participant.

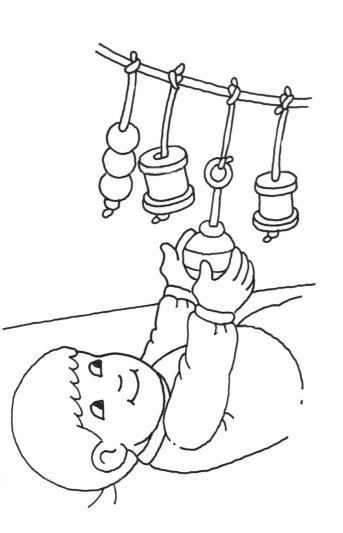

Hear My Voice, Find Me

When your baby is on his back on the bed or floor, inconspicuously move to a position several feet from where he is lying. Stoop down closer to his eye level and softly, cheerfully call his name, saying, "Jason, Jason, can you find me? Where am I?"

Give your baby time to turn his head and locate you. When he does, say, "Yes! You found me, Jason! I'm proud of you!" Kiss him and repeat the game from his other side, staying out of sight until you are positioned and ready to speak. If he does not respond at first, speak more loudly and be sure to give him time to locate you. His head movements will be limited at first, but the sound of your familiar voice will be a very strong motivation to keep trying! As he gets stronger, play the game with him on his stomach.

Your baby's confidence in his own ability is growing, along with the confidence that you are there to meet his needs. You may want to say, "Look what my baby can do! He can find Mommy! Thank you, God, for my baby!"

Roll Over

Place your baby, wearing only a diaper, on a smooth blanket or surface. Clothes will only restrict her on her first attempts to roll over. Place a fuzzy or textured cloth beside her to roll onto and cheer her on! Say, "Lana, God made you strong enough to roll over!"

Ring those Bells

Before the baby is able to put his feet in his mouth, attach jingly bells to the toes of his booties with strong thread or dental floss. He will be intrigued by his own ability to "ring those bells" as he begins to associate the kicking movements with the sound. Be *sure* to remove the bells before he is able to put them in his mouth! Tell your baby that God made his little legs strong.

I Can Get It Back by Myself

When your baby is in her dropping-toys-from-the-high-chair stage, attach twelve- to eighteen-inch yarn to the objects she is playing with and tie the other end of the yarn to the high chair tray. The yarn will allow her to learn to retrieve the toys by herself.

That Cozy Feeling

A very young baby has recently emerged from his tightly confined prenatal environment. Although he is much more comfortable with his new freedom to kick and stretch, a new baby still likes a feeling of closeness and security.

When you place your new baby on his stomach in his crib or on a sofa or bed, place a small pillow or rolled-up blanket on each side of him to make him feel warm and safe. When he is on his side, place the pillow behind his back, allowing him to freely move his arms and legs.

With pillows or blankets around him, your tiny baby will feel much more cozy in his big bed; and he will begin to develop an increasing confidence in his big new world.

Find the Toy

This activity will help your baby's memory skills develop. In addition, it will enhance her confidence in herself and you.

Show her a toy. Talk to her about it, and then place it at her right or left side where she cannot see it. If she makes an effort to turn to see the toy or to wiggle or squirm to get it, give it to her immediately. Brag on your baby's new skills that God is developing within her.

I Remember That Face!

A small financial investment will make possible a delightful, reusable memory toy for baby. Enlarge a close-up picture of baby's mother or daddy and glue it to one side of a box that is the approximate size of the picture. Cover the photo with clear adhesive paper to protect it.

Show the picture side of the box to your baby and talk about who it is. Turn the box over until the picture is out of sight and say, "Where's Daddy? Can you find Daddy's picture?" If he looks for it, praise and hug him. Tell him he is doing great to look for Daddy's picture, and be sure to show it to him if he needs help finding it.

Say a short thank-you prayer for Daddy.

Drop the Toy!

Mothers are convinced that young children are absolute masters at dropping things: Food from the high chair tray, toys throughout the house, and, before long, clothes and wet towels!

The dropping skill, however, is not an easy skill to master at first since it involves a different use of muscles from picking up or holding a toy. To help your child learn how to let go, place a bell or block in your own hand and say, "Watch . . . *drop!*" and let the object fall into your other hand. Repeat the action several times and then say, "You do it, Chrissy. *Drop* the block."

To make the game more interesting, place a metal bowl or an inverted metal lid as the catcher. It will make an intriguing noise; one your baby may enjoy more than you do!

Say, "Thank you, God, for Chrissy's hands that can drop a toy!"

The Ball Crawl

Provide a brightly colored inflated beach ball for your crawling baby to enjoy. She will push it, crawl after it, and delight in holding the elusive shape when she catches it!

Here's a New Friend

Hold your baby securely in your arms when he meets an unfamiliar person. Do not immediately hand him to the new friend. Instead say, "David, this is Mrs. Smith." If your baby seems willing, help him touch the person's hand briefly or give the stranger a favorite toy or something interesting to hand to your child.

Proceed slowly with introductions. Remember that even people *you* dearly love, like relatives or close friends, are complete strangers to your child. Meeting them is the same to him as meeting a salesperson at the door! Do not be hurt if your baby does not immediately reach for the grandpa or grandma he does not remember ever having seen before.

When your baby agrees to be held by the new person, stay within sight so that he can return to you when he wishes. Realize that he has made good progress and that his confidence with new people is growing. His developmental age and his basic temperament will have a great bearing upon how he reacts to a new friend.

The Toddler

I Can Help

A toddler enjoys picking up toys; to her it is an enjoyable game. To encourage your child's self-confidence and help-fulness, sit on the floor beside her with a plastic dishpan or a box. Drop a toy into it and hand another one to your child. Talk to her about what you are doing and ask her to put her toy in the dishpan. If she hesitates, gently guide her hand to pick up the toy and place it where you have asked her to.

Congratulate your toddler and ask her to find another toy to drop into the dishpan. She may only pick up two or three toys; but when a toddler's simple tasks are praised, she begins to have confidence in her own actions and in her ability to please the ones she loves!

Colors!

Introduce crayons to your child when he is a young toddler. Use the large pre-school crayons, and remove the paper wrappers if there are any. Tape a piece of paper to the table or the high chair tray in front of him. Give him time to get acquainted with his new object. He will probably pass it from hand to hand, show it to you, and see what it

tastes like. Crayons are nontoxic, and most young children will not chew on them long when they discover what crayons can do. (If he continues to bite on the crayon, substitute a cracker or teething biscuit, and postpone coloring until later.)

Talk with him about how smooth the crayon feels and tell him the crayon's color. If he does not inadvertently make a mark on the paper and discover that a crayon colors, take another crayon and show him how.

When your child makes a mark on the paper, praise him and encourage him to do more—but don't expect him to make a picture! Do not draw one for him at this point or he will soon prefer to watch you draw instead of color for himself.

At first offer only one crayon, but soon let him choose from several crayons that you are holding. He will be gaining confidence in his ability to use a tool for his own purpose. Tell him that God says, "Work with your hands" (1 Thess. 4:11).

I Can Be Gentle and Kind

Help your toddler learn to treat a baby doll or stuffed animal with gentleness and care. Provide him with a small blanket, baby bottle, and hairbrush. Let your child use them in taking care of his baby doll or stuffed animal. Guide his play by asking questions like these: Is your baby hungry? Is she cold? Does she need her hair brushed?

Your child will probably use these items awkardly but correctly with the doll or animal. Even though he is little more than a baby himself, these simple actions will help your child learn the pleasure of caring for someone or something else.

What Does the Animal Say?

Collect pictures of common zoo or farm animals that make distinctive sounds. Mount the pictures on cardboard for durability, and feel free to use several different pictures of the same kind of animal.

Name each animal and make its sound. Say, "You do it, Amy. Make the doggie's sound." Or ask the question, "What does the doggie say?" Amy may think your animal sound is funny at first, but she will soon delight in trying it herself.

Watch Me Draw!

With your close supervision, let your toddler use a stick to draw in the mud or dirt. Comment on whether his lines are long or short, wiggly or straight. Describe what he is making and give lots of praise for his efforts!

As an alternative, use a dusty table or steamy window or mirror for beginning art lessons. Let your toddler draw with his fingers. My own daughter's first real drawing was on a steamy church window, and I could not save it!

Carry, Pull and Push

Toddlers seem to love to push, carry, and pull. They especially love to carry big things held close in their arms. Give one of these objects to baby so that she can proudly display how strong she is as she carries it through the house:

- a squishy pillow
- a transparent sack tightly closed, full of Styrofoam stuffing
- a pillowcase stuffed with a sheet or something lightweight
- a large stuffed animal with some stuffing removed to make it floppy

From Start to Finish

Toddlers will follow a process to completion if we show them how at this age. They seem to enjoy the cleaning up and putting away as much as what we consider the fun part of the activity.

Take advantage of this stage to teach your toddler to pick up after himself and to complete activities. Keep the whole process short. Many daily activities can lend themselves to this learning skill. For example, give your toddler a whole banana, show him how to peel it, help him cut it into bite-sized pieces with a dull table knife, eat the pieces, throw away the peeling, and wipe off his hands. Finish by throwing away the napkin if you're using paper or putting it in the napkin ring if you are using cloth.

Ready, Aim, Throw

Toddlers can learn to aim and control where a ball goes by rolling and then throwing it at a stack of blocks, at a homemade target propped up against the wall, or into a box. For even more fun, your child may throw a ball or a beanbag into a large hole drawn on a piece of sturdy cardboard.

As she plays, say to your child, "Isn't God good to give Joanne strong hands? Thank you, God, for Joanne's hands."

I Can Undress

Even undressing can be a learning experience for baby. Make it easy for your toddler to undress himself by first untying his shoes and pulling them off his heels and doing the same with his socks so that he only has to tug at the toes to remove them. Praise him for the good job he is doing of undressing himself!

Unbutton his shirt and take one sleeve off, asking him to take off his shirt like the big boy he is. It would be much faster and easier to do the entire process yourself, but your child would miss a valuable opportunity to grow in confidence and independence.

Talk to your child about the wonderful little body God gave him and how much you love him as you get him dressed again.

I Can Paint

Give your toddler a plastic bucket or paper cup containing a small amount of water and a clean paintbrush or sponge. Let her "paint" on outside walls or sidewalks to her heart's content, telling her that we read in the Bible that we should "work with our hands" (1 Thess. 4:11) just like she is doing!

Stack It Up

Give your toddler blocks, boxes, sponges, spice cans, cylindrical potato chip containers, dominoes, or even large marshmallows (watch that he does not eat too many!) and show him how to stack them up to make a tower. Brag on his good job, and tell him to remember that God gave him his wonderful hands.

I Can Blow Things

Show your toddler how to blow by gently blowing on her cheek or hand. Blowing requires some mental and physical coordination in order to blow out and not suck in. Mastery of this skill brings not only hours of fun but also a real sense of accomplishment. Here are some objects your toddler might use to blow (watch out—beginning blowers are sloppy!):

- bubbles
- a horn
- a silver whistle
- a party blower
- bits of tissue paper
- feathers
- Ping-Pong balls across a table into a laundry basket
- candles on a cake or doughnut
- a straw aimed at your hair or at a tissue placed on your head

When your child is blowing on a whistle or noisemaker, turn on some quiet rhythmic music, and she may soon be keeping time with it!

I Can Balance

Let your toddler try his balancing skills on some of these objects while you hold his hand:

- a low stool or footrest
- a sturdy box
- an ironing board or table leaf suspended between two bricks
- an ironing board angled securely from a chair rung to the floor like a slide
- a street curb
- a low brick wall
- a 2″ x 4″ board

It is also fun to balance a ball by rolling it back and forth between you and your child along the suspended board.

Where Do They Go?

Save coffee or solid shortening cans with plastic lids. Cut a square shape and a round shape in each lid, large enough to allow a block or ball to go through. Make a pile of square blocks, round Ping-Pong balls, golf balls, and large wooden beads in front of your child. Supervise carefully to make sure she does not put the balls or beads in her mouth!

Let her choose where the blocks and beads go as you guide her with conversation: "Here's a round ball. Where does it go?" Show her the square and round holes. Demonstrate to her where the square block fits. Brag on her achievements and tell her you are *proud* of her! Add other containers and shapes and sizes of objects as she improves.

Open and Shut

Encourage your child's problem-solving skills and self-confidence by providing him with a clear plastic jar with a snack or toy inside and a lid loosely attached.

Show your toddler how to unscrew the lid, take if off, and remove the object that is inside. After your demonstration, put it all back together and say, "Now you do it, James."

At another time, provide a variety of containers and lids or one container with several choices of lids. Sing this simple song to your toddler to the tune of "London Bridge":

> Jesus made my little hands,
> Little hands,
> Little hands.
> Jesus made my little hands
> So that I can use them.

Clean It Up, Please

When a mishap occurs (and it most definitely will!), provide your toddler with paper towels, sponges, mop, whisk broom, and dustpan or whatever the cleanup necessitates. Show her how to use the tool or towels, and let her have a genuine part in cleaning up her own accidents. Make the cleanup time a positive time, without scolding or punishing. Accidents, spills, and toddlers inevitably go together. To err is definitely human and excusable!

Tell your child that she is helping you and pleasing God by cleaning up her own spills.

Making Choices

When your baby is beginning to feed himself, offer him two optional eating utensils—a spoon and a Popsicle stick. Show both to him and ask, "Would you like to use this or this to help you eat?" If he chooses the Popsicle stick, lovingly talk with him about how the spoon works better and demonstrate the difference to him.

At a later meal, offer your child a choice of an empty cup or one containing bite-sized food or a drink. You may also place before him choices of finger foods in a small muffin tin or the bottom half of an egg carton. Ask your child to choose what he wants to eat, and praise him for the good choice he has made.

Allow your child as many choices as possible within his daily routine, but also maintain no-choice absolutes that help to make him feel secure that someone bigger and wiser is in control. As often and as naturally as possible, let your child know that your kind heavenly Father helps you make wise choices as a daddy or mommy.

Ages Two to Three

My Own Banner

Make a personalized banner for your child from a large piece of felt or flannel. Cut out felt letters that spell GOOD BOY! (or GOOD GIRL!) and include your child's name, if you wish. Glue the words on the banner and hang it on a wall or door when your child has accomplished something noteworthy. Leave the banner up long enough for other family members to make comments to your child that will encourage him to do well again!

The banner may become an important family keepsake, and you may want to make it more decorative by adding trim or felt cutouts of pictures that interest your child. If you want to use the banner for birthdays, each year glue the number that represents his age near a picture of his favorite toy. The pictures you use may be drawings, magazine cutouts, or photographs. If you have more than one child, make a special banner for each from paper or poster board and let the other child help you color the words and glue the pictures.

Watch-Me-Do-It Walk

Take your child by the hand and say, "Let's go on a walk through our house and see what you can do, Bonnie."

As you go through each room, ask your child to do something like:

- carry a stack of pillows or an ottoman to a new location in the living room
- wash her hands by herself in the bathroom
- put the clean forks from the kitchen dishwasher into the drawer

After each job, applaud and hug her, saying, "Good job, Bonnie. Can you do more?" If she says yes, continue the game throughout the house. Tell your child that you know Jesus is pleased with all that she is able to do and so are you!

Mirror Man

Give your child a spray bottle of non-toxic window cleaner and a clean cloth or paper towel. Take him outside the front door of your house. Tell him that after you close the door he is to knock and introduce himself to you as the "mirror man" (or "mirror woman"). As the "mirror man" he is to ask if you have any mirrors in your house that need cleaning. Then let him come in and do the job.

Praise him for being such a fine worker. Ask him if God helps him do such a good job. He will probably respond with a yes! as he enjoys the good feeling of pleasing you.

It's Wash Day

Preschoolers love to wash things: walls, mirrors, the family car, the family dog, dishes, toys, baby dolls, clothes, rocks, even their own hands. Give your child the chance to wash something by first covering his clothes with a trash bag "bib" that covers the front of him and is held together behind his neck by a clothespin or masking tape.

Place a dishpan of soapy water in front of him or stand him up on a stool by the sink. Let him wash some of the objects mentioned above.

On another day you could provide your helper with a small "washing machine" consisting of a plastic container with a lid, a pair of child-sized socks, soapy water, and a toy block for an "agitator." Put the water, socks, and block in the container and close the lid tightly. Ask your little laundryman to shake the socks clean! Let him hear you sincerely thank God for your dear little helper.

It's Fun to Fold

Let your little boy or girl help you *and* grow in self-confidence as he or she folds small items such as Daddy's handkerchiefs, small hand towels, washcloths, dish towels, baby blankets, or cloth diapers.

Express your wonder aloud that God was so kind to give you such a helpful child!

This Goes with That

Play a matching game with your preschooler. Provide her with a small pile of her distinctly different socks or an assortment of Mom's, Dad's, and her socks. Talk about socks coming in two's or pairs that are just alike. Show her one sock and ask her to find the one that matches it. Do the same activity for fun with a variety of objects that can be matched, such as flatware, buttons, beans, salt and pepper shakers, or containers that are alike.

Button, Button

Ask your child, "Who gave you your hands?" Talk with him about how kind God is to have given him strong hands that can do so many things, and demonstrate a few of the things hands can do.

Make your child a simple felt vest, sewn together under each arm to fit him loosely. Call it his "clown vest" if he likes the name. Sew on three or four large colorful buttons and cut slits for buttonholes. There is no need to sew around the edges of the buttonholes since felt does not ravel; if the buttonholes become stretched out, place masking tape along each edge on the underside of the vest. Let your child practice buttoning and unbuttoning the vest on himself and then on another child or stuffed animal. Talk about your child's "amazing buttoning fingers!"

Super Helpful Supergirl!

Play a game with your child. Pretend she is a super helpful supergirl (or superboy) who spends her time looking for helpful things to do. When she sees an opportunity to help, she immediately says, "Let *me* help you!"

Let him help you with real jobs around the house or act out a couple of make-believe scenarios:

- Pretend you are carrying a heavy grocery sack in each arm and need someone to carry one.
- Pretend you have dropped a dime on the floor and cannot find it.
- Pretend you are sick in bed and need someone to bring you a bowl of warm soup.

When either parent is not feeling well, allow your child to actually perform small missions of mercy by bringing the parent what is needed and making things more comfortable. Through these real or pretend experiences, your child will learn compassion, a sense of belonging to her family, and an awareness that somebody needs her.

I Can Sing!

Make a simple mask from a paper plate by drawing facial features, cutting out holes for your child to see through and making a large round mouth! It is not necessary to tie the mask on; let him hold it up to his face by the sides and sing at the top of his voice!

If you would like to reduce the noise level a little, make a hole in the side of a cardboard box and let him fill up the whole box with his *voice* as he sings into the hole . . . or you may wish to designate a bathroom or large closet as the "singing room." Turn the light on for him and let him sing until the rafters ring. Any of these activities will help your child develop confidence in his own vocal ability.

If he is afraid of thunder, turn up the volume on a favorite Christian tape or record during electrical storms and both of you sing the clouds away.

I Can Shout!

Some children almost seem to be born with their vocal volume already turned up on high! God probably has some special future speaking or singing position already prepared for them, and they are getting in practice early for the golden opportunity.

In the meantime, if you wish to maintain your own sanity, provide a "loud place"—a bathtub with shower curtain closed, a shower stall with door closed, a well-insulated attic or basement, or a far corner of the backyard—for your child to go and let off vocal steam. Tell her that she may yell, but not scream. Explain that screaming makes a grown-up think that a child is hurt or in real trouble, and if she ever is, you want to recognize that sound. If your child begins to yell during her play, quickly usher her to her loud place.

My Work Is Beautiful!

Mom's or Grandma's refrigerator or Dad's or Grandpa's desk make great places to display a preschooler's art treasures. When we display his work, we are sending a confidence-building message to our child that his creative work is worthy of our acceptance and pride.

Here are some other ways to display your budding artist's pictures:

- Tape pictures on doors; have a display door just for his work.
- Frame pictures with an old picture frame or a cardboard one. The pictures may be changed often.
- Make greeting cards out of the pictures and send to loved ones if your child agrees.
- Make book covers, package wrapping, or place mats by covering pictures with clear adhesive paper.
- Use your child's drawing for seasonal or holiday decorating by letting him paint, draw, or color on precut paper shaped like hearts, flowers, Christmas trees, bells, or pumpkins.

Bubbles in the Wind

A young child loves to blow bubbles outside where the wind sends them sailing and soaring! She enjoys the feeling of wonder at what she and nature can do together.

Make bubble wands from bent pipe cleaners, or use the finger holes of scissors dipped in bubble solution. For larger bubbles, make a larger, circular wand from a piece of wire or bend a clothes hanger into a circle and let your child dip it in a bowl or bucket of bubble solution. If she cannot go outside, let her blow bubbles in front of an electric fan with a towel placed on the floor to absorb bubble drips.

Thank the Lord with her for the wonder of bubbles and the pretty rainbow colors we can see in them! Here is a recipe for sturdier bubbles:

1 cup water
1 tablespoon liquid dishwashing detergent
½ teaspoon sugar or 1 tablespoon corn syrup

Stir the mixture and store the unused portion in an airtight container.

Painting with Tempera

A can't-fail art project that will be suit-able for framing when dry and will bring praise to the tiny artist is car painting. It requires only a large piece of paper or a large grocery sack that has been cut open and flattened, a few drops of tempera paint, and a toy car. You will want your child to wear a pro-tective old shirt or plastic trash bag fas-tened behind his neck. Place him at a table sitting high enough to perform his work.

On the paper in front of him, place several drops of two or three colors of tempera paint. Let him "drive" his car through the paint again and again until he is satisfied with the finished prod-uct. Remove the paper for drying and replace it with a clean one to drive on!

God's Word in My Heart

A great confidence-building activity for a person of any age is memorizing Bible verses. Confidence in the mind's mar-velous ability to learn and retain in-creases through memorization. But more important, we learn to place our confidence in the one who is our only true source of strength and greatness.

Two- and three-year-olds are amazing memorizers! Take advantage of this God-given developmental stage to hide God's Word deep in their little hearts.

A Very Special Child!

Let your child know that she is a very special person in one of the following ways, but do not reserve them only for good behavior or achievements. Honor your child often simply because she is worthy of honor in your sight!

- Purchase a special plate or cup to use only at special meals of honor.
- Let your child be "queen for a meal" in a special chair or with a homemade crown.
- Tape a treat under her chair for after dinner just because she is such a delightful little girl.
- Make a special banner or flag bearing her name and display it on special days or for no particular reason.
- Prepare her favorite meal "just because," or give her a special day a month with extra-good treatment or privileges.
- If you have other children or a busy schedule, make appointments with her. During these special times put everything else aside and leave other children in your church's Mother's Day Out nursery or with a sitter. Let your facial expressions and words tell her that you think she is absolutely wonderful!

What I Think Is Important!

Little children have opinions and may come up with very good ideas if we give them a chance! Two short questions asked at appropriate times will help make your child aware that what he thinks and what he can do are of real significance.

One question to ask your child is, "What do you think?" Another is, "How should we do this?" Another statement that can really make your child feel special is "I need you," spoken when there is opportunity for your child to help you perform a simple task. All these statements can be effective in letting him know that his help and opinion are valued by you.

We're So Lucky to Have You!

Use the four fingers and thumb on your hand to give your child five reasons why you are so lucky to have him in your family!

My Own Little . . .

Providing your child with a miniature version of something you own will help give her a sense of identification with you and make her feel important. Here are some miniatures she will enjoy:

- toolbox
- sewing basket
- Bible
- purse
- wallet
- briefcase
- cap or hat like yours
- toy watch

Watch Me Jump!

Play Jack Be Nimble with your child, using a real unlighted candle and stand, a small cardboard tube, or a folded piece of construction paper for the candlestick that Jack jumps over!

Position your child on a bottom stair with the candlestick in front of him. Tell him to jump *over* the pretend candle, holding him by the hand or under his arms until he feels secure about jumping by himself.

You may let your child sharpen his jumping skills by placing other objects on the floor for him to jump over: a small pillow, a line of masking tape, a piece of string tied between sturdy objects near the floor, or a towel rolled up for a "log in the road." Graduate to a jump rope with one end tied to something solid while you gently swing the other end or hold it steady about an inch off the floor.

My Name Is . . .

Occasionally, when talking to your child, use her whole name. Say something like, "What do you want for lunch, Kimberly Dawn Smith?" Name the other people in her family, using first and last names, and discuss how she got her last name.

Pretend you are knocking at your child's door. Then say, "Hello, I'm _____. What's your name?" Pretend you are calling her on the phone and then ask her the same question. These simple activities will give your child a sense of belonging to the family unit and an awareness that she is an important person with a long, special name. Emphasize that she belongs with her family and that we all belong to God's family!

I'm Beginning to Count Things

Provide two bowls for your child, one containing a marshmallow, a potato, a strawberry, a nut in its shell, a grape, or whatever else is available, and the other containing two of the same food or object. Ask your child which bowl has one item in it and which has two. Continue to ask him questions such as "Which has more?" and "Which has less?" If you wish, increase the objects in the bowl to three in one and four in the other and do very simple addition and subtraction with your child.

Red Goes with Red

Provide your child with a sack of objects of one primary color—red, yellow, or blue—with one or two other colors included. Encourage her to find all the objects in the predominant colors and place them side by side. As she is able to distinguish well between the colors, increase the variety of colored objects and encourage your child to put them in piles that are of the same colors.

The Hairs of My Head

Play barber or beauty shop with your child and a doll or toy that has rooted hair. Pretend to shampoo, cut with pretend finger scissors, blow dry, and curl the doll's hair. Then say, "OK . . . now let's *count* her hair!" Show your child how hard it is to do by beginning to count.

Explain to your child that God already knows how many little hairs are on her head, what color they are, what color eyes she has, how big her hands and feet are. Tell her also that God gave her her beautiful smile. Make your admiration genuine and profuse! Be careful not to emphasize so much the beauty of your child's face (although every child *is* beautiful!) but the wonderful way God has designed her.

Shh! . . . You Can Do It

When your child is attempting to do something difficult or frustrating and is inclined to give up trying too soon, whisper in his ear, "Daniel, you can do it! I know you can!" or "Try it again! God will help you!" If appropriate say, "Do you want me to help you?"

This whispered conversation will probably surprise or amuse him and, hopefully, relax his tension for a moment so that he will try again. If he continues to be frustrated, encourage him to wait a little while and then try again.

One for You, One for Me

Allow your little child the opportunity to share, to help, and to learn basic number and planning skills through this simple routine.

When you are setting the table for a meal, ask her to put a napkin by each plate, then a fork and a spoon. Each time, give her the correct number of items. Emphasize to your child that there is one object for each person. (The one-to-one concept is the basis of future math skills.)

Repeat the same routine when giving snacks to friends or siblings, paper towels to each child who needs to dry her hands, or a flower to each family member.

Daddy Will Listen to Me

Let your child know that he is worthy of your full attention and that you value his words by looking into his eyes and listening carefully when he speaks. He cannot always express his thoughts adequately, and you may need to "read between the lines" and help him say what he means.

Your help and attentiveness may enable him to become a considerate listener to other people . . . a skill that will greatly enhance his future success in a vocation and in relationships.

May I Help Myself?

When your child eats lunch, occasionally place his food in small serving bowls and his drink in a small lightweight pitcher so that he can serve himself and pour his own drink. Have a damp paper towel nearby to wipe up spills or wipe off his face and fingers after eating. Show him how to dish up small amounts of food, and tell him that he may have more after he finishes these portions.

Your small child may not perform perfectly at first, but he will improve in manual coordination and good judgment as he is occasionally allowed to serve himself.

Let Me Choose, Please

When it is feasible, let your little child have a say-so in what she does. Keep the options limited, and be prepared to go along with her choice. Ask questions like these: "Do you want to have your snack or go outside first?" "Do you want to wear the red shirt or the blue one?"

Making these decisions will help her grow in confidence and independence, but make sure she understands that "Mommy must choose for you" at times.

Compliment your child and tell her that it pleases God when people make good choices!

Cheers and Songs

I am BIG! [*stretch hands high*]
I am STRONG! [*flex muscles*]
Jesus will help me
All day long!

Who makes me BIG?
Who makes me STRONG?
Who makes me HAPPY
The whole day long? JESUS!

JESUS, JESUS—HE IS STRONG!
Loves me, helps me
All day long! Yea! [*clap for Jesus!*]

To the tune of "London Bridge":

Jesus helps to make me strong,
Make me strong,
Make me strong.
Jesus helps to make me strong.
I love Jesus!

Jesus wants to make me strong,
Make me strong,
Make me strong,
Jesus wants to make me strong.
Thank you, JESUS!

To the tune of "Are You Sleeping?":

I can do this [*whatever the job*]
I can do this,
Yes, I can!
Yes, I can!
Jesus gives me power!
Jesus gives me power!
He is STRONG.
He is STRONG.

Thank you, Jesus,
Thank you, Jesus,
For your help,
For your help.
You give me the power.
You give me the power.
To do well [or *work*].
To do well [or *work*].

I can help Mom [or *Dad*].
I can help Mom [or *Dad*].
Yes, I can,
Yes, I can,
I can be a helper.
I can be a helper.
Thank you God.
Thank you God.

To the tune of "Farmer in the Dell":

The weaker that I am,
The stronger he [or *you*] will be.
Thank you, God, for all the strength
That you give to me.
[*Add* amen *if you use this as a prayer.*]

To the tune of "Twinkle, Twinkle Little Star":

I can be so many things,
Frog that hops and bird that sings,
Dog that barks, a rabbit, too,
I can even tie my shoe.
Who gives me the strength I need?
JESUS, JESUS—YES, INDEED!

To the tune of "If You're Happy and You Know It":

If you're STRONG and you know it,
Clap your hands! [or *move this chair, pick up toys, pour the milk, pick up toys, empty trash, etc.*]
If you're STRONG and you know it,
Clap your hands!
If you're STRONG and you know it
Then your hands will surely show it.
If you're STRONG and you know it
Clap your hands.

Ages Four to Five

Let's Cook

Mothers, teachers, and baby-sitters usually allow older preschoolers to lend a hand by helping cook now and then, much to the delight of the little child they care for! Here are a few quick foods to stir up with your child or to let him prepare by himself as you supervise.

- sandwich
- popcorn in a popper
- instant pudding
- toast with a topping (cinnamon and sugar, honey butter, peanut butter, jelly, or cream cheese)
- pancakes or waffles
- Jell-O made with ice cubes
- corn bread or corn pancakes
- biscuits baked in an electric skillet and flipped over to brown
- no-bake cookies (recipe below)

No-bake cookies

Mix together:
2 cups each peanut butter, honey, and powdered milk
Add:
1 cup each uncooked oatmeal and raisins
Stir in:
½ cup finely crushed nuts, if you wish.

If your child is very active and you are using an electric appliance to cook any of these treats, place it inside a cardboard box cut to the same height for a protective buffer against inadvertent bumps and burns!

May I Take Your Order, Please?

Plan to eat a meal with your child at a fast-food restaurant during a time of day when there will not be too many customers present. Midafternoon would probably be a good choice.

Let your child be your waitress, placing your simple orders and bringing the food to the table when it is ready. If the food is packaged to go, it will be easier for your child to carry it to the table, and you will be able to take any leftover food home. Ask your child to lead in prayer for the good lunch!

A Medal of Honor

Make a blue-ribbon medal to give your child for an accomplishment or for especially good behavior. Cut the round or star-shaped "medal" from lightweight cardboard and cover it with foil. Attach a short ribbon with glue, and tape or pin it to her shirt. If you let your child wear her shiny medal to the store or library, she will receive reinforcement for her good behavior from total strangers!

Let Us Make an Announcement!

Make a simple sign to place in your front yard or to tape to your garage door that reads something like this: Bobby Brown Lives Here, and We Are Very PROUD of Him!

Good-Job Trophy

For a long-term project over the summer or for an especially significant achievement by your child, order a small trophy especially for her. Most communities have trophy shops. The cost can be quite minimal, but the effect will be delightful to your child. Include the message you wish and present the trophy to your child with much fanfare. Inform your little child that she is *your* "trophy" from God!

Teacher for the Day

Let your child instruct you regarding the proper way to do something. Follow his instructions, asking questions such as, "Is this right, Son?" "Shall I do this first?"

You will, of course, feign ignorance a bit, but do not actually say that you do not know how to do something when you do! Let your child simply enjoy the role reversal that places him in the position of instructor!

I'm His Little Lamb

Preschoolers are notorious literalists. Words and terms mean exactly what they say to a young child. We often inadvertently confuse little ones with verbal expressions that seem to mean something else.

Much of the symbolism in the Bible may be reserved for later teaching, but your child can easily understand the parable of the Good Shepherd and its application, with Jesus as Shepherd and your child as his little lamb (see John 10:11). A four- or five-year old child loves to pretend she is some other creature, which makes this Bible parable just right.

Talk with her about the love and good care the Shepherd gave the lamb in the story. Relate that care to the manner in which Jesus cares for his little lambs. Remind your child that the Shepherd is much wiser and stronger than his little lamb so that he can love it, take care of it, and keep it safe and happy! If your child wants to, act out the story, with you as the Good Shepherd and your child as the lamb. Give her lots of hugs and good care!

I'm a King's Kid

Another biblical symbol that children can grasp is the symbolism of Jesus as King and his children as King's kids, or princes and princesses. (See Rev. 19:16, Rev. 20:7.) Tell your little child that when we belong to Jesus, we are his very own, very special children, He is the King of kings, and he very kindly lets us be his little prince [or princess]. Play prince [or princess] with your child.

If you feel the timing is appropriate, set the stage for your older preschool child's decision to "belong to the King." Tell him that King Jesus wants each of us to choose to become his child and that some time Jesus will gently call to each child's heart.

It's My Birthday!

Use fine dishes and silverware for a special birthday breakfast. Put one small candle in the middle of a piece of toast or a muffin, light the candle, and sing to the child or draw a heart or smiley face on the bread with a knife before toasting it. Share a special prayer of thanks for the child's growth and gifts.

Make a Circle

Place a plastic cup and a small box or block on a large piece of paper. Ask your child to trace around the shapes with a finger, then with a pencil or a crayon. Talk about the circle and square that she drew and ask how they are different.

Tell your child that God has given her a good mind to think with and that you would like her to think of what she could draw using the circle or the square. Ask her where she could put the circle in order to make the square turn into a wagon. (The circle could become a wheel on the side of the wagon.) Ask her to make a T-shaped handle for the wagon.

Your child's fine motor skills are being refined as she draws, and her confidence in her own manual ability is also growing.

Jesus Loves Me!

Tell your child the story of Jesus receiving the children from Luke 18:15–17, when he said, "Let the little children come to me." Cut around a photograph of your child standing; help him draw simple pictures of several children on a piece of paper, and let him glue his photograph in the crowd of children.

Cut out a picture of Jesus from a Sunday school leaflet or draw a simple representation of him. Let your child paste it opposite the pictures of the children. Help your child draw a colored path in between for the children to go to Jesus. Ask your child what he will do when he reaches Jesus, and talk about the truth that someday we will see Jesus just as the little children did in Bible days! Tell your child that the Bible says when we see Jesus we will bow down before him because he is our Lord as well as our friend (see Phil. 2:10–11).

Bible Helpers

Tell the story of Naaman from 2 Kings: 5. Emphasize the fact that a little child was able to help because she loved God, believed in God's mighty power, and was willing to tell somebody about what he can do!

Tell your child that she reminds you of the little girl in the story because she loves God, she believes in his mighty power, and she is a wonderful help to you! (This might be a good time to let her help you do something!)

Joining Things Together

In the sections of an egg carton, place a variety of objects such as the following:

- rubber bands
- string
- pipe cleaners
- paper clips
- transparent tape
- round binder rings
- cardboard circles

Ask your child to join together as many things as he can. Remark to your child that God gave him a good mind to think of ways to join things together. Even better than that, he joined your heart and his heart together in *love!*

You're My Jewel

Preschool children usually love rhinestone jewels. Collect plastic or rhinestone jewelry (perhaps from garage sales or craft shops), or cut out pictures of jewels and set them aside in a small box for a time when you want to give a special love message to your child. On one large cutout or drawing of a jewel, glue your child's picture. Place it under the other jewels.

Tell your child that you have a box of jewels to show her and that one jewel is the most precious of all to you! Let her open the box. Hug her when she happily discovers the *real* jewel!

Chapter 3

Introducing Your Child to Happiness

A cheerful heart is good medicine.
—Proverbs 17:22

A positive, optimistic approach to life is one of the greatest gifts we can give to our child. It will enhance every day that he lives and carry him through the inevitable hard times.

A happy spirit will make it possible for her to recover from all sorts of disappointments and discouragements. It will enable her to enjoy the simple pleasures and events of life and surround her with a circle of devoted friends.

However, helping to instill a positive attitude within our child involves more than keeping him in a consistently positive state of mind. To do so would soon become an impossible bondage for us. We could easily fall into the trap of placating his every unhappy moment, fulfilling his every whim, and softening his every disappointment with a material substitute simply to keep him "happy."

Coping with unpleasant experiences is an integral part of human existence. We cannot avoid them indefinitely, and we are better equipped to deal with life's negatives if we confront a few and adjust to them during our childhood.

To be sure, there are some babies who

seem to be born with a smile on their lips and giggle their way through childhood. Others, no less precious and suited for success in life, are simply more melancholy in their basic temperament.

Let us not make a hasty judgment regarding our child's disposition. It will go through numerous stages on her journey to maturity and happiness. However, our approach to her during her earliest years will determine, to a large degree, how much of this personal potential for happiness she will ever attain.

Parenting is a selfless task at times. Many a parent has smiled through tear-brimmed eyes or played a happy game with his child while bearing a crushing burden within. That is not to say we will never let our depression, apprehension, or negativism show to our small child. Of course we will at times, and he will survive quite well in spite of it.

However, we will find that the role of passing happiness on to our child is the very best therapy for us! As an added blessing, we may have the happiness returned someday when the child has become our own number-one cheer-giver.

God will comfort your own hurts as you endeavor to instill a positive, happy attitude in your child.

 # The Baby

We're Happy You're Ours!

From the very first time we hold our brand-new baby in our arms, we can convey the message, "We're happy you're ours!"

He does not yet understand the words, but he feels the touch and hears the kind voices and happy words and laughter as loved ones arrive to welcome him to his new world.

As the positive feelings continue to reach him after the happy earliest days stretch into months and then years (continuing even when he has later mastered the art of crying or being extraordinarily irritable!), he will generally adopt a happy attitude as his own.

Our parenting duties are performed on a daily basis; much of what we do for our child quickly falls into a pattern, a routine. Babies thrive on predictability.

In the midst of day-to-day experience our child turns from baby into toddler and toddler into young child. Because that is true, each happy day is important. We are not just passing time until he is finally old enough for preschool or school! We are shaping, molding, conditioning, and programming him every single day.

Happy Good Day

Using the tune of the familiar birthday song, sing to your baby:

Happy good day to you,
Happy good day to you,
Happy good day, dear Krista,
Happy good day, to *you!* [*gently touch the baby on the tummy*]

Talk Happy

A baby loves the sound of a voice, especially one that is becoming familiar to her. In addition, hearing us talk is necessary for mental, auditory, and verbal development and builds within her a strong silent vocabulary from which she can draw when she begins to speak.

Say directly to your child (in a gentle, lighthearted manner) as she is cuddled contentedly on your lap or on her back in her bed:

"I'm so *happy* you're right here with me, Sarah. Your face makes me happy. Your bright little eyes make me happy. The way you kick your tiny feet makes me happy. I'm so HAPPY you're my own precious baby!"

Be Happy to Music

Borrow from the library or purchase a record of happy, lively music (Christian tapes, classical, or children's music). Gently sway, bounce, or march to the music, with lots of smiles and expressions of fun and love. (My own children still love to hear *The Nutcracker Suite* that we enjoyed together when they were very young!)

Happy Face

Many newborn babies spend several hours each day awake. Instead of providing the side of his wicker bassinet as his primary view during his early weeks and months, place a picture of a smiling face there for him to see. His efforts to focus will strengthen his eye muscles, enhance his developing awareness of the world around him, and provide a friendly "companion" to see.

Glue the picture on a piece of cardboard, round the corners slightly, and later cover with clear adhesive paper when he begins to handle objects. Lay the picture on its side so that it is right side up to the baby as he looks at it, changing to a new picture from time to time. Place the picture on the opposite side of the crib occasionally to strengthen both sides of your child's neck. Eventually add faces of friendly animals to his gallery of pictures.

Happy Rhymes

Try these little simple nursery games, or custom-make your own to fit your sweet baby. Remember, baby doesn't care that we are not all poet laureates!

Clap your baby's hands gently together, as in the pat-a-cake game, and say:

Happy one,
Happy two,
Happy me,
Happy you! [*point to baby's tummy*]

Mommy's happy,
Baby's happy.
Jesus makes us
HAP-PY!

I feel good
'cause you're with me. [*point to baby, then to self*]
We're as happy [*clap your hands, or baby's, together in time*]
As can BE! [*throw arms outward*]

When baby is crying, softly say to her as you rock her in your arms:

You're my baby.
I'm *so* glad.
Baby, darling, don't be sad.

I love you when you're happy.
I love you when you're sad.
I love you, darling, all the time,
So let's be GLAD!

Happy Sounds

Make a simple tape recording of happy, pleasant sounds to play for your baby. You may use:

- pleasant music
- a gentle, cheerful voice—preferably your own, or the voices of several family members reciting nursery rhymes
- a loving voice reciting praise Scriptures (Your baby does not understand the words or concepts of traditional nursery rhymes, yet we do not hesitate to recite them to him from his early days. We need not fear that Scripture vocabulary is inappropriate for a baby; eventually the blessed words will take on meaning to him. For now, the sound of the words and the love they convey are sufficient.)

- running or splashing water
- the rhythmic ticking of a clock
- the gentle purring of the family cat or the song of a bird outside
- a music box
- voices of happy children at play
- music recorded from a church worship service
- the sound of a fan or a gentle rain or whatever you feel would make your baby's new world of sound a pleasant place to be

Happy House Tour

Take your baby on a happy tour of your home. Show him objects, lights, decorations, or pictures that make your life more enjoyable. As you approach each object, hold the baby in your arms or on your shoulder so that he can see well. Remember that a baby who is less than four months old sees best at a distance of eight to twelve inches.

Make comments such as this: "This is a light. The light helps to make our home happy and bright. Thank you, God, for the light!"

When showing a picture of a family member say, "Grandma makes us happy. Thank you, God, for Grandma!"

Conclude your tour by stating, "This is a happy, happy house!"

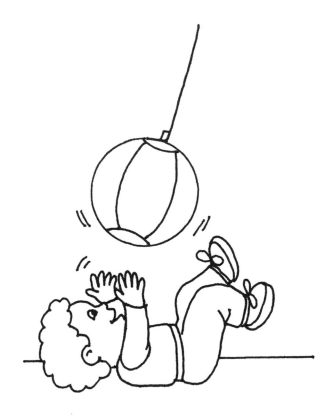

Watch the Bouncing Ball

Attach a long piece of string to the air valve of an inflated beach ball. Tie the other end of the string to a sturdy ceiling fan blade or light fixture. Position the ball to hang low enough for baby to touch, if you desire, or high enough for her simply to watch. Occasionally set the ball swinging slightly to interest and delight your baby. If she is old enough to sit alone near the ball or crawl, do not leave her unattended as she plays with it.

Talk lovingly about how happy you are that God gave her eyes to see the pretty ball. Tell her how delighted you are to have her for your baby!

The Toddler

Take a Happy Walk

On a sunny day, or on a warm rainy day under an umbrella, take a walk with your child around your neighborhood or your own yard. As you point out trees, birds, animals, houses, vehicles, or anything of interest, say something similar to this: "I'm so happy God gave us trees. Trees help to make us happy."

End the walk with a big hug, saying, "I'm so happy God gave me *you. You* make me happy!"

Happy Pictures

Keep a box of pictures of happy people and lovable animals. Round the corners of the pictures, mount them on cardboard, and cover them with clear adhesive paper. Take them out one by one as you say to your child, "Here's a happy boy. Here's a happy kitty."

When you get to the end of the picture supply, show him his reflection in a mirror or his picture and simply point and enthusiastically say to him, "And here's a happy Jason!"

The pictures also may be used for pointing out parts of the face in your other conversations with your child.

Sing a Happy Tune

Sing these songs especially when the child is not really happy.

To the tune of "If You're Happy and You Know It":

> Oh, be happy, little face,
> Give a smile.
> Oh, be happy, little face,
> Give a smile.
> Oh, be happy, little face,
> Just be happy, little face,
> Please be happy, little face,
> Give a smile!

To the tune of "Did You Ever See a Lassie?":

> Did you ever hear a giggle,
> A giggle, a giggle?
> Did you ever hear a giggle,
> A giggle from you?
>
> If I put my fingers here,
> They start to wig-gle,
> And you'll surely hear a giggle . . .
> So giggle with me!

To the tune of "Farmer in the Dell!" [*clap and sing*]:

> I'm happy, you can see,
> As happy as can be!
> Jesus makes me very glad,
> And happy as can be!

Happy Prayer Songs

These may be sung to your child at happy times or as an end-of-day prayer song.

To the tune of "Row, Row, Row Your Boat":

> Joy, joy in my heart,
> Jesus makes me glad.
> Thank you, God, for giving me
> All the fun I've had.

To the tune of "Camptown Races":

> Jesus gives me lots of joy.
> Thank you, thank you!
> Jesus gives me lots of joy.
> Oh, thank you, Lord!

Make a Joyful Noise

Use pans, spoons, lids, and other utensils to have a kitchen band with your toddler.

Say, "Jesus makes us happy . . . so let's make *music!*" With older toddlers say, "In the Bible we read that happy people sometimes played drums, blew horns, or marched to show God that they were happy . . . and we can, too!"

Listen to Happy Sounds

Tape-record family members greeting your child with brief messages such as, "Hi, Davey. This is Daddy. I love you. Have a happy day."

Between messages, include other happy sounds your child often hears . . . a sibling playing a piano tune, a family pet, a musical toy, a chiming clock, a music box, running bath water, computer sounds, or such.

To make such a recording is simple and involves only a little time. And your toddler will enjoy the familiar, pleasant sounds.

Conclude this time with your toddler by saying, "Weren't those *happy* sounds, Christopher? Thank you, God, for happy sounds to hear!"

Happy Book

Take a close-up picture of each member of your family, making sure each has a big smile on his or her face. Be sure to ask Grandma and Grandpa to send a picture, too! Or take a picture of each family member looking at your child and smiling happily at him.

Mount the pictures in a cloth book sewn together by a line of stitching down the middle of the album or place them in resealable plastic bags and sew the edges that open together to form a waterproof book. As you look at the book with your child, say, "How happy we are that God put Eric in our family!"

Happy Box

Make a tunnel by folding in or cutting off the ends of a large box that is two or three feet deep. When you are finished, set the box on its side and encourage the toddler to peek in one end. At the same time, peek at her from the other end and say, "I see you, *happy* girl!"

If she crawls through the box, say the words when she gets close to you as a gentle surprise. But don't be sudden or loud enough to startle. When her interest has waned and you put the box away, say, "We can be happy and laugh together!"

Take a Smile out of the Box

Draw a simple face on a round piece of flannel mounted on cardboard, but do not draw the mouth. Stand the face up on the couch or a chair. Let the child select a mouth from a box of construction paper mouths you have already prepared with small pieces of flannel backing on each. Repeat this game with other mouths.

If you wish, you may leave the flannel face entirely blank and let the child put on the eyes, nose, mouth, ears, and hair.

Happy Friend

Use a sock for a hand puppet. You may color on eyes if you wish, but that is not necessary. Make the puppet tell your child, "I'm here to help you be happy. I can jump up and down. I can do tricks! (Make the puppet stand on its head, make it show funny expressions, etc.) I can go away and come back! Hi, happy girl [or boy]!"

Happycise

Do these happy exercises with your child to any lively music. It is not necessary to keep time—simply create a lively atmosphere. You may choose to use no music at all.

Give these instructions:
- Make yourself as *wide* as you can! [*arms, fingers and legs outstretched*]
- Make yourself real, real *skinny*! [*arms down at your sides, feet and legs together*]
- Make yourself real, real *tall*! [*hands and fingers reaching up, standing on tiptoes*]

Repeat these instructions if your child continues to be interested. Say, "Exercise is fun!" The child will obviously enjoy your enthusiastic company!

The Smile in My Pocket

Tell your child, "I have a smile in my pocket! Watch me put it on." Pretend to take the smile out, place it in the palm of your hand if you wish, cup hand over your mouth, and come out smiling—or put your smile on directly from your pocket!

Happy Hoop

Purchase a large inexpensive embroidery hoop. Use it to roll across the room to your toddler. Although he will probably not be able to roll it himself, he will enjoy trying to catch it and bring it back to you for more.

Or you may use it flat on the floor as a "fence" to place small toys in. As your toddler begins to pretend, the hoop may become an animal trainer's ring, or a corral.

 # Ages Two to Three

Make a Happy Face

Help your child draw a happy face using your choice of the following:
- Cornmeal in a round pie pan
- Shaving cream on the kitchen table or on a large tray for easy cleanup
- Liquid starch or liquid detergent combined with tempera paint and applied to paper
- Hand lotion spread on a table top or tray
- White glue "drawn" on a paper and sprinkled with sand, cornmeal or salt
- Chalk on a sidewalk
- A steamy bathroom mirror or window

Small happy faces may be drawn, cut out with your help, and attached with tape to mirrors or over doorknobs as happy greetings to Daddy or Mommy or the child's brother or sister.

Smile Day

Tell your child early in the morning that today will be a smile day. That will mean that each time someone looks at either of you, you will smile. Explain to your child that a smile is "catching" and that to share it may make someone else happy.

Happy Hearts

Make heart shapes from Styrofoam, sponges, or wood, if there is a carpenter in your family. Experiment with your child to see what interesting designs can be made by arranging the hearts on the floor.

You can make flowers, chains, pyramids, or geometric shapes as you arrange the hearts. Your child's creativity will be encouraged, and you will have a perfect opportunity to tell him that hearts mean love and how very dearly God and you love *him!*

Merry Heart Medicine

Teach your child the Bible verse from Proverbs 17:22, "A cheerful heart is good medicine."

Play like your child (or her stuffed animal) is visiting the doctor because the patient is so sad. "Dr. Jolly" smiles, pats, musses her hair, tickles her tummy a bit, and prescribes "giggle pills." Use a container that does *not* look like a pill bottle and fill it with raisins, fruit bits, cut-up carrots or celery, or whatever you wish to use for "medicine." You may want to stress to your child that she must *never* get real medicine by herself—*only* from Mommy or Daddy, a trusted baby-sitter, or whomever you specify to your child.

Dr. Jolly then shows the child how the pills work by eating one himself and beginning to giggle. The child is encouraged to take a "giggle pill" and to enjoy a good giggle. Even if it may be a forced laugh at first, it is likely to soon become the real thing!

Create a Face

Give your child a round cracker or cookie and your choice of topping such as butter, cream cheese, cheese spread, mayonnaise, peanut butter, butter and honey, or frosting.

Provide for the child raisins, bits of dried fruit, dry cereal pieces, chocolate chips, cut-up carrots and celery, popcorn, or peanuts (if your child is old enough to chew them well). Encourage him to spread the topping on with a blunt knife or wooden Popsicle stick, and add what he wishes to make a happy face. Coconut, alfalfa sprouts, or parsley make good "hair."

You may need to coach him to include eyes, nose, mouth, ears, or any extra features you desire. Say, "*God* gives Larry his happy face, and now you've given a happy face to your cracker!"

Mr. Happy Potato

Make a happy face using a raw potato with one end slightly cut off to make a flat base for it to stand on. Use cloves, bits cut from straws, small hard candies, or whatever your imagination dictates to make Mr. Potato's smiling face!

Happy Toast

With a sharp knife, cut a happy face shape on a piece of bread. Toast the bread and let the smiling face wish your child a happy day!

Let's Have a Happy Day

Make a round happy face from construction paper and attach it to the refrigerator door with magnets.

If your child is in an unhappy mood, put the paper face upside down. Help her to cheer up as her morning progresses, and as she does, turn the upside-down face slightly toward an upright position and leave it there. Each time the child shows improvement in her mood, turn the happy face picture slightly until it is right side up—and so is her day!

If your child is habitually melancholy, check to see that her health is good, that her physical and emotional needs are being met. If you believe that she has simply developed an unpleasant habit of negativism or is using her moodiness to get undue attention, try meeting her needs by offering her a simple reward for a good disposition and happy behavior. The reward may be a smiling sticker on a small paper card, a small toy or sugarfree gum from a goody jar, or perhaps an activity or outing that she would enjoy.

Happy Handshakes

Put on a cap or hat and introduce yourself to your child. Shake his hand and say (very enthusiastically):

Hi! I'm Mr. Happy!
My hands are happy. [*shake them*]
My feet are happy. [*point to them*]
My face is happy. [*smile*]
My toes are happy. [*tap them*]
What's happy about YOU? [*encourage the child to answer*]

Happy Hi

Cover your child with a sheet or afghan as she crouches on hands and knees on the floor. Say this little happy rhyme to her:

Raindrops, [*tap your fingers on her back like rain is falling*]
Sunshine, [*rub her back in circular motions*]
Big blue sky. [*gently pound on her back with a fist three times as you say the words*]
If you hear me,
Just say Hi!

The child will respond with a Hi! Repeat the game and trade places when the child has learned the rhyme.

Happy Day Express Train

Line up kitchen chairs behind each other to become a train, with your child as the engineer. Become a passenger behind him, along with siblings, neighbors, or favorite stuffed animals.

As the train goes down the "track," make chugging motions with your arms to represent the motion of the train wheels. Say these words slowly at first and then much more rapidly, representing the sound the Happy Day Express Train makes:

> Jesus, Jesus, Jesus, Jesus
> Jesus makes us happy,
> Happy, happy, happy [*repeat*]

Happy Rhymes

Do the appropriate actions for the following rhymes:

To the tune of "Row, Row, Row Your Boat":

> Hop, hop, happy hop,
> Hop along with me.
> It's such fun to hop and hop;
> Happy hop with me.
>
> Clap, clap, happy clap,
> Clap along with me.
> It's such fun to clap and clap;
> Happy clap with me.

March, march, merrily march,
March along with me.
It's such fun to march and march;
Merrily march with me.

Jump, jump, happy jump,
Happy jump with me.
It's such fun to jump and jump;
Happy jump with me.

Pray, pray, pray to God, [*fold hands*]
Pray along with me.
I'm so glad that we can pray;
Pray along with me. [*Say a brief prayer of thanks to God for our strong bodies and this happy day*]

Hug, hug, happy hug,
Hug along with me.
I'm so glad God made you mine,
Hugging happily.

Happy Helper

Encourage your child's help during the day with simple tasks that she can do. Explain to her that her help makes you happy and that it makes her happy, too.

Later in the day show her a box with a closed lid. Tell her that you have a helper in the box. Mention some of the tasks this helper willingly performed that day. Then say, "Let me show you this helper." Remove the box lid to reveal a mirror. Hold it up and say, "The helper is Toni! I'm very *proud* of her!"

Happy Handprints

Paint one or both of your child's hands with tempera paint. Show him how to press down on unrolled white paper, repeating the procedure again and again to make gift wrapping paper.

Handprints may also be placed above a tree trunk already drawn on the paper to form "leaves" on a tree. When dry, the picture may be taped to his door for an attractive addition to his room.

The child's handprint might also be used to decorate a card for someone, along with this little poem:

> Right now I'm little,
> My hands are small;
> But it will be no time at all
> 'Til childhood days
> Will all be past.
> This card may help
> The memory last.

The prints of your child's hands also may be made with acrylic paint and applied to an apron for Grandma or Mother. If acrylic paints are used, wash the child's hands immediately and blot the dried handprints with vinegar to set the print before washing the apron.

Following the String

Wind a piece of string or yarn through the rooms of your house for your child to follow on a treasure hunt. At the end of the string, place a happy face, a happy box containing fun items, or a page of colorful stickers for your child to enjoy.

This happy treasure hunt is an excellent activity for a baby-sitter to begin as soon as you leave the house. Tell the children they may have a treasure hunt as soon as you leave, and the baby-sitter and children may follow the string or the happy faces that you have placed in various rooms and numbered from one to five.

Happy Box

Collect a box of items that will make your child smile:

- a feather to gently tickle the child on chin or feet
- a funny picture (perhaps one taken of a family member, or one you drew)
- a funny noisemaker (duck call, birthday party blower, toy sound box imitating an animal's voice, waxed paper over a comb, etc.)
- a paper on which is written a funny joke on the child's level
- a silly puppet
- a funny-looking toy
- a funny hat, fake nose, or glasses

Use your imagination and what is handy at home, or check for items at costume shops or in discount stores during the month of October.

Take each item out and use it to promote smiles and laughs. Then say, "Isn't God *good* to us? He loves for us to smile and laugh!"

Happy Hats

Keep a collection of hats you have saved from your own outdated wardrobe, from Grandma's closet, garage sales, party shops, or some you have made or decorated together. All ages of preschoolers love to change their identity instantly by putting on a hat!

The Giggles

Grab every chance to really laugh with your child. If we look for the bright, humorous side to daily occurrences, we will usually find it—and enjoy it together.

Manufacture "giggle moments" with your child. It isn't necessary to tickle in order to giggle. Just make a funny face or silly word and say, "Let's laugh!" Or just start to laugh a phony, corny, childish sort of laugh that will soon turn into the real thing! (Did you ever notice how a young child who has just enjoyed a really hearty laugh tries so hard to fake it, making the laughter continue as it begins to fade away? All ages find a good laugh such fun and so refreshing!)

Happy Apples

Make happy-face apples by cutting a slice out of a red apple to form the mouth. Place whole cloves for eyes and nose or stick on raisins with peanut butter or cream cheese for the "glue" to hold them in place.

Spread a small amount of peanut butter or cream cheese in the mouth and let your child put marshmallow "teeth" in place. After the happy apple has shared its smile on the kitchen shelf for a while, tell your child it wants him to eat it and enjoy its good taste!

Thank God for yummy red apples!

 # Ages Four to Five

Happy Face Meal

On a roll of wide white paper (available at discount stores, restaurant supply stores or teachers' supply stores), let your child help you draw many happy faces. Use the happy paper for a tablecloth and invite a friend to join you or just enjoy a favorite meal or snack for the two of you.

For a breakfast happy meal serve hot cereal with a raisin, marshmallow, or chocolate chip happy face arranged on it and carve a heart on a slice of bread before toasting. For lunch, make heart-shaped sandwiches, or open-faced "happy-wiches" with features made of pickle slices, olives, alfalfa sprouts, or toppings of your choice placed over a favorite spread.

Talk about happy experiences you have had with your child at church or discuss upcoming trips and events. Don't forget to thank God for the happy times he lovingly allows us!

Happy Huddles

Football teams huddle together frequently to discuss immediate plans, promote unity, and rev each other up for the next play! Why not do the same for your children?

Frequently gather them together with the words, "Time for a huddle!" (or "Time for a cuddle huddle!"). With arms around one another's shoulders, say something like this: "OK, guys, . . . the sun is shining . . . we have food to eat and great toys to play with . . . and Jesus is our friend . . . so let's be happy and *play!*"

A little rough-and-tumble fun is certainly in order!

Happy Hammering

Provide a tree stump outside or a block of wood and large nails for your child to do some happy hammering. Position the nails in the features of a happy face, if you so desire.

Tell her how happy you are that God gave her strong hands to hammer, as you closely supervise her during this activity.

Happy Day Parade

Turn an ordinary day into a celebration—have a parade!

Attach streamers to tricycles and kiddie motorcycles. Tie toy trucks, skates, or even old kitchen pans to the vehicles and put stuffed animal passengers inside. Dress the passengers as much as you wish with paper hats, lace around their necks for collars, jewelry, construction paper crowns, or whatever your child's imagination suggests.

If the weather is bad outside, stage your parade in the garage or in a large inside room. Include lively background music or have a live marching band with kitchen instruments or hands cupped to represent imaginary horns.

Your parade can go down the street to the house of a friend who may wish to join the festivities. A delightful end to the procession could be at a shut-in neighbor's house for a cheery hello.

Happy Hunting

Stage a happy hunting treasure search, following numbered happy faces or smiles taped throughout the house or yard. You or your child may put the happy clues in consecutive order, and the successful treasure hunter will find a treat of some sort at the end of her search—or she may find a smiling brother or sister who enthusiastically shouts, "Have a happy day!"

Happy Hunting Grounds

Four- and five-year-olds love to pretend, and playing Indians has long been a favorite of children!

Pretend to be a family of Indians preparing to go hunting. You may wish to use only imaginary props; or you may dress up, make a teepee out of brooms and mops tied together by their handles and draped with a sheet, and build a "campfire" from twigs and red paper flames.

As a part of your Indian activity, let one child be a laughing hyena and the others be braves in a hunting party. Tell the hyena to stay hidden and to laugh at intervals so that the hunting party can locate him. When they do, encourage your squaws, braves, and hyena all to have a good laugh together!

Happy Hair Sculptures

In the bathtub or at the sink while washing your child's hair, let her make happy hair sculptures with her own hair or a brother's or sister's. Be sure to have a mirror nearby for viewing the masterpieces!

Few children can resist heartily laughing when they see the magnificent hair designs created with sudsy hair that stays right where it is swirled or twisted or smashed. No-tears shampoo is a must!

Exercise as You Sit

Say this simple rhyme as you sit with your child. Extend your arms out front, then touch your shoulders, out front, touch shoulders, and repeat until the rhyme is finished.

One-two, one-two,
Jesus, Jesus, I love you!

[*Next stretch your arms to the sides, touch shoulders, to the sides, touch shoulders, etc.*]

Three-four, three-four,
Jesus, yes, I love you more!

[*Now touch your shoulders and then reach straight up with your arms, touch shoulders, reach up, etc.*]

Five-six, five-six,
Jesus helps me when I'm sick.

[*Repeat the actions from the beginning.*]

Seven-eight, seven-eight,
Jesus, Jesus, you are *great!*

[*Repeat the arms stretched to the sides, touch the shoulders, and to conclude with an outstretched grand finale.*]

Nine-ten, nine-ten,
Jesus, Jesus, come again!

You may also play this game facing your child, clapping your palms against his and then clapping your hands together once, palms together, clap hands, and repeat until finished with the rhyme.

Happy Humming

Hum a familiar tune to your child and ask her to identify it. Hum or sing the tune together if you wish. If you alternate humming and guessing tunes with your child or if you hum several different tunes, conclude with a tune about Jesus. Remark how happy you are to know about Jesus!

Happy Tunes

To the tune of "Camptown Races":

> Jesus gives me lots of joy.
> Thank you, thank you.
> Jesus gives me lots of joy.
> Oh, thank you, Lord.
>
> Jesus puts a song in me.
> Tra la, tra la.
> Makes me happy as can be,
> Oh, happy day!

Happy Helper

Use this simple rhyme to make any helpful activity more fun:

> I'm happy when I'm helping.
> I'm happy when I'm good.
> I'm happy when I smile and share,
> And do the things I should.

Breakfast Kabob

A happy way to start a morning is with a breakfast kabob. This early-morning answer to a dinner shish kabob is sure to bring a smile to your child's face and increase his chances of eating a healthful breakfast.

On a skewer (with warnings to be careful of the sharp end and instructions not to put it in his mouth) or on an uncooked fettuccini noodle (or two of the uncooked noodles together for added strength), place grapes, cheese squares, round dry cereal pieces, bacon bites cooked in a ring shape, bites of toast or doughnut, apple, or other fruit, and whatever else you have handy for your child to eat.

Your child's happy day will begin with a smile and a nourishing breakfast!

Watch Happy Me!

Nothing is more delightful to a preschooler than seeing herself being funny! On those special occasions when you rent a video camera or at in-between times for no special reason, videotape your child performing her own brand of humorous activity.

Play her comedic monologue back for her thorough entertainment, but without an audience. Use props that will encourage playful creativity, and you may find that your just-for-fun tape turns out to be a real treasure!

Happy Fishermen

Tell your child this simple version of the Bible story of the fishermen and Jesus (see Luke 5:1–6):

Simon and his friends had been fishing from their boat all night long and had caught no fish at all.

The next day Jesus was talking to Simon, and he said, "Go out into the deep water and put your fishing nets back in the water."

Simon said to Jesus, "We've worked hard all night and haven't caught a single fish. . . . But because you told me to, I'll put my nets back in the water," and he did.

This time the nets were so full of fish that Simon called his friends to help him pull the heavy nets into the boat!

Talk about how fishermen in Bible days (and many even today) used nets rather than poles and hooks. Act out the Bible story with your child, using a cloth diaper or dish towel for the net and cardboard cutouts or sponge shapes for the fish.

Emphasize to your child that Jesus can make a happy day out of a sad one, and he can put smiles on gloomy faces!

Happy Surprise Trip

Wake your child with the good news that today you are taking him on a surprise trip just because he is so precious to you! Do not tell him the night before, nor make him wait too late in the day before you go.

The trip can be a breakfast at a favorite restaurant, a playground, a picnic, a museum, a petting zoo, or something similar. Take advantage of places or events of special interest in your town.

Know Why I Am Happy?

This is an especially good game to play in the car or while waiting your turn for an appointment.

Alternate taking turns giving one reason why you are happy: "I'm happy because the sun is shining" or "I'm happy because the rain is giving a drink to the plants and animals."

If you are home or somewhere with plenty of room, play the game like charades and act out what makes you happy. Some good ideas would be a hug, the falling rain, the birds flying and singing, a small kitten, your friendly puppy, drawing a picture, playing ball, or going to church.

Color Me Happy

As an alternative to telling or acting out what makes you happy, take turns with your child drawing a simple picture of something you enjoy. If you do not have drawing paper on hand, cut open an empty grocery bag to use for your art work.

If you wish to save the happy drawings as a later reminder of happy day fun, staple the papers together or punch holes and tie them together with string on the side or top to form a what-makes-me-happy book.

Happy Secret

If you have several children, play this game like the whispering game, Telephone. Whisper something happy in one child's ear and let her whisper it to another child, who says the happy statement aloud. Alternate whispering happy statements to one another. The closeness with your child is as good as a hug!

I Love Everybody in This House

This happy little tradition can accomplish a great deal in five seconds.

Someone in the family who suddenly feels a surge of loving emotions toward the dear ones God has placed in his home says loudly and rapidly, "I love everyone in this house!" The other family members try to be the first to repeat his words, "I love everyone in this house!"

Everyone is a winner in this love contest, and many a smile will be shared through the years each time those words are spoken.

Happy Toe Touch

Do a simple stand-up-touch-toes exercise with your child as you say this simple rhyme:

One-two, three-four,
Jesus knocking at the door.
Five-six, seven-eight,
Let him in and do not wait!
Nine-ten [shout] Let him in!

Cup your hands around your mouth like a megaphone as you shout the last three words.

PART TWO

Introducing Your Child to Godly Relationships

Chapter 4 _____

Introducing Your Child to Kindness

Be kind and compassionate to one another.
—Ephesians 4:32

A very small child thrives in the care of a parent or grandparent who speaks to him lovingly, holds him tenderly, and demonstrates kindness in daily life. He may not yet understand the concepts at work, but he responds to them. As this fortunate child grows and develops, he will begin to emulate those qualities.

However, a wise parent must also correct the tendencies toward unkindness and a lack of consideration for others that will inevitably arise within a child. Our positive example will never be all that is necessary to instill kindness in our children, but it will help immensely.

Studies show that children retain 10 percent of what they hear, 50 percent of what they see, and 90 percent of what they *do*. As a child learns to show kindness toward other people, she will begin to understand the true meaning of living the Christian faith and message in daily experience. Even little children delight in doing good to other people. What little child does not love to bring a flower to Mother or Daddy, repeating this kind gesture countless times during her early years? Why? Because she feels *good* when she is kind! A brief trip to visit an elderly friend, a sick neighbor, or a family with a new baby can be a much more effective way to teach our child the scriptural principle of kindness than many lectures on the subject.

Kindness assumes many forms. It manifests itself as helpfulness, compassion, good manners, polite words, and concern for people who are elderly, have handicaps, or are ill. Kindness extends to people of other nationalities, to neighbors, to grandparents, to people in financial need, and even to the natural world of plants and animals. A kind child experiences the additional benefit of enhanced self-worth and the good feeling that comes from giving of oneself, whether two years of age or ninety!

Jesus Christ personified kindness. His was the *ultimate* tender touch, kind word, loving look, and helping hand. His whole life centered on manifesting God's infinite love in the human realm of needy, hurting, suffering people. We cannot properly introduce our child to God without revealing the matchless compassion God has for every human being and without impressing upon our child the truth that it pleases God for us to be Christlike in kindness, as well.

As you incorporate some of the following suggestions into your child's daily life, remember what God is like toward us: "For he is gracious and compassionate, slow to anger and *abounding in love*" (Joel 2:13, emphasis added).

 # The Baby

Please Handle with Care

A baby is born with no innate awareness of the people around him. He first must begin to realize that other people do exist, that they are separate entities from him, and eventually, that those other people have feelings and needs as he does. The baby's transition from his totally egocentric world to one in which he recognizes the needs of other people and tries to meet them with consideration and kindness is a *big* step!

Since a young baby is unable consciously to relate to people in a kind manner, the way he is handled and cared for will largely determine how he later treats those around him. He will not recall, "My daddy was kind and gentle to me as a baby, so I'll be that way to you," but those positive qualities are being etched in his little subconscious mind.

Your kind interactions with your spouse and other people will determine much about how kind your child becomes. But even before that time, he will be absorbing your messages of love and kindness. None of your parental kindness care is in vain!

Kindness Is Familiarity

A baby is fascinated by every new sight and sound, but familiar experiences are the foundation for her developing memory. Her mother's and father's faces, voices and smells, the sound of running water at bath time, the telephone's ring, and the barking of the family dog all soon become a part of her everyday world and help to make her feel secure.

We may encourage this sense of well-being in our baby by making sure that some aspects of her life are the same from day to day. Do not constantly change the toys surrounding her in bed, the crib mobile above her, the pictures on the wall, or the furniture arrangement in the room. Establish as much routine as possible, and use the same phrase each time you describe an activity. Begin bedtime traditions when your child is still a baby—the approximate time she goes to sleep and the activities that precede bedtime. Include soft music and a very simple bedtime story, if you wish.

Introduce changes and new routines gradually, giving your baby plenty of time to enjoy the security of the familiar before you try something new.

Kindness Is a Quiet Time

Babies need times of solitude, just as we all do at any age. Since many of baby's waking moments are spent being bounced, jiggled, coaxed, patted, and played with, she simply needs times of stillness and quiet. Many times we bounce and vigorously rock our crying baby in an effort to quiet her. And as she increases her vocal intensity, we increase the speed and vigor of our bouncing—an uncomfortable combination we might not enjoy if we were in baby's tiny shoes.

Our homes are full of loud, continuous noises. Air conditioners, central heating blowers, refrigerators, fans, televisions, radios, stereos, hair dryers, telephones, doorbells, and dozens of other sounds fill a baby's day. When the electricity suddenly goes off, we are acutely aware of the unusual quiet.

Sometimes our babies deserve to hear no talk, no music, no electrical motors—just stillness. Too much play and noise will make her tense, or she may later feel the need for constant amusement when we would love for her to play quietly by herself.

Kindness Is Letting Me Crawl

A baby's great curiosity soon creates in him the need to be mobile and to explore his fascinating new world. When he becomes a skilled traveler, provide crawl-through places and tunnels for him. Open-ended cardboard boxes and sheets draped over back-to-back chairs are interesting additions to his world. Get on the other end and encourage him to crawl to you. Praise and cheer him when he does!

Show your baby how to push a toy car through an open-ended round or square box. Show him that the car can go in, be hidden for a moment, and then magically reappear!

Kindness Is My Surprise Bag

Make a simple drawstring bag from an old pillowcase by cutting two slits close together at the hemmed end of the pillowcase. Thread a cord in one slit, through the hem tunnel, and out the other slit, and then tie the ends together. If you do not have an extra pillowcase, use any bag or basket that can be closed to conceal its contents.

Each night without your baby's seeing you, place in the bag an interesting toy, stuffed animal, childproof plastic jar containing beans or macaroni to shake (double-check the lid for safety, and do not leave the baby unattended as she plays with the shaker), a book, a laminated picture of a family member or pet, a round plastic mirror, or something of similar interest to your baby.

Place the bag beside your baby's bed, and as you greet her in the morning, change her diaper, and welcome her warmly to the new day, say, "What's in your bag, Sara?" Place her close to the bag as you open it and enjoy the object together. You will be helping to develop her memory skills and demonstrating kindness as you provide nice surprises for her within the secure structure of a familiar daily routine.

Pat-a-Kind

Play this game as you would pat-a-cake with your child, substituting these words for the more familiar ones:

> Be ye kind,
> One to another,
> Kind to your sister,
> Kind to your brother.
>
> Be ye kind,
> One to another,
> Kind to your daddy,
> Kind to your mother!

Kindness Is Finding a Surprise!

For an activity your older baby will enjoy, crumple up white paper or paper towels or a lightweight bath towel in a bucket. Hide a ball or small toy in it as he watches. Say to your baby, "Be kind and find the ball for Mommy."

Play the game several times if he seems interested, and then be kind enough to let him continue to play with the ball on his own.

The Toddler

Speak Kindly to Me, Please

Sometimes we bemoan the fact that our children seem unable to remember statements of common courtesy such as please and thank you, but we fail to notice how we speak to them:

"Sit down!"

"Get over here!"

"Be quiet! Hush!"

"Put that down!"

"No! Don't touch that!"

Little has as much effect on our child's spoken manners as our own patterns of kind and polite talk. If we speak to her from her early days as a treasured friend, being kind but firm when necessary, she will very likely mimic our example with occasional reminders.

When we must speak firmly to our child, our tendency is to make our voice louder for emphasis. However, our words are often more effective if spoken quietly, firmly, close to her face, and with direct eye contact, than if they are yelled from across the room. It necessitates a little more legwork, but a kind, cooperative child is worth the effort!

Puppy Care

With a stuffed animal and empty plastic dishes, pretend that your child is caring for a pet. Talk with your toddler about an animal's need for food, water, bathing, brushing, affection, and a place to sleep.

Tell your toddler that God "said" in the Bible that boys and girls and mommies and daddies are supposed to take care of animals and be kind to them (see Gen. 1).

Kindness Toss

With a large rubber ball or beanbag, play a game of catch with your child or grandchild. Use this common activity for an opportunity to teach your child to be kind.

Make comments like these: "Be kind and throw the ball gently, Bret. If you throw it too hard, I might not catch it." Praise him for his good throwing and catching and tell him that you like to play with him because he is *kind* to you.

Return the Kindness, Please

While sitting near your toddler, tell her that you are going to do some kind things to her and you want her to do the same kind things to you.

Pat your toddler's face gently and say, "Now you pat Mommy's face, Dawn." Next, kiss your toddler's hand and say, "Now you kiss *my* hand, Dawn," and extend your hand toward her. Clap your hands and say, "I'm clapping my hands for you, Dawn. Now you clap your hands for me, please." As you give her a hug, say, "I'm giving you a big hug, Dawn. Will you please hug me back?"

As you conclude the game, say, "Do you know why I want to be kind to you, Dawn? Because I *love* you!"

Be Kind to Plants

Let your eager little toddler help you water indoor plants or those in your yard. Tell your child that God is pleased when we take good care of the beautiful flowers and plants he has made. With a big hug, let your child know that the most *wonderful* thing that God has made is *Katie!*

Handy the Puppet

Use a sock or mitten for a hand puppet. You may add button eyes and other features if you wish, but they are not necessary. Give the puppet a voice and a personality and make it do a whole variety of kind things to your child.

Say things like, "Oh, oh, your hair is a little messed up. May I smooth it for you, please?" or "You must be hungry. Here's a cracker for you." Make the puppet say to your child, "God says, 'Be kind . . . to one another.' Would you be kind and hug me, please?" (Put your hand and puppet near the child's neck where a hug comes naturally!)

You May Sit in My Chair

Make believe that you and your child are caring for a teddy bear. Put him in the high chair, let your child bring him a plastic bowl and cup of food and drink, and be sure to fold his paws and lead him to pray before eating. Ask the teddy bear if there is anything else kind that you can do for him.

Tell your little boy or girl that you both are being kind to the teddy bear because you *love* him and because God wants you to be kind.

Share the Ball, Please

Have your children sit on the floor in a circle with their legs spread apart and feet touching the others. Say to them, "We have only one ball. Everyone can play and have fun if we share! I will share the ball with Jeffrey." (Roll it to him.)

Jeffrey then rolls the ball to another child, and as the game proceeds say, "Jeffrey shared the ball with Lindsey. Now Lindsey is sharing the ball with Mommy. Jesus is pleased when we share!"

Kindness Is a Morning Surprise

Babies and young toddlers need routine and familiarity, but by the time your child nears his second birthday, he also begins to enjoy the element of surprise in his life now and then. Pleasant and unexpected experiences stimulate his budding imagination and make his day more fun!

Frequently after your toddler is asleep at night, set up a play scene for your child to enjoy as soon as he awakes in the morning. It may be a large empty box or laundry basket, or it may be a road drawn on a piece of poster board or a cloth that has been taped to the floor with toy cars parked nearby. It may be a stack of small boxes with a toy standing at the top, a plastic tea set all arranged, or a tunnel made from a blanket draped over two chair backs.

Vary the scene often, and your child will begin to anticipate the fun that awaits him as he awakens. Greet him with a paraphrase of the wonderful Bible verse: "This is the day the Lord has made, Tyler . . . let's enjoy it together" (see Ps. 118:24).

Kind Care for Baby Doll

When you show your toddler how to care for a baby doll gently, he will be more likely to treat a real baby with tenderness. However, he is little more than a baby himself and will have to be supervised carefully when he is with a younger child.

Make his doll's bed from a round oatmeal box, cut in half lengthwise. Glue the lid on one end to form a headboard. If you wish, let your toddler decorate the bed by coloring its sides or attaching stickers. Show your child how to place a hand towel or handkerchief inside the bed for a blanket. Use a small doll or stuffed animal for the baby, and help your toddler give it good care!

As you demonstrate kind care, sing this little song to the tune of "London Bridge."

Jesus wants me to be kind,
To be kind, to be kind.
Jesus wants me to be kind,
I'll be kind to Baby.

Be-Kind-to-Family Book

Enlarge snapshots of the faces of family members and put them in a small photo album for your toddler to keep in her room. Look at the album with your child, talking about each person, patting his picture and remarking that "we want to love and to be kind to one another because Jesus tells us to! It makes Jesus happy when we are kind." (Make sure the photographs are protected by plastic covers in the album.)

God Is So Kind

When it is raining, and especially if your child is apprehensive or unhappy about the weather, hold him where he can see the falling rain and lovingly talk about God's kindness to the plants, the animals, the farmers, and *us!* Tell him that we do not have enough water to give everything, so God helps us by sending the rain we need. You may want to use Acts 14:17, "He has shown kindness by giving you rain from heaven."

The early positive impressions we leave with our child may help make a difference whether he later enjoys or dreads rainy days.

Ages Two to Three

Our child's needs and demands often seem trivial in the light of our own heavy adult cares. But a tiny bump on the head, a dot of blood on her scraped knee, a broken toy, a ball that cannot be found, or an unexplained shadow on her wall are vitally real to her. It is kind of us to show her genuine concern and helpfulness; our actions demonstrate to her a minipicture of the compassion of a great God who condescends to meet the needs of finite humanity. Our kindness, too, will better equip our child to become a compassionate, caring person. "Whoever welcomes one of these little children in my name welcomes me" (Mark 9:37).

Flower for a Friend

Paint a clean flowerpot with colorful acrylic or enamel paint before your child begins his part of the project.

When the flowerpot is dry, provide a small container of white glue and a paint brush or several cotton swabs for your child to paint small sections with the glue. Then let your child stick on beads, bits of rickrack or lace, buttons, sequins, or yarn strips. Continue doing small sections until the pot is completely decorated.

After the flowerpot dries, you or another adult can spray it with clear lacquer. When the lacquer is dry, let your child fill it with potting soil and plant a flower to give to a shut-in, neighbor, or sick relative.

I-Love-You Baskets

Help your child make a fancy basket from a round doily reinforced with construction paper. Fold the doily in half carefully but avoid creasing the fold. Staple or glue the right and left sides together to form the basket. Attach a handle made of ribbon or yarn to its corners.

Fill the pretty doily basket with real or artificial flowers to express "I love you" to someone. Tell your child that the Bible says, "Be kind to one another," as you and she deliver the basket or hang it on the doorknob of the lucky recipient's house.

Kindness Sack

Attach phrases such as "Give Daddy a big kiss" or "Help Mommy do a job" to pieces of gum, stickers, small toys, or other treats and place them in a small paper sack. Let your child keep the treat after he performs the deeds of kindness. Act as delighted with his display of kindness as if he had thought up the specific deed himself.

As an alternate method, place in the sack phrases such as:

- I love you.
- You're nice.
- You have a pretty smile.
- You're my friend.
- You may go first.

Your child may want to pick a phrase from the kindness sack each morning and say it to someone that day. Reward all kind words with smiles, hugs, applause, or looks of happy approval. Let him know that you notice what a kind child he is! "An anxious heart weighs a man down, but a kind word cheers him up" (Prov. 12:25).

Heart Book

Make a heart book for Grandpa and Grandma or someone else who loves your child. Cut out several heart shapes from construction paper; make them larger than the standard snapshot size. Staple the hearts at the top or the side to form a booklet. Let your child glue a picture of himself on each page and send the heart book to a loved one.

Another idea for a heart book is to fill it with family pictures such as birthdays, holiday observances, and trips or outings. On the front cover, if you wish, glue a small amount of cotton for padding and then cover it with a heart smaller and a different color from the cover. Glue the edges of the smaller heart to the cover to form a cushiony decoration. You may also glue a small bow in its middle, with small hearts or stickers attached to the ends of the ribbon. Real fancy!

God Gives Us Treasures!

Take along a sack to fill with God's treasures when you go on a walk with your child. To a tiny child, every acorn, colorful fall leaf, and smooth stone is a treasure worth saving, so let her! If you have no place in the house to keep her findings, keep a treasure box in the garage to hold her valuables when she tires of them.

When it is possible, acquire an extra special treasure from a shop—a polished stone, a piece of fool's gold, or a lovely abalone shell.

Fingers Can Talk!

Cut the fingers from gardening gloves to make finger puppets. Add facial features with a fine-tip marker or pen and make hair with some yarn and glue. Any extra touches such as clothes, animal ears, or tails can be cut from snips of cloth and glued in place.

Use the puppets on your own fingers, or place one on your finger and one on your child's finger to act out kindness events such as:

• One finger puppet greeting the other kindly and politely
• One falling and the other helping him up
• One crying and the other saying, "I'm sorry you're sad. Let me hug you."

Be Kind to Mother

Let your child help you clean something with water. Water play is a favorite of small children, and you can turn a fun time for her into an expression of kindness and helpfulness.

Let her sponge off the kitchen table, wash a few plastic dishes, clean bathroom fixtures or walls, or wipe smudged doorjambs with your careful supervision.

Tell her that you are so glad that she is kind to her mother!

Candy Jar

Purchase a glass jar with a wide cork lid. Let your child put white glue on the top of the cork lid and arrange on it small jelly beans or other candies. Encourage your child to glue several layers of candy for a piled-high effect.

When the glue is dry, fill the jar with candy to match the lid, and take your child along as you present the candy jar to someone who is sick or alone. Tell your child that when we do kind things for other people, it makes God glad, and we feel happy, too.

Kindness Tree

With your child, find a small branch that has fallen from a tree and place it in a pot containing liquid plaster of paris. When the plaster is set, tie wrapped pieces of candy to the branches as you talk with your child about whom you will give the kindness tree to.

Deliver the tree with the following message attached, or help your child memorize it so she can repeat it to the recipient:

> I have a little gift,
> It's sweet to eat, that's true.
> But even though it's tasty,
> It's not as sweet as YOU!
> I love you!

Kindness In a Nut Box

Have your child cover a small box with glue, one side at a time, and then press on different kinds of nuts in their shells. Allow each side to dry completely before beginning another. Your child may arrange the nuts in rows or however he wishes.

When the whole box is dry, give your child shelled nuts to fill it. Deliver the box to someone just to be kind, especially to someone who may be sad or discouraged. Stress to your child that Jesus was always kind to everyone he met.

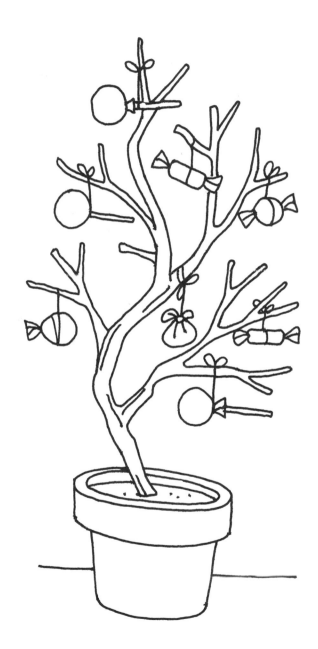

Kindness Congratulations

Make kindness awards by gluing large circles cut from poster board to the top fold of doubled-over blue ribbons and then affixing gold stickers to the circles.

Near the end of each day for several days give out kindness awards, pinning the ribbon on your child if she has performed acts of kindness that day. Inform her ahead of time to be looking for kindness opportunities, and point them out to her when they arise: "Johnny needs someone to be kind and help him put on his shoes. Here's a good chance to be *kind!*" Recall specific kindnesses your child has done and lead in a spontaneous prayer of thanks to God for giving you this kind child!

Kindness Circle

Sit on the floor with your child, repeat this rhyme, and do the actions:

Kindness, kindness [*pat hands on floor four times*]
Yes, we say! [*clap three times*]
We'll do [*hands tap head two times*]
kindness [*put cupped hands over heart*]
Right away! [*slide hands together three times*]

Speed up the game for more fun.

Songs and Cheers

"Oh, Be Kind," to the tune of "Oh, Be Careful":

Oh, be kind, little child;
Help someone.
Oh, be kind, little child;
Help someone.

Jesus wants us to do good
And show kindness, as we should.
Oh, be kind, little child;
Help someone.

Kindness Cheer

Be a kindness cheerleader with your child as you enthusiastically cheer each other on to kindness. Clap or jump as you repeat this cheer:

> Kindness, kindness,
> Yea! Yea! Yea!
> Let's show kindness
> All the day! Yea! [*jump*]

"I'll Be Helpful," to the tunc of "Are You Sleeping?":

> I'll be helpful,
> I'll be helpful.
> I'll be kind.
> I'll be kind.
>
> I will help my mother,
> [*teacher, Daddy, Grandpa,* etc.]
> I will help my mother.
> I'll be kind.
> I'll be kind.

Kindness Meal on Wheels

Let your child be an active participant in preparing and delivering a meal to a person who is bereaved or sick or to a new family down the street. As you do, talk with your child about the kindness Jesus showed to people, the kindness Mary, Martha, and Lazarus showed to Jesus in their home, and the fact that when we do kind acts to other people, we are doing them because we love Jesus and want to be like him.

Let your child help you carry the food to the people and discuss their needs on the way home. Make sure that you and your child pray for them occasionally after your visit.

Shop with Kindness in Mind

Each time you grocery shop with your child, let him pick out one nonperishable item to keep in a box or basket to help other people. When a need arises, contribute the food to a church or community project, or locate a newly-settled refugee family and take your food basket to them yourselves.

Be a kindncss scout. Always try to notice your child's deeds that are praiseworthy. Stop immediately and give credit when it is due!

Kindly Feed the Can

To encourage your small child to be kind to Mom by picking up after herself, draw a large face with a permanent marker on the hinged lid of a plastic waste receptacle. Draw eyes and a large nose and let the lid and flap opening be the mouth. Remind your child to "please feed the can" when she needs to discard anything. Tell her that picking up trash is a kind deed for Mom and it pleases God, too.

Shall I Be Kind?

Interesting kindness gifts may be made by cutting a cardboard picture frame the size and shape to fit a photograph you have. To be sure you make the frame the proper size, draw around the photograph, positioning it in the middle of a piece of cardboard, leaving equal borders all around. Cut out the center space, making it one-fourth inch smaller than the photograph you wish to frame.

Let your child apply glue to the picture frame and cover it with small seashells that he has collected. When the shells are dry, turn the frame over and tape the photograph in place inside the frame. Take it to someone who treasures your child's friendship!

Be Kind to People Who Are Blind

Take your child on a blindfold walk in the house or outside. Cover her eyes with a bandana or give her dark glasses covered with black paper to wear, or ask her to keep her eyes closed. Tell her that the walk is a little like how it feels for a person who is unable to see, who is blind. When you are in an elevator with your child, let her feel the braille numerals and explain how people can read with their fingers. Tell your child to be kind and helpful to everyone, including people who cannot see. Be sure that your child understands that being blind affects seeing, not hearing. It is important that we speak in a normal tone of voice. Tell your child that Jesus was always kind to everyone and that we want to be, too.

Kindness Is Good Manners

Stress to your child that having good manners is a nice way to be kind to others. Good manners include speaking in such a way that our words will make another person feel happy, eating in a manner that lets other people at the table enjoy their food, letting another person have a chance to talk when it is her turn, and responding politely to someone's question or compliment to us.

Here is a kindness activity that encourages good manners on the phone. Let your child make practice calls with a toy phone or a real one that is disconnected. Teach her how to answer the phone, how to call someone else to the phone, and how to say good-bye.

Kindness Is Forgiveness

With teddy bear in hand say, "I'm going to pretend that Teddy has just broken my best vase. He is sorry, but it cannot be put back together. What shall I do to Teddy?" (If your child suggests some type of punishment rather than remuneration for the broken vase, tell him that Teddy was not being careless or disobedient but that he simply had an accident.)

Name some other hypothetical accidents or misdeeds that Teddy may have done, such as leaving the gate open and allowing the dog to get out of the yard, spilling his milk when the glass slipped from his paw, or forgetting to water the flowers when he really meant to.

Let your child help you think of ways you can help Teddy do better, but in each case stress to your child that you need to forgive Teddy and pray for him.

Kindness Flowers

Let your child place white flowers, preferably carnations, in glasses containing water colored with food coloring. When the flowers turn pastel colors, remove them from the water and tie a ribbon around them. Go with your child to take his kindness bouquet to someone who'll enjoy the custom-colored flowers.

Is It True?

Ask your child to sit on the floor in front of you. Tell her that if what you say about kindness is true, she should quickly stand up. If it is not true, she should sit down. Your child may not be able to think immediately of the proper response and do it. Help her by repeating the game several times in a row until she gets the hang of it. Use these sentences or make up your own:

- It is kind to smile at people. [*stand*]
- It is kind to say thank you and please. [*stand*]
- It is kind to push and hit. [*sit*]
- It is kind to grab toys from other children. [*sit*]
- It pleases God when we are kind. [*stand*]
- God will help us to be kind. [*stand*]

Who Is It?

When you acknowledge your child's deed of kindness, you may wish to use this quick game. Say: "I see someone who has done something *kind!* He has brown hair and blue eyes. He is wearing cowboy boots. He is very sweet. He has just [*mention his good deed*]. Who is it?"

All children need to know that we notice and appreciate their deeds of kindness. When adequate attention is given for positive actions, their need for attention through negative behavior is greatly lessened. And our praise takes so little time to give!

Magic Plant

Select a plant in your house or a bush in your yard to be the magic plant. Let it "bloom" occasionally and unexpectedly with small treats attached to its branches.

Let your child pick one or several treats as a reward for kind and loving behavior. Tell her about the specific good deeds she performed and the attitudes you observed that caused the sudden outburst of blooms!

Be Kind to Grand Folks!

Here are three simple activities that may help your child remember that grandparents and other older people deserve our kindness.

1. *Listen to Grandma.* Teach your child that one of the nicest ways of showing kindness to people, especially to grandparents, is to listen very closely to their stories, their instructions, and their words of wisdom. When Grandma or Grandpa speaks, direct your child's attention to her face, gently lifting your child's chin, to insure a listening young ear!

2. *Take a Drink to Grandpa.* When Grandpa, or anyone else you observe, has worked up a thirst toiling in the yard or house, encourage your child to be sensitive to his needs and take him a cool drink of kindness in a paper or plastic cup. If little hands spill some on the way to the recipient, the accident is of little consequence in comparison to the importance of his deed.

Tell your child that Jesus sees every good deed and is pleased with the kindness he showed. You may want to quote the following verse at some point: "Anyone who gives you a cup of water in my name because you belong to Christ will certainly not lose his reward" (Mark 9:41).

3. *Take a Treat to Grandma and Grandpa.* When visiting grandparents, ask your child to help you prepare a kindness basket for them containing their favorite goodies: dried or fresh fruit, some type of nut mix, brownies, a crossword puzzle book, magazines, and so forth.

Let your child deliver the basket and tell Grandma and Grandpa that when the basket's contents are gone, it means it is time for them to come visit *you!* Make sure you give equal kindness treatment to both sets of grandparents.

Be Kind to Animals

If you have a pet that is almost a family member himself, you may wish to celebrate his adoption day just for fun. Let your child help you fix a special meat bone for the pet.

Your child may ask to buy pet toys every time you pass the pet section at the grocery store. Tell her to wait until the special be-kind-to-Rover day and then she may pick out an inexpensive squeeze toy or rawhide bone for the celebration.

Make sure you discuss how kind God was to make Rover and to let him live in your family; tell your child that God loves all his creations, including the animals. Go on to say, "Rover does not really know about God like we do, but God expects us to take good care of animals, and we will!"

Be Kind to Birds

Give your three-year-old a bowl containing seeds, diced scraps of meat and fat, croutons or bread crumbs, cracker crumbs, nuts, and dried fruit or dry cereal. Use whatever similar food items you have at home in whatever proportion you wish.

Ask your child to mix the ingredients together as you add melted bacon fat or lard. Let him use a large spoon to stir the mixture until it cools, and then he may knead and mix it thoroughly with his hands. Spoon the mixture into empty plastic margarine or yogurt containers and push a knotted piece of yarn or string into each container. When the mixture hardens, remove it from the containers and hang outside by the string to be kind to the birds.

Also ask your child to drop cracker or bread crumbs and seeds on the ground for ground-feeding birds.

Explain to your child that God sees when even the tiny sparrow falls (see Matt. 10:29), and you know that it pleases him when you are kind and feed his birds.

Bird Menus

Birds enjoy eating fruits like raisins and cut-up bits of oranges and apples. Mockingbirds like bread crumbs; chickadees prefer mixed seeds; and cardinals love sunflower seeds and peanut butter. Spear apple slices onto the branches of a tree for the birds' eating convenience.

Express the Bible thought that God gives food to us (see Ps. 136:25) to your child, and tell him that our heavenly Father gives us food to share with the birds.

We Welcome You!

Be a welcoming committee of parent and child in your neighborhood. Begin with your own street, making cookies with your child's help and letting her carry them to the homes of new families who arrive.

Watch for sold signs on houses and take the opportunity to welcome the new residents. Follow up your initial visit a few weeks later and invite your new neighbors to church. Most important, talk to them about their relationship with Jesus Christ.

So Glad You Are Here!

When family members return home or when out-of-town friends visit, help your child extend a warm welcome by putting fresh flowers in their room, hiding love drawings or notes in drawers, and placing mints on their pillows. Let the notes tell your guests that you are *so* glad you are able to have them with you.

Ask your child to make a smiling drawing of his own face and write under it who it is and why he is so happy!

Happy Birthday Kindness

Here are two ways your child can show kindness to another on her birthday:

1. *Happy Birthday Collage.* Let your child make a festive placemat to be used by each family member when she has a birthday. On a large sheet of construction paper or poster board, ask your child to spread glue sparingly with a brush or cotton swab. On the glued area, she may arrange paper shapes you have cut from various kinds of wrapping paper, bits of confetti, or pieces of shiny foil paper. Include in her collage pieces of ribbon and a flat balloon.

Cover the collage with a piece of waxed paper and place under heavy books to flatten it. When the collage is dry, cover it with clear adhesive paper on the front and back.

Make the placemat for another person's birthday first, just to be kind, but let your child enjoy her collage creation or make another when her own special day arrives.

2. *Turn-about Birthday.* Help to foster a spirit of kindness by beginning a tradition that the birthday child is to give a small, inexpensive, wrapped gift to his brothers and sisters. This gesture of kindness is to be a way of saying, "I'm glad we're in the same family!"

In order not to let the tradition dwarf the birthday celebration itself, keep the gifts *from* the birthday child smaller and less significant than the ones to him. Remind your children that *every* good gift we receive comes from God, and encourage your child to say or listen to someone else pray a thank-you prayer before or after the gifts are opened.

Be Kind to New Baby

Let your child go with you to pick out pink or blue balloons to welcome baby home. Let her choose for herself an extra special congratulations balloon for the occasion of becoming a big sister. Make a banner together to tape over the front door or on the garage to let baby know you are glad she is in your family. Let your older child pick out a special gift bear or Bible that can be later referred to as "what sister gave you the day we brought you home."

Make sure that baby, too, has a very special surprise gift for sister as baby's first act of kindness and the beginning of the bonding process between the siblings. Take pictures of your older child by herself on the special day and mount them on cardboard or in an album over the caption "This is Joy on the day Anna came to live with us." Take pictures of her with the new baby and make extra copies for her to keep where she can handle and look at them as often as she desires. Place them, if you wish, in a Joy and Anna book for her own use.

Anna's arrival will be no less significant because she had to share the attention and limelight on that special day, and the extra love showered on big sister may pay off in the jealousy-prone days ahead, especially if she is to continue to feel special to her family.

 # Ages
Four to Five

Kindness Is Giving Me!

By this age your child can understand that the very *best* form of kindness comes not in the wrappings of a gift but in the present of undivided time and attention lavished on someone else.

Give your child an opportunity to give of himself as you visit people who are elderly, shut-in, or alone. If possible, bring a lunch to share with the person you visit, and let your child bring a toy or book to show. Be sure that you also give the gift of undivided attention to your child at home. You will be demonstrating to him how to give of himself to another.

Little-Deeds-of-Kindness Sack

Ask your child to draw on a small paper sack a picture of someone performing a kind deed. Tape the sack to the back of a chair. Place inside the sack slips of paper on which are written suggestions for kind deeds:

• Pet the dog and give her a dog biscuit.
• Fold clean clothes for Mom.
• Do something helpful for Dad.
• Call Grandma and tell her that you love her.
• Pray for a friend who is sick or sad.

Bluebird of Kindness

Your bluebird may be any color, but he has an important message of love and kindness to convey!

Make a bird's body from the left half of a paper heart laid on its side. Use a smaller heart for the bird's head with its point for a beak. Use the right half of another heart for a wing. Let your child give the bird an eye with a crayon or marker.

If you want the bird to carry a message, slit its beak and insert a ribbon through it, securing the ribbon with tape on the backside of the bird. Glue several small hearts that carry messages such as "I love you" or "You're nice" to the ribbon. Let your child "fly" the bluebird to someone who needs or deserves some kind words.

Kindness Words

Print the words *Be ye kind* inside a heart drawn on a piece of white paper. Hold the message behind a clear glass or jar of water and see how the words get larger!

Tell your child our kind deeds grow, too, when we show kindness. The people who receive our good deeds also feel like sharing kindness, and the kindness grows and *grows!*

Kindness Means Looking in Your Face

A child who receives a lot of attention may begin to take it for granted and start responding to other people in a careless, disinterested manner. If that occurs, encourage him to be kind enough to stop, look at the speaker, listen, and respond politely. Kindness means giving all our attention to someone during the short time she is kind enough to talk with us.

Kindness Is a Daisy Chain

Help your child make a chain from daisies or other flowers to give to someone she loves. Pick daisies with stems about four or five inches long. Cut a small slit near the ends of the stems with your fingernail or a small knife. Show your child how to thread the stem of another daisy all the way through the slit until it stops at the flower.

Repeat the same threading action again and again through the slit in the stem of each daisy until the chain reaches the desired length. Use a paper clip to fasten the two ends together, and accompany your child as she delivers her kindness chain to a friend.

A Pretty Plate

Press flowers and leaves by placing them between two pieces of waxed paper and laying them under a heavy book.

After several days, when the flowers are flat, instruct your child to pour a small amount of white glue into the center of a plain white plate or saucer and to spread it around with his finger, a paint brush, or a cotton swab. Give him the pressed flowers and leaves to arrange on the plate.

Allow the decorated plate to dry completely. Stick an adhesive hanger on the back of the plate and give it as a kindness gift from your little child. Tell your child that he did two special things God tells us to do in the Bible: he worked with his own hands (see 1 Thess. 4:11) and he was kind (see Eph. 4:32).

Would You Kindly Fix a Snack?

Let your child fix a fun snack for other members of the family and herself. An easy combination that your child can mix together herself, and that siblings will especially enjoy, is a combination of some of the following: dry cereal, raisins, small crackers, nuts, miniature marshmallows, diced dried fruit, M&M's candies, or chocolate chips.

Other snacks that can be fixed with a limited amount of help from you are drinks from concentrated juice or packaged mixes, cheese slices and crackers, many fruits, or popcorn in a popper (you will need to supervise and do the cooking, and she can finish the job by adding salt and melted butter. Then she can share the finished product with the family).

Placemat for Grandma's House

Provide for your child a piece of unbleached muslin approximately twelve-by-eighteen inches. Ask your child to use crayons to color a favorite activity he does with Grandma or Grandpa. Ask him to make several placemats if he enjoys the activity. Place a piece of waxed paper or cloth over the placemat, and iron over the design to make it more permanent. If you wish, your child can draw with waterproof felt-tip markers. Show your child how to pull threads from the edges of the fabric to make a fringe.

Let your child present his masterpiece of love to Grandma or Grandpa with a big hug!

My Drawings-for-You Book

Collect eight or ten of your child's drawings that will be significant to the special person who will receive them. Let your child mount them in a photo album, a scrapbook, or a homemade construction-paper book that you have stapled or taped together.

Take your child to present her book of originals to someone who loves her and will appreciate her artwork. Your child will enjoy the experience of giving something she has personally created to someone of importance to her. Tell her, "It is more blessed to give than to receive" (Acts 20:35).

Kindness Cards

Start early to encourage your child to send his thanks for little and big deeds of kindness done for him. He may dictate his sentiments to you, or you may compose the message and read it to him for his approval. If he enjoys copying a brief printed message, let him write his thanks by himself. Include a drawing that represents what your child received or how happy the kindness made him.

Tell your child that it is kind to say or send our thanks. Relate to him in your own words the story of Jesus and the ten lepers (Luke 17:11–19).

Tongue Twisters and Songs

Try these mouthfuls with your child:

Kindness causes kids to care.
Caring and kindness create
the correct kind of kids.

To the tune of "The Farmer in the Dell":

The kinder that I am
The happier I will be.
So I'll be kind to everyone
And show God's love from *me!* [*point to self*]

To the tune of "Are You Sleeping?":

I am trying,
I am trying,
To be kind,
To be kind.

Then I'll be like Jesus.
Then I'll be like Jesus.
He is kind.
He is kind.

To the tune of "London Bridge":

I'll show kindness to my friends,
To my friends, to my friends.
I'll show kindness to my friends
'Cause that pleases Jesus.

I'll be kind to those who aren't,
Those who aren't, those who aren't.
I'll be kind to those who aren't,
I'll be kind like Jesus.
[or, 'Cause that pleases Jesus.]

Kindness Verse

Here are some verses related to kindness that you may wish to read and explain to your child, or ask her to explain them to *you:*

Proverbs 12:25
Proverbs 14:21
Proverbs 14:31
Proverbs 19:17
1 Corinthians 13:4
Ephesians 4:32
1 Thessalonians 5:15

Be Kind to Your Child

Each day as you serve your child his breakfast, tell him, "I have a message from my *heart* for you!" Place before him a small paper heart on which you have written a love message to him, or whisper the message in his ear, if you prefer. You may use some of the following statements or make up your own:

- I think you're *wonderful!*
- You make me so happy!
- You're my favorite little child in all the world!
- I'm so glad God made you!
- You are so nice.
- I love you with *all my heart!*
- You make my heart *happy!*

Adopt a New Friend

For a day, "adopt" a new friend—a foreign student or someone who is handicapped or elderly or without transportation.

Let your child accompany you as you take your adoptee anywhere she needs or wants to go. Go shopping, go on a sight-seeing tour, or eat a nice lunch together at a restaurant or in your home.

Holiday times are great opportunities to adopt a student or a single or an elderly person who has no family nearby. Your little child will long remember the adventure in kindness, and your simple gestures to accommodate new friends may make a more profound impression on your child than you dreamed possible!

Kindness Charades

Take turns with your child acting out kind deeds for the other to identify. Some suggested deeds are picking up toys and putting them in a box, making a bed, hanging up a coat, and pretending to divide Play-Doh or a cookie with another child.

End the game with a hug and kindness cheer:

I'll be kind. [*clap*]
I'll be good. [*clap*]
I'll help others! [*arms outstretched*]
Yea! [*clap*]

My Helping-Hands Ticket Book

Draw around your child's hand on two thicknesses of construction paper and cut along your outline. Use the hands as front and back covers for a booklet. If she is able, let your child cut out matching handprint pages for tickets. Place the tickets between the covers and staple or tie all the pieces together with yarn at the wrist. On each page, write a kind deed that your child suggests doing for the booklet's recipient. Some suggestions might be:

- water plants
- dust table
- sweep porch
- sing a song
- say a prayer
- feed pet
- pull some weeds
- tell a story
- bring some homemade cookies
- sit down and talk for awhile

Ask your child to take the booklet to someone he sees often with the suggestion that the tickets may be cashed in for kind deeds. Be sure to follow through by letting your child do what the tickets promise he will.

It's Time to Show Love!

Make a small paper plate into a clock with hands cut from construction paper and secured with a paper fastener in the middle of the plate. Ask your child to glue small hearts around the edges of the clock to represent the numbers. Writing numerals on the heart shapes would give him good writing practice, or you may write them yourself as he watches you.

On the face of the clock write the statement, It's TIME to Show Love! Refer to the clock often, reminding your child with a hug that it is time to show love. Make sure he knows that Baby, Daddy, Grandma, and whoever is nearby deserves to be included in the loving, too.

Kindness to Company

Let your child make a welcome sign to put on your door when you are expecting visitors. She may copy the message, Welcome, Friends! or something similar, edging the message with flower drawings, cutouts, or decorative stickers.

Her kindness will be noticed and enjoyed by the guests, which will encourage her to keep on showing kindness!

Garage Full of Kindness

Let your child help you have a garage sale with several purposes in mind:

- To share the proceeds with someone less fortunate
- To let your child pass out Bible tracts or invitations to church
- To give the items that do not sell to someone who can use them
- To share God's love through friendly smiles and conversation and, when possible, to witness about his love

After the garage sale, go with your child to purchase *new* gifts or clothes for a family with special financial needs. Take your child with you to present the gifts (and include food items, too, if needed by the family) to the people you have selected. If it is Christmastime, wrap the gifts and let your child experience the *real* joy of the season.

Kindness Calls

Make a brief call to someone each day or each week just to be kind. Talk with your child before you place the call, stressing the importance of sharing kindness with other people. Let him talk with the person you call, too.

Children enjoy talking on the phone. They can use their maturing linguistic skills and share God's love at the same time.

Be Kind to Animals

Plan a zoo outing with your child. The day before you go, help your child make a simple book of pictures of common zoo animals cut from an old children's storybook or from animal magazines. Paste one picture on each page.

Take the book along to the zoo. As your child observes each animal, write on its page some ways that she observes that zookeepers have been kind to the animals. Some suggestions might be:

- They keep the animals' cages clean.
- They provide fresh food and water every day.
- They create a suitable habitat for the animals.

When you go home, place a picture of your child's own pet at the end of her book. Write down her ideas about ways she can be her pet's own kind zoo-keeper.

Animal Likenesses

Cut a large piece of poster board into two halves. On each half draw a circular or oval shape the size of your child's face and cut out the center. Around the edges of the circle (with the poster board positioned vertically), your child may draw the ears, mane, fur, or whiskers of the animals of his choice. If there is room on the poster board, ask your child to draw a small body of the animal for identification and for fun. Make four different animals by using both sides of both halves of the poster board.

Take turns with your child holding the animal drawings up to your face and making appropriate sounds as you contort your face into the animal's features. Pet, hug, and talk nicely to the animal, telling him that God made him and that you are going to take good care of him. Pretend to feed, water, and groom the animal because you know that kindness pleases God.

Kindness to Daddy

Your child does not need to wait until Father's Day to be kind to Daddy! Make this interesting gift for any day:

Cut a piece of construction paper the size of an empty tin can. Let your child apply glue to the paper and wrap it around the outside of the can—before or after decorating.

When the paper has dried slightly, ask your child to paint glue with a brush on one small area of the construction paper. He may then sprinkle in the glue one kind of seed: sunflower seed, bird seed, grass seed, melon seed, or spice seed. Allow the glue to dry for four or five minutes. Repeat the process with different kinds of seed until the entire can is covered.

Your child will enjoy giving his handmade gift to Daddy to hold pens and pencils on his desk. Teach your child this important verse: "Honor your father and your mother" (Exod. 20:12).

Kindness Hearts

Your child may wish to cut out pink or pastel-colored hearts and write "I love you" on each in her own fancy writing. Provide lace, ribbon, or rickrack for her to glue around the edge of the heart.

When the pretty project is completed, your child may take her kindness heart to someone who is special to her.

I'm a Servant!

Tell your child that Jesus said it is very good to be a servant, to be willing to help and serve people and to be last rather than first sometimes.

Invite a younger sibling's friends over for lunch, and let the older child serve the food and help them in their play. Make sure the lunch menu includes food that will be a hit with the children; too many complaints from those being served can discourage even the kindest "server"!

At other times, encourage your older child to serve the younger by fixing his toy, making a drawing for him, or helping him wash up or change his clothes. Tell your servant that he not only is helping you, but he is pleasing Jesus, too. Let your own servant spirit be a positive example that your child will want to imitate.

Shell Kindness from the Sea

With your child, select a large, flat seashell such as a mussel or abalone for this project. Glue three marbles or beads on the outer curve of the shell, positioning them as legs. Make sure the legs are steady and allow the glue to dry thoroughly.

When the glue is set, turn the seashell over and ask your child to fill it with potting soil. Let her place in the soil several small plants and give it to someone as a kindness garden. If you prefer, place decorative soap in the seashell instead of plants. As she presents the gift, she may say, "I'm giving this to you because I love you and because I love Jesus."

Your child's gift and message may be used as a witness to an unsaved friend, neighbor, or relative.

Caramel Kindness

Let your child make three or four smiley-faced caramel apples and decide to whom he would like to give them, just to be kind. It would be ideal to give them to people in your neighborhood and teach your child the words of Jesus, "Love your neighbor as yourself" (Matt. 19:19).

Melt caramel candies in a double boiler. Let your child push a Popsicle stick into a clean, dry apple or pear. Dip the fruit in the melted caramel and place it upside down on a piece of waxed paper to dry.

When the caramel is soft set, let your child hold the fruit by the Popsicle stick as she makes a face from candy pieces or miniature marshmallows. Coconut makes good hair as a finishing touch. Perhaps you might tie a bow around the stick to serve as a tie.

Kindness Posters

Provide paper and crayons or markers for your child to draw posters depicting kind behavior toward all sorts of people—family members, police officers, teachers, mail carriers, or others. Tape the posters on doors inside or outside your house as reminders to the whole family to "be . . . kind to one another" (Eph. 4:32).

Playing a Game with Siblings

Ask big brother to entertain his little brother Mikey for a few minutes while you complete a job. Tell your older child how much you will appreciate his kindness and offer him some suggestions for activities that he will probably enjoy, too. Here are some possible ideas:

• Provide a paper cup, a bowl of water, and a small sponge. Your older child will show Mikey how to dip the sponge in the bowl and squeeze water into the cup. Make sure there is a towel under the whole setup!

• Place a bowl on the floor across the room. Ask your older child to help Mikey do one or both of the following: (1) Scoop up Ping-Pong balls or marshmallows one at a time in a spoon and deposit them in the bowl across the room.
(2) Pick up cotton balls one at a time with salad tongs and carry them to the bowl.

• Provide paper cups and small paper plates. Ask your older child to help Mikey build a tower by stacking them in an alternating pattern: cup, plate, cup, plate, and so forth.

• Ask big brother to play with Mikey using toy cars on a wooden board or ironing board ramp that you have elevated with one end on a pillow.

• Give both big brother and Mikey inflated balloons. Tell your older child
to explain the rules of the game to
Mikey: They must throw their balloons into the air and laugh while the
balloons are airborne, but they must
stop laughing immediately when the
balloons touch the floor.

Do not expect to get much accomplished during this time. Try to complete one very short job for which you
can credit your older child's kindness in
entertaining Mikey for you. The object
of this activity is to encourage kindness
in your child, and any effort made in
that pursuit is time well spent.

Hurt Folks Need Kindness

In order to help your child be sympathetic to the needs and problems of people who are handicapped or injured, put your child's good arm (the one she uses to color with) in a dish-towel sling.

Ask your child to draw or color a picture for you, using only the arm that is *not* in the sling. She will soon sympathize with the difficulty some people really face each day. Remind her that God wants us to show kindness and love to everyone.

Mephibosheth

Tell your child the beautiful story of King David's kindness to Jonathan's crippled son, Mephibosheth (see 2 Sam. 9). Act out the story, asking your child to play the part of Mephibosheth as you play the part of David. Trade roles for the second enactment, if he wishes. Take Mephibosheth to the kitchen table for a tasty snack of king's food. While he is eating, discuss the funny name in the story and the fact that no one you know has that name. Continue the conversation by mentioning to your child that although there are no *Mephibosheths* in your town or neighborhood, there *are* people who are crippled and cannot walk, or cannot walk well.

Talk about how to be kind to people who appear to be different, and that you should be careful not to stare or laugh at anybody. Encourage your child to be a kind, caring friend and arrange a fun outing with someone who uses crutches or a wheelchair.

Give Baby a Party

Let an older sibling prepare for baby's first birthday party. A four- or five-year-old can be a help by making placemats or name cards for the family, decorating, making paper hats, helping to bake a cake, or making a happy birthday banner with words or pictures to commemorate the special occasion.

Your older child can also invite Grandma and Grandpa to come over for cake and ice cream. Let her make a birthday book of drawings of the cake or presents that baby received.

Explain to your child that the Bible says, "Whatever you did for one of the least of these brothers of mine, you did for me" (Matt. 25:40). Tell her that when we do something for someone small like baby, we are doing it for Jesus, too, and he is pleased.

Chapter 5

Introducing Your Child to Obedience

When I was a boy in my father's house, still tender,
and an only child of my mother, he taught me
and said, "Lay hold of my words with all your heart;
keep my commands and you will live."
—Proverbs 4:3–4

An obedient child is a beautiful sight. He may be active or docile, outgoing or shy, but when he is given an instruction by someone in authority over him, he obeys. His reaction is not one of trepidation or of mindless robotic prgramming; he responds to instructions with an attitude of affirmative cooperation. A child who is lovingly taught to obey is a happy child. His world has order and security in the awareness that someone larger and wiser is in control of him and the events that affect him.

Obedience, however, must be taught, demonstrated, and encouraged. Certainly, some children seem to arrive on the domestic scene with a compliant spirit, while others, equally precious to their parents and to the heavenly Father, are more prone to arch their tiny backs in a show of self-will. We can be sure that no child simply begins at a certain age to obey the scriptural admonition, "Children, obey your parents in everything" (Col. 3:20). By the age of six or seven, the patterns for self-will are so firmly established that a child will have great difficulty making the transition to obedient behavior even if she desires to. It is our responsibility to lovingly and carefully train our child from her early days to obey our words.

That is our goal in introducing our child to obedience: to train him to obey our voice, our words. Many scriptural admonitions include the phrase "obey my voice," "obey my words," or "obey the voice of your Father." Deuteronomy 32:46–47 says, "Take to heart all the *words* I have solemnly *declared* to you this day, so that you may *command* your children to obey carefully all the *words* of this law. They are not just idle *words* for you—they are your life" (emphasis added).

Our goal is to train our child to obey our voice, not our anger or our threats, but our *voice*, in preparation for her to easily, naturally, willingly obey the voice of the heavenly Father.

Formula for Obedience

What a new parent wouldn't give for a fail-proof, three-easy-steps method to insure obedience from his young child! Training a child to obey while leaving his self-esteem healthy and strong is a delicate operation that requires a cou-

pling of our efforts with the wisdom and divine expertise of the Creator. His Word contains many admonitions and assurances to guide us as we teach our children to obey.

Here are some practical guidelines that may prove helpful as you train your child.

1. *Keep the number of prohibitions to a minimum.* Give your child much freedom to explore and investigate, but when you declare a boundary, stick with it firmly and consistently.

2. *Make sure your child understands her limits and the meaning of your instructions.* Sometimes, disobedient behavior results from a lack of adequate communication by the parent or a lack of comprehension by the child.

3. *Let genuine praise abound!* Give your child the benefit of the doubt each time that it is appropriate. Try not to reprimand him for every childish mistake or minor infraction of the rules. Much positive input is required to produce in a child a confident, yet compliant, spirit.

4. *As often as possible, take the positive approach.* Try to make your answer and attitude yes! a majority of the time.

5. *Be careful to save face for your child.* If at all possible, do not embarrass her in front of others. Keep discipline a private affair.

6. *Let your words convince your child*

that he is an obedient and pleasing individual. In your conversations about your child, especially those within his hearing, emphasize his good qualities. *No one* wants to have his less-than-perfect behavior broadcast to other people! Vow to remove from your conversations these very common remarks:

"He's a mess!"

"He's so hyper!"

"What am I going to do with her?"

"She's driving me up the wall!"

"You ought to see how she is at home!"

"I feel sorry for her teacher!"

"I can't do a thing with him!"

7. *When your child hears and understands your words and willfully disobeys or disregards them, do something to help her obey, and do not be afraid to spank her, if necessary (see Prov. 13:24).*

- Reserve a spanking, administered in love and with control, for rebellious, defiant, or deliberately disobedient behavior.
- Make a spanking an event rather than frequent angry barrages of swats.
- Do not hesitate to show profuse love and affection after the spanking has been administered. To hold and hug your child will not undo the benefits of the correction; it will reassure him that your correction was done because you value him so greatly.
- Explain the reasons for the spanking and pray with your child for God's strength and forgiveness.

- Restore your child to immediate full fellowship with you.
- *Never ever* use the biblical admonitions to use the rod of correction as an excuse for abusive behavior toward a child. To abuse a child in *any* manner is absolutely contrary to the Word and nature of God.

But if anyone causes one of these little ones who believe in me to sin, it would be better for him to have a large millstone hung around his neck and to be drowned in the depths of the sea! (Matt. 18:6)

The activities in this chapter will not eliminate the need for discipline, but they will prove to be a positive influence as you introduce your small child to godly obedience. Help is always available from the only One who was perfectly obedient to the words of his Father: "He humbled himself and became obedient to death—even death on a cross!" (Phil. 2:8).

The Baby

Hold This Rattle, Please

When your baby is able to grasp and hold a toy for several seconds, give him this loving command, "Hold this rattle, please, Tim." Hand him a pretty rattle that you know he can easily hang on to. As he holds the toy, softly praise him for obeying you and tell him how very proud you are of his wonderful accomplishment.

It may seem strange to give a command to a tiny baby, but you will be beginning to establish the earliest foundation of obedience to your words. You are instructing him to perform a task he has done successfully before.

Never reprimand a tiny baby if he does not comply. These instructions are only the beginnings of his listening and comprehension skills. He does not understand what you say at this point, but very soon he will.

Please Drink Your Milk

When baby is hungry and ready to be fed, just before she begins to drink, say, "Please drink your milk, Dianne." Then say, "Thank you, God, for Dianne's milk to drink."

At first you may feel awkward talking this way to your new baby, but she will be drinking in your loving voice as her physical hunger is met. Soon conversations like these will seem much more natural to you.

Since your purpose in speaking the instruction is to condition your baby to respond to your voice, speak the command only when you are sure she will drink willingly. You will be using a natural activity to begin teaching the concept of doing what Mommy says on occasions when you are certain she will not do otherwise.

Eating Good Food

After he has tried a food and you know he likes it, say to him lovingly when he is hungry, "Here is your yummy cereal. Eat some, please." (Use words that seem natural to you.)

When he does eat, tell him how proud you are of him and how glad you are that God gives us good food to eat. *Do not* scold him if he does not eat, and do not insist that he do so when he has refused! A young baby is obviously un-able to consciously understand and obey.

Your goal is to begin teaching obedience so that it becomes a habit. Lovingly and consistently encourage your child to obey until it becomes second nature for him to comply with your words.

Go, Doggie, Go!

Let a stuffed animal demonstrate obedience to your baby through these simple games.

Say, "Go, doggie, go!" and make the animal run alongside your baby's crib or playpen. Then say, "Stop, doggie, stop!" and make the animal abruptly stop running. Repeat the commands and actions. Say, "Good, doggie, good! You obeyed me!"

As the baby grows older, add more commands to the animal such as "Roll over!", "Say Bow-wow!", and "Lie down!"

Obeyercise

Gently exercise your baby's little arms and legs as you give her her first lessons in listening and responding. Lift her arms up and down slowly, one at a time, saying, "Lift your arm, Kari. Now put it down. Lift your leg, sweetie. Now put it down." After a few repetitions say, "Good! You're stretching your little arms and legs!"

Go to Sleep, Little One

When you lay your baby in bed for his nap or as you rock him in your arms, say lovingly, "Go to sleep, little baby. Mommy says go to sleep, darling." You may wish to add, "Jesus wants you to get your rest, and I do, too."

Obviously, a baby is unable to consciously understand and obey your instruction to sleep. No punishment or reprimand should be given if he does not comply. The purpose in your words should be to acquaint him with instructions that eventually will have meaning to him.

Look at That Sweet Face!

Place a baby-safe mirror in front of your baby or toddler. Say, "Look at that sweet face! Why, that's Rachel!" As you point to the reflection in the mirror, the baby's eyes will follow your finger.

Say, "Look at Rachel's eyes!" (Point to her eyes in the mirror.) "God helps Rachel to see with her eyes."

"Look at Rachel's tiny nose." (Point to it.) "God made Rachel's nose so she can smell."

"And look at Rachel's happy mouth! God gave Rachel a mouth to smile and eat and make happy sounds!"

Remember, an obedient child is one who is learning very early to listen to your words and do what you ask of him. A baby is very limited in his ability to understand and comply, but you need to lay the initial foundation of obedience.

Touch the Bear

Place a stuffed animal near your baby. Talk with her about its eyes, nose, ears, and mouth, its soft fur and round tummy. Tell the baby that you want her to touch the bear. Say, "Isn't he a cute bear, Chrissy? Now Mommy wants you to touch the bear."

Gently place the baby's tiny hand on the bear and repeat, "Touch the bear, please, Chrissy. Isn't he soft?" Do not force her hand if she resists or pulls it back. And be sure to praise her: "Good girl!"

The Toddler

Speak Nicely, Please

As you give instructions to your very small child, as often as possible say please and thank you to him. Offer the same polite respect you would offer an adult friend. Polite talk will become a part of his hidden vocabulary before he can even speak. When he is able to talk, you will be pleased to hear him say the words you have spoken to him.

Eat This First, Please

Give your toddler a piece of cheese, a bite of dry cereal, or a small piece of cracker or fruit. Say with a smile, "Eat this first, please." Then as she finishes the bite, say, "Now eat this next," alternating foods.

You will be making snack time a natural lesson in obedience. It will be a happy time if you are kind with your words and free with your smiles and praise.

Whisper, Whisper

Toddlers enjoy the closeness and sound of a whisper. Give your child a simple whispered command, and praise him in a whisper after he obeys. Give him other commands, one at a time, if he seems to enjoy this activity.

Obedience Basket

Place an empty laundry basket in front of you. Tell your child, "Please put a book in the basket." Point into the basket as you speak. As she does so, say, "Good! Now put a (familiar toy) in the basket."

Praise her each time she follows your instructions. Play the game as long as she is willing, and ask for objects she can recognize and carry.

Give her a big hug as you tell her that you and Jesus both love your precious, obedient girl!

Beanbag Duet

Make simple beanbags by sewing two circles of fabric together, leaving an opening for filling with beans, popcorn, or macaroni. Sew it up securely when finished. Make two beanbags and give one to your child and keep the other for yourself. Instruct your child to copy your actions.

Some activities you and your toddler each may enjoy with your beanbag are putting it on your head; holding it in your upturned palm; putting it on your foot or the floor; throwing it up into the air.

Say, "This is fun! Thank you, God, for letting us have fun with beanbags!"

O Is for Obey

When your child is eating an O-shaped breakfast cereal, show her an *O* in the spoon and say, "*O* means obey, Janie. Obey means to do what Mommy and Daddy say."

Sing to her this little song to the tune of "Farmer in the Dell":

O is for obey.
O is for obey.
O means doing what we should.
O is for obey.

Listen to the Tape

Take a few minutes to tape brief instructional messages from several people whose voices your preschooler will recognize. Mommy may say something like this: "Hi, Sam! This is Mommy. I want you to do something for me. I want you to please pick up your ball and put it in the toy box. Thank you!"

Stop the tape between messages and help your child carry out the instructions. Daddy might say: "Hi, sweetie! This is Daddy. Would you please go kiss Mommy (or some other family member) for me? Thank you!"

Let your toddler know you are proud he obeyed every command and that he pleased Jesus, too!

Jump, Little Frog

Tell your older toddler that you and she are going to be frogs. Show her a picture of one, if possible. Tell about the strong legs God gives the frogs and how strong he has made ours, too. You may wish to make round green paper lily pads, or hop from pillow to pillow on the floor, or simply pretend.

Show your child how to squat down with hands on the floor and hop like a frog. If you are using lily pads, and if your child is old enough to comply, tell her to jump from one pad or pillow to the next. As she does, say often, "Hop, little frog, hop!"

Remember that obedience is simply doing what you ask her to. You are training her through natural, enjoyable activity to follow your instructions. When she tires of the game, reward her for her efforts with a hug. Tell her that she is a very obedient little frog and a good hopper, too! Remind her that God is pleased when little frogs do what their mother says!

Ages Two to Three

Stop and Go!

Position your child across the room, facing you. Give him the command "Go!" He must then proceed to walk or run toward you until you say, "Stop!" He must go and stop at your command until he reaches you for a big hug!

Repeat the game if your child seems interested. The next time ask him to crawl or jump to you.

This game is also called Red Light, Green Light.

Obey When I'm Not Looking

Play this game the same way you did Stop and Go, with one variation.

Stand with your back to the child and give the command "Go!" When you say stop, turn around to see if she is in the process of doing as you instructed.

Tell her that she is to obey your words and stop and go as soon as you tell her to. (Do not indicate that you caught her moving when she is attempting to stop. It is not easy for a preschooler to get her little body to respond quickly!)

Look Up, Look Down!

This activity is a simple exercise in obedience as well as an introduction to the concept of opposite words. The game can be played while traveling in the car, while waiting for a doctor's appointment, or whenever you need something to do.

Give your child commands such as these:

- Look up . . . look down.
- Point up high . . . point down low.
- Look happy . . . look sad.
- Put your hand *over* my arm . . . put your hand *under* my arm. [*Hold your arm in front of him and show him what you mean if he needs help.*]
- Clap very softly . . . clap very loudly.
- Say "I love you" slowly . . . say "I love you" fast!

Tell him with a hug that you really do love him and that he does a good job of obeying what you say!

Pegboard Obedience

With a pegboard or similar child's toy or blocks, make a short row of pegs, alternating two colors.

Talk with your child about what you have done and ask her kindly, "Will you please make a row of pegs to match the one I made?"

Obedience Pictures

Tell your child that you are going to give him some things to do so he can make a pretty picture! Cover his clothes with Dad's old shirt or pin a towel around his neck to absorb spills.

Lay a piece of white paper on the table in front of him. Hand your child a small bottle of food coloring and a clean medicine dropper, and tell him to put a drop on the paper. Give him a straw and show him how to blow through it toward the drop of food coloring.

Give him other bottles of coloring, one at a time, saying the name of each color and asking him to blow toward the drop with the straw. The picture he makes will delight you both.

Let him know that the pretty picture was made because he obeyed your words and that you and God are both pleased.

Let's Treat Our Guest Royally

When company is coming, involve your child in preparing for the arrival. Give him one simple instruction at a time to carry out. Ask your child to hang up hand towels, place new soap in the holder, place flowers in the room, or a candy mint on the pillows.

Listening Day

At the beginning of the day, tell your child to listen really well to everything you ask her to do that day. Encourage her to do what you ask, and when she does, she can put a star or gummed sticker on a paper poster you have placed on the refrigerator door.

You may decorate it if you wish, or leave it plain. If you do not have gummed stars handy, show your child how to draw a star each time she obeys you.

At the end of the day, she may receive a small reward for her good obedience. Be sure to remind her that her behavior has pleased you and Jesus, too!

Please Pack the Picnic

Nothing helps increase a child's self-esteem more than when she accomplishes a task by herself and receives genuine praise from her beloved parent or teacher.

Plan a backyard picnic with your child. Set out on the kitchen table all the items and food your child will need to pack the lunch herself. Even a small child can place cut-to-fit pieces of cheese between crackers, spread mayonnaise or soft peanut butter on bread, cut soft fruit with a blunt knife or Popsicle stick, or place potato chips or cookies in plastic bags.

Everything can then be put into a basket or grocery bag and taken outside or spread on a sheet in the kitchen for an inside rainy-day picnic. As she prepares lunch, gently give her instructions one step at a time and tell her that the result of her obedience will be a yummy lunch. Reward her with a hug for a job well done!

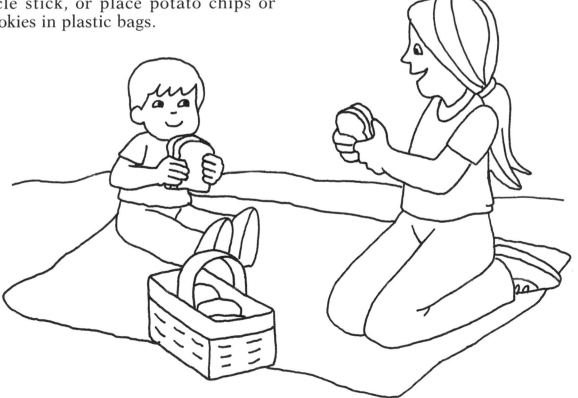

Mirror, Mirror

Instruct your child to look at himself in a large mirror and see what happens when he moves his arms or changes the look on his face. Point out to him that the mirror face, the reflection, does exactly what his face does.

Perform several simple actions such as clapping your hands, jumping up and down, acting like a monkey, rubbing your tummy, slapping your sides, or marching like a soldier.

Ask your child to be like the face in the mirror and to obey what you do by doing the same thing. Use the word *obey* to impress upon him that obedience is a positive, enjoyable activity.

Tell your child that we are to act like mirrors of Jesus and do kind and loving things.

Where You Lead, I Will Go

Play this game like Follow the Leader, but do not give spoken directions as you play. Instead, tell your child to follow you and do what you do. Wind your way through the house or yard, jumping, hopping, waving your arms, clapping over your head, and doing other actions she can duplicate.

When you have taken turns being the leader and the game is finished, kneel on your child's level and look right into her eyes. Say with a loving hug, "God wants us to follow and go where he leads us. We always want to follow God."

Obedience Train

Talk about trains with your child and show a picture of one, if possible. Explain how all the parts of the train must follow the engine. The boxcars cannot go off the track in any direction they want to. If they did, they would not be a train anymore.

Play train, with you as the engine and your child as a boxcar holding around your waist. He must imitate the *chug-chug, ding-ding,* and *all aboard* sounds, and follow you as you move.

As you play, say this little rhyme and encourage him to join with you in repeating it:

Chug, chug, hey, hey,
Jesus wants me to obey.

Invisible Rope

When you go shopping with your child, take a walk outside, or play this game in the house, tell her that you have an invisible rope. Explain that *invisible* means you cannot see it. Ask her to hold on tightly to one end of the rope as you hold the other. Tell her that will keep her from getting lost.

After your game, pretend that you are jumping with your invisible rope and then hand it to her to jump. The rope can also become a tightrope. Whatever the rope is used for, it must be used only by an obedient child: the tightrope walker must try very hard to stay balanced on the rope.

Obey a Whisper

Whisper pleasant instructions in your child's ear, such as:

"John, go find a book, and I'll read it to you."

"Find Mommy's mirror in the bathroom drawer, and I'll show you something great in it!" [*Show the child his own face and compliment him as you do*: "God gave you those beautiful brown eyes, John," *or* "I love how God gave you a smiley, happy mouth, John."]

Whisper to him how pleased you are that God helps him to obey Mother and Daddy. Tell him in a whisper that the Bible says, "Children, obey your parents in the Lord, for this is right," and that he *does* obey!

Chants and Songs

Jesus, Jesus,
I'll obey Him!
Jesus, Jesus,
Yes, I will!

J [*pause*] E [*pause*] S-U-S.
I'll O [*pause*] B-E-Y!

To the tune of "Camptown Races":

I'll obey the Lord my God,
Yes, sir! Yes, sir!
I'll obey the Lord my God,
Oh, yes, I will!

To the tune of "Row, Row, Row Your Boat":

I'll obey the Lord,
I'll obey His Word.
Jesus tells me what to do.
I'll obey my Lord!

To the tune of "Are You Sleeping?":

[*Mother*] Where's a boy [*girl*],
Where's a boy,
Who'll obey,
Who'll obey?

[*Child*] I'll be very glad to!
I'll be very glad to!
Yes, I will!
Yes, I will!

Obedience Necklaces

Using O-shaped breakfast cereal, tell your child that *O* means "obey!" Explain that obeying means doing what Mommy and Daddy say, and let her string the *O*'s on a shoelace or on a piece of yarn with tape around one end. Tie the finished product around your child's neck for a necklace to remind her that obeying pleases God and makes Mommy and Daddy happy!

Obedient Ollie

An important concept that will help motivate your child to obey is the truth that he will be happy when he does.

Make Obedient Ollie on a plate for lunch or a snack. His body can be a canned peach or pear half, flat side down. His arms and legs can be carrot or celery sticks, and his head can be a hard-cooked egg. He can have a pimiento or radish-slice mouth, raisin or olive eyes, and alfalfa-sprout hair. Make him look as happy as possible.

Obedient Olivia can be made with a lettuce-leaf skirt over her pear body, and she can have grated cheese or cottage cheese for hair. Either Ollie or Olivia can be made from whatever items you have in the refrigerator that day.

As your child enjoys his lunch friends, talk pleasantly about the times he obeys you so well and how much that pleases you.

Boom, Ding-a-Ling, Click

Play this listen and obey game with your child. You will need two lids and two spoons, two bells, and four sticks or pencils.

Say, "This is like a drum; it goes boom, boom [*demonstrate by banging lids with spoons*]. This is a bell; it goes ding-a-ling [*ring bell*]. These are rhythm sticks; they go click, click [*clack sticks together*]. Now, please listen and obey, OK?"

Divide the instruments. You and your child each take a lid, a spoon, a bell, and two sticks. Turn and sit with your back facing your child as she sits with her back toward you. Play an instrument and ask her to obey you and play the same sound. As she does so, say, "You're a good listener, Barbara!"

Sing this little song to the tune of "London Bridge" and play along with an instrument, if you wish:

Jesus wants us to obey
All the day, all the day.
Jesus wants us to obey.
Will we mind him? YES! [*Shout last word*]

Ages Four to Five

Listen and Do

Explain to your child that you want him to listen to a recording that you will play.

When the music is loud, you want him to clap his hands. When it is quiet, you want him to put his finger to his mouth and say, "Shh!" Select music that has a variety of loud and soft sounds, or adjust the volume control to make the music loud or soft at will.

After your child has responded to the music, allow him to operate the tape or record player while you listen and obey.

Ready, Set, Go

Tell your child that she is a soldier and you are her commander. Explain that a commander tells a soldier what to do and the soldier must obey him.

Give the child one command as she stands like a soldier in front of you. She must listen carefully and then proceed only when you say, "Ready . . . go!"

Praise her for obeying correctly and tell her that she is ready for a harder command. This time give her two orders to obey before returning to her soldier position. She may soon be ready to obey three commands at a time.

Be sure to praise her for her good obedience and tell her how important obedience is to God.

Traffic Policeman

Let your child help you make traffic signs on red and green construction paper. Cut four-by-five-inch circles from the paper, print the words *Stop* and *Go* on the appropriate colors, and attach the circles to flat sticks or rulers. You may wish to make only one sign, with red on one side and green on the other.

Pretend that your child is the police

officer and that you are driving your car down the road. Make the sound of the motor, turn the steering wheel, and stop and go as he holds up the traffic signs. Take turns being the driver and the police officer.

If you want to drive a more visible car, make a simple drawing on cardboard or poster board and carry it under your arm or in front of you as you obey instructions.

Little Boy Careless

Make up a simple dialogue about Little Boy Careless, using a hand puppet or stuffed toy for the actor. Tell how Little Boy Careless never thought it was important to obey his mother and daddy. He cared much less than he should about obeying, and that is how he got his name.

Show how he does not take his medicine or wear his jacket or boots [*shake the puppet's head NO!*] and gets very sick [*make the puppet curl up on his side as if he does not feel well*]; he does not feed his pets, and they run away [*make him fold his arms and turn his back toward your child, and then pretend he is crying*]; and he does not listen to his teacher in class and then he cannot answer her question [*cover the puppet's ears with his hands and then shake his head as if embarrassed*].

Contrast Little Boy Careless with Little Boy Careful. Repeat the situations, making the puppet respond appropriately to the name *Careful* in each one. Show how happy Little Boy Careful is by making him jump up and down and clap his hands together when he has been obedient.

Do-What-It-Says Cards

Write simple commands on several small cards. Lay them on the floor or table facedown and let the child pick one and perform the command as you read it to her.

You may wish to make the cards more appealing by cutting them in heart shapes or by using several different colors of paper.

King and Servant

Four- and five-year-olds love role-playing and pretending, especially when you are involved in the action!

Tell your child that you are going to be a good king and that you would like him to be your servant. Drape a colorful towel over a chair to represent your throne. A long-handled spoon makes a good scepter.

Instruct your child to bow obediently as he approaches you. Give him one or more simple instructions to follow. After his successful responses as your obedient servant, trade roles with your child and let him give the commands to you.

Mention that there were some good kings and some bad kings in the Bible. The good kings were the ones who obeyed God. Tell your child that he is a good king because he knows how to be a servant as well.

Obey the Customer

Play restaurant with your child, using simple props such as a table setting, centerpiece, and folded-paper menu or use only your imagination. Be the customer first and let your child be the waiter or waitress with pencil and pad in hand to scribble down your order.

Have her pretend to obey your requests for getting a drink of water or a clean fork, lighting the candle on the table, bringing you ketchup for your french fries, pouring more iced tea, and so forth.

Change roles and be an obedient waiter, answering her requests with a polite, "Yes, miss."

When the game is finished, ask her if she thinks it really *is* important to obey in real life. If she seems interested, continue the discussion by asking questions such as "Why should we obey?" "Who should we obey?" or "How should we feel as we obey?"

Stress that we obey because God says it is right, because we want to be pleasing and kind, and because it even makes *us* happy!

Obedience Match

Place two grocery sacks side by side. Make a hole slightly larger than your child's hand in each sack. Put identical objects in each sack. You may use items such as forks, spoons, spools of thread, pencils, rolled-up socks, or whatever you have handy.

Tell your child to reach into the hole in one sack and find an object, leaving it in place. Ask him to listen and obey your next instruction: "Now find a matching object in the other sack. When you think you have found it, remove both objects through the holes, and we'll see if you are right!"

Continue the game until he has matched all the objects. If you wish, you may use this game to emphasize left hand-right hand identification.

Be sure to tell him that he has listened and obeyed well. Remind him that obeying is important to you and important to God!

Obedience Flowers

Create an experience in obedience while planting seeds, plants, or blooming flowers with your child. Her listening skills will be enhanced, and she will begin to recognize the correlation between listening, obeying, having a pleasant experience, and enjoying a successful end result.

Divide the planting process into several steps: select the planter or spot to plant, dig the hole, add fertilizer, place the plant in the hole, add dirt, and water.

Keep your instructions simple and pleasant. Resist the urge to correct her every move—no beginning planter is a perfect planter! Activities such as this enhance or undermine your child's self-esteem. Plan your planting for a time when your patience is at a high point. Remember that a valuable lesson in obedience and a time of strengthening your relationship with your child is more important than a manicured flower garden.

I Will Obey

Play this game like Mother, May I? facing your child as she stands across the room or yard.

Tell her what kind of steps she must take to come toward you (hopping, crawling, giant, jumping, and so forth) and how many she is permitted to take. End each instruction by asking, "Will you obey?"

She responds by saying "I will obey" and proceeds as you have instructed her to do. When she reaches you, give her a big hug or vigorous handshake and tell her how proud you are of your obedient child!

Tell her that it is fun to obey and that it pleases God, too!

Spin a Command

Use a spinner from a children's game or make one from cardboard or poster board and use a paper fastener to secure the arrow loosely in the middle of a circle.

Print simple instructions around the edges of the circle. Take turns with your child at spinning the arrow and performing the action toward which it points. Some instructions you may wish to include are:

- Pat your head three times.
- Shake hands with a friend.
- Sing a song about Jesus in your best voice.
- Tell Jesus you love him.
- Wink at someone.
- Clap your hands five times.

Obedience Bowling

Collect three empty cylinder-shaped potato chip or tennis ball containers. Cover them with different colors of construction paper.

Make three Bible verse markers to match and place them in a Bible at verses that teach obedience.

Place the paper-covered cans several feet away like bowling pins and space them approximately eighteen inches apart.

Instruct your child to knock down one can at a time with a ball. Each time he succeeds, ask him to find the colored marker in the Bible that corresponds to the color of the can. Read the verse to him and very briefly explain what God says about obedience in that verse. You may wish to use some of these: Exodus 20:12; Proverbs 3:1, 12; Proverbs 4:1; Proverbs 4:20; Proverbs 7:1; Ephesians 6:1; and Colossians 3:20.

Obedience Puzzles

Find a picture of a child doing a kind deed or performing a job, or use a picture of a Bible story character who obeyed what God commanded.

Mount the picture on cardboard or poster board and cut into puzzle shapes. Then see if your child can put the puzzle together. As he does so, discuss the picture and how important it is to obey God.

Lights Off!

Tell your child to begin waking around the room until you flick the lights off and on. Tell her that she must freeze right where she is when that happens, listen to what you tell her, and then do it.

You might instruct her to bend and touch her toes, to scratch her head, to put her hands behind her ears and wiggle them, to act like she is vacuuming, washing her face, praying, and so on.

Repeat the game of lights on, lights off several times. Praise your child for her good obedience, and then let her give *you* the orders several times.

As a well-adjusted adult in years to come, she will need both to give and to receive instructions. This game allows her to practice both.

Get Free!

Children this age love pretending. Tell your child to pretend that he is walking through a muddy forest and before he knows it, he is stuck in the mud! Act it out with him.

Tell him that you will help him out, but he must obey your instructions very carefully! Throw him an imaginary rope and tell him to catch hold, pull his right leg out, then his left leg, and before he knows it, he is free!

Now, parent, it is your turn to get stuck!

Obey the Sign

On your child's back, tape a piece of paper that carries the instruction *Act like a (familiar animal)*.

Instruct your child to ask questions that can be answered by a simple yes or no such as:

Is this animal fierce?
Does this animal make a loud noise?
Is this animal small?
Does this animal eat meat?

You may give additional clues until she identifies the animal. She must then act like the animal usually does and make its sound.

Applaud your child's good obedience and fine acting skills. Tell her that God is pleased when animals obey people (Genesis 1:26 says that we are to rule over them), and God is very pleased when *we* obey him!

Guess What!

Tell your child that you have four items in a paper sack, and as you remove each one you will tell him what he is to do with it.

A spatula and a bean: Instruct your child to place the bean on the flat spatula and carefully carry it across the room and back without dropping it. If the bean slips off the spatula, he must put it back on, step back three paces, and go forward again. Applaud his obedience when he reaches the designated finish line.

A small orange or ball: Show your child how to hold the orange under his chin (or between his knees if he cannot make the orange stay) and walk across the room in that position. Tell him that was a hard trick and that you are proud of his obedience even when it is hard to obey!

A penny or other small coin: Place a penny on your child's nose. Instruct him to carry the penny across the room and back, dropping it into a bowl at the finish line. Give that little nose a kiss for an obedient job well done. Explain to him that a child who obeys well in fun times can obey well in serious times, too. That pleases you and his heavenly Father, too.

Noah Was Obedient

Tell the story of Noah from Genesis 6–9. Stress his obedience to God's command even when other people did not obey.

Act out the story of Noah on a sofa "ark" with stuffed toys for the animals. Tell your child that there were two of every animal, even though you probably only have one each of a few kinds.

You be the reverent voice of God, calling to Noah, played by your child. (Make it serious, not silly.)

Say, "Will you obey what I ask?" (Noah answers, "Yes.")

Tell her to get a lot of gopher wood. (The child pretends to get wood.)

Tell her to cut it into boards. (The child obeys.)

Instruct her to nail the boards together to make a boat. (She can pretend to hammer.)

Request that Noah put tar on the inside and outside of the boat, so that it will not leak.

When you are finished, talk with your child about how good it was that Noah obeyed God and that we always must, too.

Classroom Obedience

Children usually like to play school, especially if you join them in the pretend classroom. Pretend that you are together in a schoolroom or a Sunday school class. Let your child and some of his stuffed animals be the pupils, and you be the teacher.

Give the students directions such as "Take out a pencil, please." "Write your name, please." "Please stand." "Stand in a line, please."

Praise your child for his good obedience. If he is not obeying your instructions as well as you wish, discontinue the game, making sure that he knows that obeying a teacher is very, very important! Stop the game as soon as he loses interest.

Let your child go outside for recess or let him play inside with you as a reward for his good obedience in class!

Chants and Songs

I'll listen with my ears [*cup hands around ears*]
And in my heart I'll say [*place hands over heart*]
"I'll do what Daddy (Mommy) asks me to . . . [*shake finger determinedly*]
All . . . this . . . day!" [*clap as you say each word*]

I'll mind you when it's morning;
I'll mind you when it's night.
I'll mind you every single day,
'Cause minding you is *right!*

Teach your child to say this to you as parents and occasionally as a prayer chant before bedtime!

To the tune of "London Bridge":

I'll obey what Jesus (Daddy, Mommy) says.
Yes, I will!
Yes, I will!
I'll obey what Jesus says,
I'll obey him (her)!

To the tune "Mulberry Bush" as the child performs an assigned task:

This is the way I mind my mom (dad),
Mind my mom,
Mind my mom,
This is the way I mind my mom,
I'm happy to obey!

To the tune of "Farmer in the Dell":

I love to mind my mom,
It makes me feel so good.
I like the way the day goes when
I do the things I should!

Obedient Octopus

Draw a simple picture of an octopus as large as a piece of construction paper. Give the octopus a smiling face, and on each side of his eight legs, write a description of obedient behavior that your child can perform. Each evening, let your child put up a sticker or star on the appropriate octopus leg.

You may wish to use some of these statements:

• I obeyed my mommy's words.
• I obeyed my daddy's words.
• I obeyed my teacher's words.
• I obeyed my baby-sitter's words [or Grandma's].
• I obeyed Jesus by being kind.
• I obeyed Jesus by praying.
• I obeyed Jesus by sharing.
• I obeyed by doing my work.

As you let your child put up his stickers, talk more specifically about his good behavior during the day, and do not forget to mention that it pleases God!

Rope, Rope

Tie a rope or ribbon taut between the backs of two chairs. Ask your child to perform various rope tricks by listening to you and obeying your instructions. This activity is a good one to help her learn word concepts as well.
• "Put your back to the rope."
• "Put your nose on the rope."
• "Put your hands *over* the rope."
• "Crawl *under* the rope."
• "Walk your fingers along the rope."

Sheep and Shepherd

Talk with your child about the job shepherds did in Bible days and still do in some countries today. Tell him that shepherds are often children who help and obey their father by taking care of the family's sheep.

Emphasize the importance of the sheep following the shepherd and ask your child why he thinks a lamb should obey when the shepherd calls. (The shepherd will keep the lamb from danger, lead her to grass and water during the day, and direct her to the sheepfold at night.)

Take turns with your child roleplaying the shepherd and the sheep. As you do, tell your child that Jesus is sometimes called the Good Shepherd and you want *always* to obey him.

Obey and Toss

Place five different colors of construction paper on the floor. If you wish, you may write a number on each to help your child learn to recognize numbers. Tell her to listen, please, and obey your words. Give her a beanbag or a child's sock filled with beans and tied shut. Instruct her to toss the beanbag to the colors (or numbers) you name, one at a time.

When finished, commend her for her good job of listening and obeying! Tell her to keep up the good work!

Place Them in the Basket, Please

Place two baskets, boxes, or sacks in front of your child. Let each one represent a category such as summer and winter, animals that fly and animals that swim, hard objects and soft objects, or heavy objects and light objects. If you wish, tape or draw a picture on the outside of each basket to represent its contents. For instance, use a snowflake for winter and a sun for summer. Place objects in front of the baskets that belong in either of the two categories.

Ask the child to listen to your words and do as you say:

"Pat, please find what you might wear in the winter and place it in the winter basket. Now find a shirt that you would wear in the summer and place it in the summer basket." Continue the game until each item is in its proper basket.

Whom Shall I Obey?

Make a simple envelope by folding in half a piece of typing or construction paper and gluing or taping shut the side edges. Write the words *Whom shall I obey?* on the front of the envelope.

If possible, find pictures of a police officer, a teacher, a doctor, a parent, a grandparent, and perhaps a minister and place them in the envelope. Include also a picture of Jesus. You may wish to use actual photographs of people whom your child will be expected to obey. If you cannot find pictures, write the name of each authority figure on a separate square of paper instead.

Ask the question "Whom shall I obey?" See if your child can name someone she is expected to obey, and after she has done so, let her reach in the envelope and pull out the name or names of someone she should obey.

You may wish to sing this little song to her and encourage her to learn it (the tune is "The Farmer in the Dell"):

Whom shall I obey?
Whom shall I obey?
I want to do the things I should;
Whom shall I obey?

Sack of Commands

Tape a small sack to the back of a kitchen chair. In it, place strips of paper with a command written on each. Some possible commands are:

- Please straighten the pillows on the couch.
- Please make your bed.
- Please dust the table.
- Please give me a hug.
- Please say a short prayer for someone.
- Please sing me a song.
- Please do a trick for me to watch.

On each paper, if you wish, tape a small reward that your child may have after he obeys the instruction.

Place the paper strips with commands that have already been obeyed in a separate container, and encourage your child to make periodic checks to see how many obedient deeds he has already performed.

Let him know that you are delighted with his good obedience!

Chapter 6

Introducing Your Child to Honesty and Purity

Whatever is true, whatever is noble, whatever is right,
whatever is pure, . . . think about such things.
—Philippians 4:8

"A man of integrity," "a loving, gracious woman," "a faithful husband and father," "a devoted wife and mother," "one whose conduct is above reproach"—all statements a caring parent longs to have spoken one day about his own dear child. In order for our children to have high moral standards as adults, we must have an active part in their early character development. Occasionally, an individual rises above a lack of early training to mani-fest qualities of honesty and purity in adulthood, but in the majority of cases, early patterns set the norm. We must live and teach what we want to see pro-duced in the lives of those in our care.

As we begin rearing our child to be honest and pure in her life-style, we must remember that the job is not in-stantly and easily completed! We should not be appalled when our sweet child one day tells a lie or takes some-thing that is not hers. We are not to make her think that she is simply a bad girl who has betrayed our trust. Instead, with God's wonderful help and wisdom, we are to encourage the development of a good self-image while making sure that we do not condone or allow improper behavior from our child. The delicate balance *can* be maintained. In addition, our child must become aware that all of us, parents included, have a tendency to do wrong and that we need God's strength and forgiveness in order to do right.

There are many Scriptural guidelines that give us wisdom as to how to handle the situation when our child does something wrong. After the wrong has been dealt with, we must quickly grant forgiveness and restore him to the same full fellowship he enjoyed before the incident. He is not permanently tainted; he is a little child just learning how to conduct himself in the manner God desires of us all. He, too, is verifying what the Scripture clearly says is true of all of us. "There is no one righteous, not even one. . . . For all have sinned and fall short of the glory of God. . . . But God demonstrates his own love for us in this: While we were still sinners, Christ died for us" (Rom. 3:10, 23; 5:8).

The Baby

A baby is just becoming aware of the world around her. Any parent knows his little baby has absolutely no consciousness of what is morally pure and honest; that knowledge must come later in her development. Even then, we must proceed very carefully and with God's wisdom in order that we not discourage her blossoming imagination and creativity in the name of "always telling only the truth," nor cause her to think of her beautiful God-given little body as shameful or a cause of embarrassment.

When introducing honesty and purity to our child, we should begin when she is very young and in a very natural, loving way as we take care of her needs in our home each day. She will not yet understand what our words mean. Remember, this is *only* the initial introduction. Use the following ideas as a loving, enjoyable part of baby's play and conversation times, much as you would use nursery rhymes or games. At some unknown point in her preschool years, the concepts of honesty and purity will begin to have meaning and take root in her little life.

Clean Little Baby

As you bathe your baby, say, "I'm washing baby's hands. Please, dear God, keep baby's hands always doing what is right and good." As you wash his feet, pray "Please help these little feet to go only where you would be pleased."

Wash your baby's tiny ears, eyes, and mouth, praying that God's strength will keep your baby pure, clean, and pleasing to the heavenly Father. As your hand gently feels your baby's heart beating, pray, "Lord, may this little heart always beat with pure love for you." Make prayer an integral part of your daily practice as long as God gives you life. Your child, now a baby and one day an adult, will never outgrow the need for a parent's prayers.

Prayer for Baby

As you talk to your baby, say something like this as the prayer of your heart: "You're Mommy's (Daddy's) sweet little baby. Your little eyes shine with God's pure, bright light. His bright sunshine is coming through the clean window glass. Dear God, please help my baby's life to stay clean and pure and always pleasing to you. Amen."

God's Sparkling Light

Hang a mirror in your baby's room where the sunlight can dance off it onto the walls and ceiling as it turns and moves, perhaps near an air vent or an open window. Your baby will enjoy the moving reflections.

Tell her, "Jesus wants our life to shine for him with a clear, pure light."

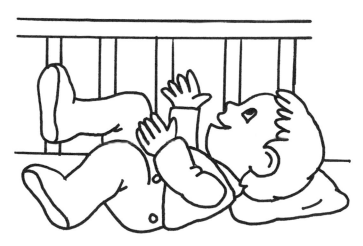

Clean, Pure Water

Set a clear glass of water where your baby can see the light shining through it. Put it out of reach on a table or shelf near your baby's bed or playpen. Or hold your baby near a running water faucet and let him feel the water on his hand and try to grasp it, as older babies try to do without success!

Talk about God's wonderful gift of water and give the baby a drink from a cup or bottle. Tell your baby that water is clean and pure and crystal clear, and that's how Jesus wants him to be all his life. Give him a hug and a kiss!

Don't Say "Yuck!"

As you diaper your baby, be careful not to convey by your facial expressions or words that any part of her little body or any normal bodily function is dirty or disgusting. Instead, be very matter-of-fact as you take care of her diapering needs, talking and singing to her as you perform this job that is not always pleasant!

Our ultimate purpose is to develop within our child an attitude that God has perfectly designed every part of her physical body for its own marvelous purpose, and has instructed us through his Word and by our own Spirit-led conscience to use our body in the proper manner for his glory and honor. "Therefore honor God with your body" (1 Cor. 6:20).

 # The Toddler

Yummy Good Drinks

Make one of the following nutritious fruit drinks with your child's help, or use any concentrated juice drink that he can help you mix. Tell your child that he is making (or drinking) the good, pure drink God wants him to enjoy! Talk about God's kindness in giving us our bodies and about his desire for us to keep our bodies clean and pure.

Give your little child a pat on his sweet little tummy or back when you are through.

Fruit Crush

½ cup strawberries, fresh or frozen
¼ cup strawberry (or other fruit) juice or water
½ cup nonfat dry milk
Sugar (or sugar substitute) to taste

In a blender, mix all ingredients. Add crushed ice or ice cubes and again blend well. Serve your child, and have some yourself! Don't forget to thank God for the fruit he gives.

Tangy Apple-Grape Juice

Apple juice
Grape juice
Frozen lemonade concentrate, thawed
Lemon-lime soda

In a pitcher or large jar, mix all ingredients in whatever proportions you wish. Let your child help you stir, and add juices, pouring in the soda as the tangy final touch.

Apricot Refresher

1 large can of apricot nectar
12 ounce can of frozen lemonade concentrate, thawed
1 large bottle of lemon-lime soda

Mix the juices and soda for a refreshing drink. If you have an apricot or lemon on hand, show it to your toddler, letting him taste the fruit as you explain that the good juice came from that kind of fruit. Thank God for the tasty drink!

Love Rhyme

As you hold her close, rocking your dear little toddler, say this loving rhyme to her:

Thank you, God, for my sweet girl,
Keep her pure and full of joy!

Or say:

Here's my sweet Sarah,
I love her so.
Help her pure and good to grow!

You're Absolutely Beautiful to Me!

Regardless of a child's physical features, he is a marvelous work of *beauty*, and he deserves to be told so by those whose opinions matter to him! While parents should not make physical attractiveness a primary emphasis, we do want to build up a kind of insulation in our child to help protect him later from the unkind taunts of classmates that inevitably come to most children.

Always stress your child's inner qualities of beauty and call attention to them, but occasionally compliment his physical appearance, too. Use a mirror as you talk about him or simply point to each facial feature and say something like, "Isn't that a cute little button nose! It can sniff." (*Show him how.*) "It can wiggle. It can sneeze." (*Demonstrate each ability.*) "And it can smell yummy food and sweet perfume! Thank you, God, for Sammy's cute little nose!"

Talk about Sammy's eyes, ears, mouth, hands, and feet in a similar loving manner. If he is too wiggly to let you proceed through all his physical features at one sitting, talk about his wonderful physical qualities at other times in a natural manner.

As you conclude your assessment of his beauty, say, "What do we have when we put him all together? A beautiful, wonderful boy!" Grasp his hands and dance around in a happy circle with him!

You're So Valuable to Us!

When you must correct your toddler's behavior, explain to her that Daddy and Mommy must say no sometimes because she is so *valuable*, so *precious* to you. She will understand those words in time as you occasionally use them to reinforce her sense of self-worth.

Tell her that you cannot allow her to do something that would hurt her in any way or that would not be good for her to do. Repeat, "You're so very *valuable* to me," with a hug and a facial expression that shows love!

Pat-a-Cheer

Play a pat-a-cake game with your toddler, saying this cheer as you clap his hands together:

God cares what I say,
God cares what I do,
God cares what I think,
And Jesus, I do, too! Yeah! [*Stretch his arms out to the sides for a grand finale!*]

Let the Light Shine Through!

Let your toddler shine a flashlight through clear things—a magnifying glass; a windowpane with someone standing on the other side; the windshield of a car; a clear drinking glass, dish, or vase; a piece of clear plastic; or a piece of plastic wrap.

Place your hand on the opposite side of the clear object and show your child that the light shines through on you. As he enjoys shining the flashlight, talk about how the object must be clear and clean for the light to shine though it. Mention that we must be clean and pure for God's light to shine through us, too.

Do not be concerned that he does not understand the concept of personal purity. Remember, we are only making introductions! Someday, he *will* understand.

Clean and Clear

Let your toddler clean windows or mirrors with a spray bottle filled with water. Show her how to wipe the surfaces clean with a cloth, sponge, or paper towel. Talk with your child about how clean and clear she is making the glass.

Tell her that Jesus wants us to be a clear glass so that his love can shine through us. Talk about how good "clean" feels!

Let's Clean Up!

When your toddler is especially dirty, use her cleanup time for more than just a scrub-up! As you wash her hands, fingernails, face, and ears, play a happy funny-words game with her. Make up your own words, if you wish. They do not need to rhyme.

Scrub, scrub, scrub!
Mommy's scrubbing Tammy's hands!
Use them, God, to do good things!
Scrub, scrub, scrub!

Wash, wash, wash!
Mommy's washing Tammy's face!
Shine her face with your pure love.
Wash, wash, wash!

Soap, soap, soap!
Mommy's soaping Tammy's feet!
Help her walk the way you please.
Soap, soap, soap!

Clean, clean, clean!
Mommy's cleaning Tammy's ears!
Please keep watch o'er what she hears.
Clean, clean, clean!

Swab the Deck!

Toddlers love busywork. Give your child a scrub brush, a sponge, or a wide paint brush and a bucket containing a small amount of soapy water. Show him how to scrub the sidewalk, driveway, garage door, or brick wall outside your home. Plan on his having wet clothes, but think what a great deal of fun it will be for your child!

Tell him that Jesus makes us clean and washed when we ask him to. Sing "What Can Wash Away My Sin?" which is based on Hebrews 9:22. Some day your child will understand the concept of sin and Jesus' wonderful forgiveness. Today he will experience the happy, fun feeling that comes from making something clean and from being outside with *you!*

All of Me

As your little toddler stands undressed before or after her bath, play this little all-of-me-is-important rhyming game. A child who has grown up with a healthy concept of her own worthiness is less likely to engage in later activities that are harmful or impure.

Here is your head, [*knock gently on her head*]
Eyes, nose, and chin; [*quickly point to each*]
Here is your mouth, [*touch it*]
That the food goes in. [*walk fingers along her cheek toward her mouth*]

Here are your shoulders,
Elbows, hands, too; [*point to each*]
Here is your tummy,
Pat, pat, koochy, koochy, koo. [*pat and tickle gently*]

This is your bottom, [*pat her little backside*]
These are your knees, [*tap each knee*]
These are your feet, [*touch them*]
Now tickle them, please! [*do so!*]

Ages Two to Three

Color Me Pure!

Trace around your child as he lies on a large piece of butcher paper or several grocery sacks flattened and taped together. As you draw around his ears, say, "Jordan, what we hear should be pure and right, like pretty music, the songs of birds singing, good stories, and good words." As you trace his hands say, "What we do with our hands should please God, too, like waving at somebody or hugging a friend, making a pretty picture to give away, or opening our Bible to read."

After the outline is complete, ask your child to add features and hair to the face and to color where the shoes and clothing should be. If he needs help, show him where everything belongs on his face and body.

As you discuss his feet, talk about good places we should go—to church, to help somebody, or to get something Daddy needs. When your child draws his mouth, tell him that "our mouths should say kind, true, and pure things and should sing songs to God to say we love him."

If your child remains interested, discuss his eyes and what he sees. Tell him that his brain is inside his head, and mention that it makes him *think.* God wants us to think good, pure, and kind thoughts. That makes God glad! "Whatever is true, whatever is noble, whatever is right, whatever is pure, whatever is lovely, whatever is admirable . . . think about such things" (Phil. 4:8).

Whisper Good Things

When another child whispers something to our child in our presence, we usually wonder if the message is one that we should hear and squelch! We suspect that the children are up to something, and they may be!

Tell your child when she is alone with you that when we whisper something to someone, we must be sure that we whisper good things, loving and *pure* things.

Suggest some good things to whisper: "I like you," "Let's help your daddy," "Let's obey your mommy," or "Let's surprise your grandma and sing her a happy song!" Remind your child that Jesus hears us even when we whisper, and he is *so* pleased when we whisper good things. Find many opportunities to whisper good things in *her* ear!

What Goes in Your Mouth!

Play I'm-thinking-of-something-good-to-put-into-your-mouth. Name a food, a drink, a toothbrush and toothpaste, a horn, a whistle, a piece of gum, and so on. Ask your child after each item if it would be good to put into her mouth. As you name the good things, occasionally interject something bad like a sharp object, a marble or other tiny toy, or too much candy. Include other substances that your family does not approve of your child drinking, eating, or using by mouth.

Praise your child for her wise choices in this game, and then tell her that there are some things that should not come *out* of our mouths either—crabby talk, bad words, things that are not true, and words that are not kind. Tell your child that Jesus loves her and is pleased with good talk. Sing lovingly, "Oh, Be Careful, Little Mouth, What You Say."

Pure Water

Tell your child the Bible story of David and the sheep as you paraphrase Psalm 23. Especially emphasize the importance of clean, pure water for the sheep. Tell your child that the shepherd took the sheep to still water because sheep are afraid of water that is moving like a rapidly flowing river or stream.

Share a cool drink of water from the kitchen or the garden hose if you are outside. Tell your child that Jesus is *his* Good Shepherd who takes good care of him!

True Tree

Trace around your child's hand on paper and cut duplicates from several different colors to represent leaves. On each leaf write a statement that is either true or false. If you are playing this game in the fall, talk with your child about the beauty of God's changing foliage.

From brown adhesive paper that has the appearance of wood (available at most grocery or variety stores), cut a simple tree trunk and branches, and let your child help you stick it on paper which you can hang in his room. Place the handprint leaves in a box and let your child pick one at a time for you to read aloud.

If your child believes the statement that you read is true, let him attach the leaf to his tree limb with a circle of masking tape on the back. Continue to add true leaves to the tree. If you wish, let your child stick the leaves that are not true under the tree, as though they have fallen there.

Sing this simple song about truthfulness to your child and encourage him to join you in singing it a second time (the tune is "London Bridge"):

> Jesus wants me to be true,
> To be true,
> To be true.
> Jesus wants me to be true.
> I'll be true for Jesus.

Piano Drama

Make a musical story for your child's listening and learning pleasure. It is not necessary that you know how to play the piano, nor that you use a melodious tune or chords. The keyboard sounds will simply help you emphasize what you are trying to illustrate to your child.

Begin your story with a small child skipping happily along (skip your fingers along the upper keyboard). As he does, someone comes along who wants him to take some bad medicine or drugs (with a fist, make discordant, but not scary, sounds on the lower half of the keyboard). Ask your child what the boy should do. (After he answers, pound twice on the upper notes with your fist as you say, "No! No!" Then skip the boy happily away because he made the right decision. Pound the bad guy off the keyboard to your left and pretend that he is gone.)

Tell a similar story using any kind of improper behavior that you want your child to avoid. Talk with your child about bad strangers or even friends who would want him to do wrong things (be as specific as you think wise). Encourage your child to always say no, to get away from that person, and to tell you about it even if that person told him not to.

Car Wash

Let your child help you wash the family car or her own tricycle. As you work, talk about how clean and shiny the car is becoming as the dirt is washed away! Tell her that sometimes we do wrong things like disobeying parents, saying unkind words, or hitting someone. When we do wrong, we must tell God we are sorry, and he washes the dirt away and makes us clean again. "If we confess our sins, he is faithful and just and will forgive us our sins and purify us from all unrighteousness" (1 John 1:9).

Pure as Gold

Place a brass candle holder on the floor, or use a vertically folded piece of yellow or gold-foil paper to represent a golden candlestick. Take turns with your child jumping over the candlestick, as in the nursery rhyme "Jack Be Nimble." Quote this rhyme as your child jumps:

> Stacy, be nimble,
> Stacy, be quick,
> Stacy, be pure like a
> Golden candlestick!

You can share the following verse with your child, "They made the lampstand of pure gold" (Exod. 37:17). Explain that gold candlesticks were made to go in the tabernacle (church).

Sweet Smells

Let your child enjoy a fragrance such as spices, a spray of perfume, or a scented candle. As he smells the fragrance, tell him that little boys and girls and mommies and daddies who do good things are like a sweet smell to God! (See Exod. 30:34–35, 37.)

Gold Star Words

Make four stars out of poster board or cardboard covered with gold foil. On three of the stars, print the following words and be prepared to explain their basic meaning. Hang the fourth star on a piece of yarn.

- true
- pure
- honest

Turn the stars facedown so the words cannot be seen, and ask your child to turn them over one at a time. Or you may want to use a stick, string, and magnet—attach a paper clip to each star and let your child fish for a star.

After the game is over, ceremoniously hang the blank gold star around your child's neck and announce that she is a gold-star child because she does what the words mean. Mention specific instances of good behavior your child has performed and tell her that she is a golden girl to God, too.

Go for the Good!

Help your child make boots from small or medium paper sacks. Have him step into the sacks, tie them around his ankles with string or yarn, and fringe the top edges if your child wants Indian moccasins. As you are making moccasins, talk about the importance of where our feet go—they can take us to good places and bad places. Help your child think of some good places our feet can take us:

- to church
- to a friend's house
- to do a kind job for someone
- to play with a friend
- to hug and kiss somebody

Ask if your child can think of any places our feet should not take us (anywhere Mother or Daddy would not like, anywhere dangerous, anywhere that would not please God).

I'll Be Like a Prism

Purchase a prism from a toy store or use a crystal portion of a chandelier or glass doorknob to catch the direct rays of the sun. Show your child the lovely rainbow colors they produce. Tell her that Jesus wants us to shine God's love in a beautiful way like a prism does!

 # Ages
Four to Five

God's Warrior

This may be a good activity for a child who likes superheroes.

Make a warrior's helmet from an inverted small paper sack, folding over the edges several times for reinforcement. Ask your child to color it grey or silver. Explain to him that a mighty warrior is a fighter for good and for God. Emphasize that a warrior must be pure and honest. He must be trusted to mean what he says and to do right. Tell your child that you are both God's mighty warriors!

March as you sing "Onward, Christian Soldiers." Talk with your child about the courage and strength God gives his warriors such as Gideon, Joshua, and David.

Clean and Shiny

Let your child help you clean and scour copper or aluminum pans until they shine. Or give him a polishing cloth and a silver-plated tea set to polish for you. Talk about the gleaming beauty of the metal when it is clean and shiny. Remark that we are clean and shiny for Jesus when we do good things, say good things, and think good things.

Where's the Gold Ring?

This is a game for three or more players.

Players sit in a circle on the floor. One player has a gold ring (foil wrapping paper around a small cardboard circle works well). The player with the ring walks inside the circle with the ring in her fist. She taps her fist on the upturned fists of the seated players and secretly deposits the ring in one of their hands, repeating this rhyme as she goes from player to player.

> Gold ring, pure ring,
> Who has you?
> I'll be pure
> In all I do!

The other players try to identify which player now has the gold ring. The one who received the ring then becomes "it," walking from player to player as the game is repeated. To conclude the activity, repeat the verse together and briefly explain its meaning.

Pure Speech

Give your child a tube of toothpaste and a small plate or dish. Ask him to squeeze some toothpaste into the dish and put the cap back on the tube. Tell him that you would like him to repeat that action two more times. Then ask him to put the toothpaste *back* into the tube, and let him make an effort to do so!

As your child realizes that he cannot put the toothpaste back into the tube once it has been squeezed out, you might use this situation to say the following: "Our words are like this toothpaste. When we say them, we cannot put them back in our mouth. That is why we must be very careful to say nothing that would hurt anyone's feelings or that would be unkind or untrue. God wants our talk to be pure and good, and he's happy when it is. Good talk makes us happy and other people, too!"

Be Careful What You Say!

Let your child hammer large nails into a board. After she has done so, help her remove them with the claw end of the hammer. Show her the holes that the nails made in the board and use them as an object lesson for your child.

Tell her that saying unkind or impure things is like hammering nails into the board. When the person who said the unkind words is sorry and says so, that is like pulling the nails out of the board. Then ask your child to make the holes in the board go away. When she states that she cannot do so, explain to her that even when we are sorry for bad words, we cannot take them back, just as the nail holes cannot be removed. Tell your child that you and she must always be careful to say pure, kind words.

Pure Religion

The three following activities may help your child to understand and put into practice admonitions given in James 1:27: "Religion that God our Father accepts as pure and faultless is this: *to look after orphans and widows* in their distress and *to keep oneself from being polluted by the world*" (emphasis added).

1. *Visit the widow.* Visits to rest homes, convalescent homes, grandparents' homes, and elderly neighbors' homes serve a double purpose. They teach children to be kind and unselfish, and in return they receive grandparent-style love and affection. Many children do not live near grandparents, and *no* child can have too much of that very special kind of love! Make opportunities for your child to visit and help dear widowed women and other elderly people.

2. *Visit the orphans.* Take advantage of opportunities to help children who live in children's homes, children who live in foreign countries and have little to eat or wear, and children whose fathers or mothers are in prison or away in military service. Sponsor such a child with financial aid, letting your own child earn money to share. Or take

a child on an outing with your family or invite him to share a special meal with you and your family.

What an unforgettable experience will be your time spent with an orphaned child! Repeat the kindness as often as possible. Your show of love and attention may help to fill the void in the life of a needy child, and it certainly pleases the heavenly Father.

3. *Keep yourself from being polluted by the world*. Put a white shirt on your child one morning before he begins his play. Tell your child that you want to have a contest with him. The object is to see if he can keep his shirt clean all morning without getting a single smudge on it! If he can, you will reward him with a treat.

If he gets a spot, tell him that you have a way of making the shirt look like there was never a spot on it. Let your child help you wash or bleach the shirt until it is clean again.

Explain that when we sin or do wrong, it is like getting a spot on our heart, but when we tell Jesus we are sorry, he forgives us and makes us clean again! Tell him, "Now you may have the same reward as though the spot never happened!"

Crystal Clear Objects

Take turns naming things you can see through, such as clear plastic wrap, a window, ice, a magnifying glass, cellophane, bath water, binoculars, a swimming pool, a telescope, a glass of water, or a prism.

Say to your child, "Did you know that Jesus wants the way we act to be as clean and pure as that window? He wants his love to shine through us just like sunshine."

Pure Hearts

Help your child make a decorative heart in one of the following ways:

• *Salt dough*. Mix two cups salt and one cup flour with approximately one cup water. Flatten the dough and cut out a heart shape with a small hole at the top. Bake it at 325° until hard. When cool, paint it white and tie a ribbon or string through the hole for a hanger.

• *Styrofoam heart*. Provide craft glue, sequins, beads, and small strips of ribbon for your child to use in decorating a Styrofoam heart. You can purchase ready-made heart shapes at a craft supply store or cut them out yourself from the foam trays used to package produce and meat. Be sure to wash them thoroughly first.

• *Heart cookies.* Let your child help you make heart-shaped sugar cookies. Ask him to help frost them and decorate with colored sprinkles, if you wish.

• *Paper hearts.* Cut various sizes and colors of paper hearts and let your child glue them on a sheet of white paper. A doily makes a pretty background for a paper heart, too.

• *Fuzzy heart.* Provide for your child 1½-inch squares of tissue paper, a piece of 8½-by-11-inch construction paper on which a large heart has been drawn, a pencil with an eraser, and a bottle of white glue. Instruct your child to spread glue on a small section of the heart. Show him how to press the squares of tissue over the eraser end of the pencil and then press them down on the glue so that the ends stand up making a fuzzy effect. Proceed around the heart until the whole shape is covered.

As your child makes a heart, say, "Jesus wants our own heart to be clean and pure like this pretty heart. He will help us do what is right, say what we should, and keep our hearts clean and pure for him."

Pure Eyes

Let your child make a sun visor from a moon-shaped piece of poster board or paper plate. Ask your child to color it as she desires; then attach the visor to your child's head with yarn or ribbons.

Play a game with her as she is wearing her visor. Tell her that you will say some pretend activities. If the activity mentioned is one that would be OK for her to look at or enjoy, she should raise her visor or look up; if it is an activity that she should not watch, she should lower the visor or look down. Use the following statements as examples:

- A beautiful sunset can be seen in the sky.
- A child is acting very naughty in class just to get everyone to look at him.
- A child is trying to get dressed privately.
- Your pastor is praying in church.
- A violent television program is on at a friend's house.
- A friend wants to show you a drawing he has made.
- Beautiful red flowers are blooming in a yard.

You might also share this verse with her: "Your eyes are too *pure* to look on evil" (Hab. 1:13, emphasis added).

My Body, God's Temple

Play this silly, familiar game with your child: Pat your head and rub your tummy at the same time! As you do, chant this rhyme together:

> I'll keep my body clean.
> I'll keep my body good.
> I'll keep my body pure,
> And do the things I should.

Smudges

When your child has smudged a window or mirror with his own sweaty fingerprints or a sidewalk with muddy footprints, tell him that smudges do to objects what sin or wrong actions do to us. They make us dirty!

Help your child clean up his own dirty smudges. Explain that Jesus graciously erases our sin spots when we ask him to do so and that he makes us clean and pure with no smudges!

Keep Your Heart Clean

This activity may seem a bit strange to you, but it will likely be a hit with your child and will help her to long remember the visual lesson. That is our purpose.

Some evening when she is ready for a bath, rub a little hand lotion on her chest and draw a heart shape on the area with eyebrow pencil or lipstick! (The lotion will make removal easier.) Put your child in the bath with her heart still on and tell this story to her:

Once there was a special girl who tried very hard to do what is right and keep her little heart clean and pure. One day someone came along and said to the girl in a whisper, "How would you like to steal something?"

"No!" said the girl as she covered her clean heart. "I won't!"

"All right then," said the person, "how about disobeying your mother and daddy and running away with me?"

"No!" said the girl. "I won't!"

Finally, the bad someone left her alone with her clean, pure heart and there it is! [*Point to your child.*]

Input Guard

You will be inevitably confronted with the question, *Why can't I see that?* When your young child wants to watch a television program or movie or look at some book or magazine to which you object, you need to remind yourself of this fact: A child is most secure and least confused when he knows that his family has reasonable standards of conduct that are consistently enforced. He may push against the standard at times, but inwardly he finds safety in knowing that the standard is firm, even when he seems unhappy at the prohibition.

Explain to your child that his mind is a computer much *more* valuable than any other computer in the whole world. (Make a simple drawing to illustrate your words, if you wish.) Tell him that a daddy and a mommy are supposed to help guard their precious child's mind from pictures and ideas that would not be good for him to see.

My Lips Shall Speak Pure Words

Select a large white or light-colored envelope, cut out mouth shapes from red paper, and let your child glue them on the envelope.

In the envelope, place good statements that a young child should heed, such as:

- I will tell the truth.
- I will talk nicely to grown-ups.
- I will not make jokes about God or Jesus.
- I will not tease anyone about his or her body.
- I will not laugh when someone acts naughty.

Instruct your child to choose a statement each morning and to try very hard, with God's help, to do what the paper says that day. At the end of the day, help the child with a brief assessment and let her know God's love and help are always available.

Oh, Be Careful, Little Child, What They Say!

Warn your child to watch out when someone makes statements like these to him (and to be sure to tell *you* about it, too):

- "Come on . . . everybody's doing it!"
- "What's the matter? Are you scared?"
- "What are you . . . a *baby?*"
- "Don't tell your mother or daddy about this!"

Teach your child that "God is faithful; he will not let you be tempted beyond what you can bear. But when you are tempted, he will also provide a way out so that you can stand up under it" (1 Cor. 10:13).

Pure-Thinking Game

Play this word-association game with your child, using it as a springboard to a conversation about right and wrong behavior. Ask your child to tell you what ideas or pictures come to her mind when you say these words:

bubbles
cheating
clean
detergent or soap
dirty clothes
lying
pure
stealing
truth
washcloth
washing machine
water

Try to help the child understand the symbolic meaning of cleanliness.

Pure Fragrance

You and your child can make a sweet-smelling fragrance-hanger to spice up the atmosphere. Ask your child to help you press whole cloves into a small orange, covering the orange as completely as possible. Attach a pretty ribbon for a hanger. Or make a potpourri wreath instead. Glue dried potpourri to a small Styrofoam wreath and hang it where it can be seen and enjoyed.

As you work with your child on either project, mention to him that what you are making will remind you to be a pure, sweet-smelling fragrance for Jesus! "For we are to God the aroma of Christ" (2 Cor. 2:15). If you wish, talk about the perfumes the wise men brought as a gift to the Baby whose life would always be pure and fragrant with God's love.

God's Commandments Are Pure

Make a flattened tablet from clay, baker's clay, or salt dough (two cups salt to one cup flour to approximately one cup water). Explain to your child that in Bible days, God gave to Moses clay tablets upon which he wrote ten very special rules, or commandments.

Give your child a pen or other pointed instrument with which she can carve her own hieroglyphic writing on the tablets. Tell her that she can pretend to write actual letters or words as you tell her some of the commandments God gave to Moses and to us. Paraphrase the commandments to help your child understand them (see Exodus 20):

"You must only worship the true God."

"You must not make a statue and call it your god."

"You must not use God's name in a bad way."

"You must remember to keep God's day special."

"You must obey and be kind to your father and mother."

"You must not kill."

"You must be faithful and true to your wife or husband."

"You must not steal."

"You must not lie."

"You must not want to have something that belongs to someone else."

Hide the BIG Words!

Write these big important words on poster board or cardboard and hide them one at a time (your child may want to take a turn at hiding the words, too):

• Modesty
• Honesty
• Purity
• Integrity

Give a simple definition of each word as your child finds it; see if he can explain the words to you at the conclusion of the game.

Modesty: Dressing and acting like Jesus wants us to, because we know that God made all of our body wonderful and just like he wants it and that some parts are more *private* than others, so we are careful not to show them off in any way that wouldn't please God.

Honesty: Telling and doing what is true and right.

Purity: Being careful not to do anything that would hurt the body that God gave us.

Integrity: Being the kind of person that other people and God can trust.

Crown of Purest Gold

Help your child make a crown in one of these ways:

• Invert a small paper bag on top of your child's head and fold up the edges of the sack's opening several times for reinforcement. Ask your child to make the crown fancy by using crayons, gummed stars, or glitter.

• Cut gold foil paper into strips approximately eight inches long. Arrange the strips like spokes on a wheel and staple at the hub or center. Glue or staple a small round piece of paper over the center of the strips where they are all connected, like a jewel on top of the crown. Staple the other ends of the strips at even intervals to an additional paper band that has been measured to fit your child's head. Gently shape the paper strips to allow the center "jewel" to rest near or on your child's head. If it will not stay down, secure the jewel to your child's hair with a bobby pin.

• Cut a crown shape (the lower edge flat, the upper edge zigzagged) from a strip of poster board measured to fit your child's head. Let her decorate the crown with crayons, markers, gummed stars, and glitter, and tape the ends together to form a ring. Let your little queen enjoy the crown.

Explain to your child that in the Bible we read about crowns. They were made from purest gold and often with beautiful, glistening jewels. Share Psalm 21:3 with her and tell her that Jesus says someday there will be a beautiful crown for people who love him and stay pure for him!

A Kiss Is Very Special

Draw or paste a mouth shape on paper. Under the mouth, print the words *A kiss is very special.* Explain in your own words what that means. Elaborate as much as you wish, but be sure to tell him that "one of the nicest gifts you can give somebody is a kiss." Because that is true, he is to give a kiss only to those people who are very special.

If you wish, explain to your child that when he is older and likes a special person, he still must be careful not to give out kisses too often because kisses mean "I like you" or "I love you very much." Smile and say, "And I *do* love you very much! So, here!" (Give him a big kiss.)

Let's Be Ladies and Gentlemen

Pretend with your child that he is a "gentleman." Occasionally call him by that title when you address him at other times. Act out how a lady and gentleman should act, and play the opposite role if you only have children of one sex. The role play may become a little funny if Daddy temporarily must be a lady or Mommy must be a gentleman.

Stress to your child that we should treat each other with politeness and good manners in the way we talk and act. Help the child know that God made both girls and boys to play together, talk together, and enjoy each other's company.

Parents—whether married or single—must be careful to treat the opposite sex with respect in conversations and attitudes in order for children to recognize their own worth and the value of other people. A child who has learned appreciation and proper conduct toward people will be less likely to use or abuse them later in life.

Aren't You Glad You're You

When it seems appropriate, take spontaneous opportunities to stress to your child how delighted you are that she is a girl (or that he is a boy)! Talk about the wonderful characteristics you like about your child's sex.

Emphasize those specific traits that you see in your child: "I like girls because they are strong and playful but they still are able to be gentle." Or, "I like girls because they can be gentle and quiet, but they can also run and play and have great fun!" Let your child know you are glad to be the sex you are, especially if your child is of the same gender as you. Tell her how glad you are that God made her just like she is!

Prayers and Songs

Make me careful what I say.
Make me careful what I do,
'Cause I really want my life
To count, dear Lord, for you!

Keep me clean, Lord Jesus,
Keep me pure.
Help me be your very special little
Good Deeds *Doer*!

To the tune of "The Farmer in the Dell":

I want my mind to think,
I want my hands to do,
I want my feet to only go,
Where you would want them to.

When I must make a choice
If I'll do bad or good,
I'll choose to do what Jesus says.
I'll do the things I should.

When someone says bad words,
So near me that I heard,
I'll put *good* thoughts inside my head
And say *good* words instead!

To the tune of "Mulberry Bush":

God can see me when I'm shy.
God can hear me if I lie.
He sees all the things I do,
So I'll do good for Jesus!

Chapter 7 ———————————

Introducing Your Child to Witnessing

Even a child is known by his actions.
—Proverbs 20:11

People observe people. The elderly person observes the young, the child observes the teen, and the youth observes the other youth. Each person who is watched has a sphere of influence, sometimes extensive, sometimes limited, but influence nonetheless.

Probably no person is more often noticed than a young child. Few people can pass an unsteady toddler or an active preschooler without a smile or word of greeting to her. In our home a little child is a source of great attraction. We are usually fascinated by a child, and what she does and says has a strong impact upon us. Our daily adult lives are influenced by the children in our families.

Children also influence other children. An observation of how rapidly negative behavior is passed from one child to another verifies that!

Conversely, with guidance and encouragement from us, our child can exert a strong influence for good and for God upon other people.

The activities that follow are designed to help insll in our very young children the guiding principle that what they do and say and how they act and react may help to draw people to the Lord Jesus Christ and his Truth. May God bless you with wisdom as you help your young child learn to be a positive influence upon others.

 # The Baby

Because babies and toddlers are in the initial stages of self-awareness and have no concept of the needs of other people, fewer activities are included for those age groups than for middle or older preschoolers.

Peek-a-Boo Baby!

While holding your baby on your lap or facing him as he lies in bed, say slowly:

"Peek-a-boo!" [*cover and uncover your eyes as you speak*]
"Peek-a-boo!" [*repeat the action*]
"Someone's watching *you!*" [*point to baby and touch his tummy gently*]
"Someone's watching *you!*"

Mommy's Listening

When baby is making contented cooing sounds, say gently to her: "Mommy's listening, darling. Tell me more."

Stand By

Sing this little song to baby as he lies quietly in bed (the tune is "The Farmer in the Dell"):

You (name) are my friend.
Your smile makes me smile, too.
I love to stand by baby's bed
And watch the things you do.

Share a Smile

As you introduce your baby to another baby and the two face each other, say to your baby: "Share a happy smile with Jimmy, darling!"

The Toddler

Pass It on!

Tape or tie a long empty wrapping paper cylinder to the handrail on a stairway. Give your toddler a rubber ball small enough to roll through the cardboard cylinder, and position him at the top end of the cylinder. Tell him to "pass the ball down the tunnel to Mommy, please." If he does not understand, demonstrate how to place the ball in the cylinder. Catch the ball each time he rolls it, and repeat as often as he has interest in the game.

As you play with your child, tell him lovingly that "Jesus wants us to pass his love to other people like Christopher is passing the ball to Mommy!"

Share the Good News!

Let your child crawl through a large box that you have opened at both ends. If you do not have a box handy, make a tunnel from a table covered with a large sheet.

Say, "Crawl through the tunnel to Daddy! I have good news!" Keep repeating the words as your child crawls toward you.

When she crawls out at your end of the tunnel, say, "The good news is . . . Jesus loves you, Erin!"

My Face Reflects God's Love!

Hold a hand mirror to your toddler's face. Talk about each feature and what God made it to do. Point to your child's eyes, nose, mouth (teeth, tongue), and ears as you discuss the purpose of each.

Say, "Jesus smiled with his love and made Jimmy's sweet face! Now Jimmy's face will smile for Jesus!" (Give that smiling face a kiss!)

I Can Make Music for Jesus!

Let your toddler "play music" on toy instruments or kitchen pots and pans. Provide recorded music to accompany her or sing along as she plays. Say, "Ellen can make beautiful music for Jesus that Mommy can hear!"

Fruitful Trees

"By their fruit you will recognize them" (Matt. 7:16).

Cut a simple tree trunk and branches from a piece of brown felt. Cut out several apples, oranges, and bananas from colored squares of felt.

Make a simple flannel board from a cardboard square you have covered with flannel or felt. You may use a sofa cushion for a flannel board instead, if you wish.

Place the trunk on the flannel board and let your toddler put fruit on the tree branches. As he does, tell him that Jesus wants us to share the fruit of his love with other people.

Praise your child for his good job of putting fruit on the tree!

Ages Two to Three

Indian Peace Circle

"If it is possible, as far as it depends on you, live at peace with everyone" (Rom.12:18).

You may make this activity as simple or as elaborate as you wish. Help each child in the family make a feather headdress, a vest, a blanket, or moccasins made from paper sacks tied around the ankles. You may put on "peace paint" or simply pretend!

Sit in a circle on the floor.

Shake hands with your child and ask her to pass the handshake on to the next child. Do the same with a pat on the back, and then let your child initiate an action to pass on, if she would like to. With four- and five-year-olds, try speeding up each activity as you pass it on.

Pass on statements such as, "Let's be friends" or "The Bible says make peace"; and then, as you count to three, all together shout, "Yea!"

We Need Others

"None of us lives to himself alone" (Rom. 14:7).

In a small box or in a sandbox outside, make a cave from a small empty cardboard tube by covering it with sand or cornmeal. Leave one end of the tube, the entrance to the cave, uncovered.

Ask your child to place a small toy animal inside the cave. Explain that the toy animal lives all alone and has no friends. He has no one to keep him company, to eat with him, to play with him, or to help him when he is hurt or sad.

Say, "That's why God gives us our family and friends, so let's give our animal some friends." Place other animals around the outside of the cave. Make the cave animal come out to meet his new friends and have him jump up and down excitedly.

Tell your child, "We can help each other, laugh and play, and even be sad together . . . and God is *always* with us, too!"

Fruit Sharing

Your child can be a wonderful encouragement to a homebound person. Let him take a colorful fruit basket to a person who needs some love and attention.

Or pack several pieces of fruit on a small paper plate and cover it with plastic wrap and a colorful bow. Go with the little one to deliver such fruit plates to residents of retirement homes and tell him he is bearing fruit for Jesus.

Something Very Special

Tell your child that you have something very special clasped tightly in your hand. You want to pass it on to her.

Put the object (something good to eat or play with) in her hand and let your child keep the object.

Remark to her that the most special thing we can ever pass on to someone else is Jesus' love!

Influencing Neighbors for Good

"Each of us should please his neighbor for his good" (Rom. 15:2).

Plan several good-neighbor activities in order to help your child spread a spirit of neighborliness on your street while learning to be helpful himself. Here are some possible activities:

- Pick dandelions and weeds from the side of your yard nearest to your neighbor's to keep them from spreading to his lawn.
- Offer to shovel your neighbor's sidewalk in winter or do so when he is not expecting you to. Let your little child help as much as possible with his own shovel or scoop.
- Take cookies to someone.
- Put paper baskets (made from open manila envelopes or construction paper rolled into cone-shaped containers and stapled or taped) of flowers on doorknobs.
- Call a person who is ill. Run an errand for him with your child.

Spread a Little Son-shine

Tell your child that smiles are "catching!" Explain that when we share one with somebody, she usually will give it back to us and, perhaps, share it with someone else, too.

Smiling can spread and spread, making many people happy! Since Jesus makes us happy, we want to share his joy with other people!

Make a grocery store trip a "sharing Son-shine" outing. Tell your child ahead of time that you and he are going to smile at people and try to spread Jesus' happiness all around. Even a shy child can usually muster a coy and absolutely irresistible smile.

Enjoy the fun that sharing the Son-shine brings!

Put on a Bead

Make a necklace of beads, macaroni, or O-shaped cereal. String the pieces on yarn that has been reinforced at one end with a small piece of tape wrapped around it.

After your child strings a bead, he must pass the yarn to you to add another. You then take turns stringing the beads. Include as many children in this activity as you can.

Tell your child that when we share God's love with each other like we are sharing the necklace, we make something *beautiful!*

What's in a Name?

Discuss your child's name with her. Include her full name—first, middle, and last—in your discussion. Talk with her, too, about the names of family members.

If you know the meaning of your child's name, explain it to her. Tell her how she measures up to the positive character trait her name implies.

Tell your child that when we have Jesus' love in our heart, we have his name, too. We never ever want to do anything to hurt Jesus' wonderful name!

A Pretty Light

"You are the light of the world" (Matt. 5:14).

Let your child dip the bottom two inches of a candle into white glue and arrange pressed flowers, beads, sequins, or other flat decorative objects on the glued area. You may also wish to sprinkle a little glitter on the glue for him. (Two-year-olds are too young to use glitter themselves; it can easily be transferred from their hands to their eyes.)

After the pretty candle has dried, set it somewhere as a reminder that we are to shine for Jesus.

Explain to your child that we shine brightly for Jesus when we are kind, obedient, and helpful.

Shine like Stars!

"You will do well to pay attention to it [Scripture], as to a light shining in a dark place" (2 Pet. 1:19).

Few of us sleep outside or have a bedroom skylight that permits us to enjoy starry nights. Let your child make her own stars appear on the ceiling of her room.

With a pencil, punch holes in the bottom of an empty oatmeal box. If you wish, arrange the holes in the configuration of the Little Dipper constellation.

Place the box over the end of a flashlight and secure it with masking or strapping tape. Let your child lie back, turn it on in her darkened room, and enjoy an evening with the stars!

Quietly tell your child that she is Jesus' little star that shines for him! Be sure to make her feel that she is the light of *your* life as well!

Salty Sidewalks

Let your child spread a little salt in your neighborhood some winter morning by shaking rock salt on neighbors' icy sidewalks and steps. This is inexpensive. Keep a supply handy for this special purpose.

As your child does her good deed, remind her that Jesus wants us to be his salt in our world and that you are so glad that Darcy is sharing her salt with her neighborhood!

Salt Garden

This interesting activity is sure to be a hit with your preschooler, but do it when you do not mind his hands being temporarily stained.

Fill a bowl or cake pan with crushed ice or ice cubes. Let your child sprinkle the ice with salt from a shaker and then add drops of food coloring of different colors. Watch interesting ice shapes form as the salt melts the ice.

Tell your child that Jesus said we are to be like salt—to make our world an interesting and beautiful place to be!

Greenhouse Giants

Plant birdseed on a wet sponge or in a shallow container of soil. Place a "greenhouse," an inverted small glass jar, over one section of seed. You will soon notice that the patch of grass in the greenhouse grows faster and taller than the grass not enclosed by the greenhouse.

Explain to your child that God has put her in a greenhouse, too. Her greenhouse is the family, friends, and church that love and protect her so that God's love can shine brightly on her.

Express your confidence that she will grow straight and tall and strong to shine God's light on other people.

I'm Like a Pendulum!

One pendulum can set another swinging. Here is how to demonstrate that to your child.

Cut two pieces of string about eighteen inches long and press a ball of modeling clay about an inch and a half from the end of each string. Tie a large knot or a button on the end to keep the clay ball securely in place.

Tie another string tightly between the backs of two chairs and place heavy books on the chairs to hold them steady (or you and your child may each sit in one!).

Tie the pendulums to the string between the chairs and hold one still as you set the other swinging.

Carefully let go of the second pendulum, allowing it to hang down motionless. It will immediately begin to swing with the other clay pendulum.

Tell your child that other people do what we do, just like the pendulums. If we do what Jesus wants us to—mind our daddy and mommy, talk kindly, and be gentle to other children and pets—others may behave that way, too. (Include the special kinds of behavior you want to impress upon your child.)

Spread the Good Word

Children love to write on steamy windows and mirrors. In this activity, the child writes upon a mirror before the steam arrives!

Guide his hand to write a special message to Daddy on a bathroom mirror. Dip the tip of a cotton swab in liquid soap and print the letters with the thin, nearly invisible film of the soap. Place a message (such as "Jesus loves you!") and a happy face drawing on the mirror where it will not obscure Dad's view.

When the mirror steams up from Dad's shower (or on a window on a cold day), the happy message will appear.

Who's Peeking at Me?

"Even a child is known by his actions, by whether his conduct is pure and right" (Prov. 20:11).

Explain this Bible verse to your small child. Demonstrate to her by peeking out from behind your hands that people watch us to see what we do and say. If we love Jesus and act like he wants us to, other people may, too.

Make a peek box with your child as a reminder of this truth. On one side of the inside of a cardboard shoe box, glue a picture of your child. Place a lid on the box.

Make two round holes on the opposite side of the box, large enough and spaced far enough apart for your child to peek through. If it is too dark in the box to see well, cut some small holes or a slit in the lid for light to shine in.

Sing the following song to your child as she peeks at her picture:

To the tune of "Are You Sleeping?":

> Someone's watching,
> Someone's watching,
> Watching me,
> Watching me.
> I'll be very careful,
> I'll be very careful,
> What I do,
> What I do.
>
> Someone's watching,
> Someone's watching,
> Watching me,
> Watching me.
> I'll be very careful,
> I'll be very careful,
> What I say,
> What I say.

Naaman and the Little Girl

Tell the Bible story from 2 Kings 5 in a manner your young child can understand such as the following:

In the Bible there is a story about a very sick soldier named Naaman. He could not get well, and he was sad about being sick. One day a little girl told him that God's preacher, Elijah, might help him. Naaman went to see Elijah. Elijah said that God wanted Naaman to dip under the water in the Jordan River seven times. One . . . two . . . three . . . four . . . five . . . six . . . seven! [*Make your hand dip as you count.*] When Naaman did as God wanted him to, he was well again! Naaman was so glad the little girl had helped him know what to do.

Use a waterproof toy character for Naaman. Take your child and Naaman to the bathroom sink. Fill the sink with water and permit your child to dip his toy under the water seven times. Make the toy character excited over his good health!

Emphasize to your child that someone small can be a wonderful help to big, grown people.

Someone's Following You

Trace around your child's feet or shoes on felt squares or on an old rug you do not mind cutting apart.

Using the cut-out feet as a pattern, make ten more of each foot. Place the footprints through the house and take turns being the leader as you and your child follow where they go. Ask her to make the footprints go somewhere, but do not worry if they are not in perfect left-right sequence.

As you follow her, explain that people follow us where we go, and so we must be careful to go to good places and do good things.

We don't want people to follow us somewhere dangerous, like into the busy street or away from Mommy when we are in a store.

But we *do* want them to follow us to the dinner table when it's time to eat or to the toy box to put our toys away or to church with us.

Ages Four to Five

I Want You to Love Jesus

Many Christian families share the common burden of having an unsaved spouse or unchurched parents and friends.

A little child is often a great influence in their coming to know the Savior personally. A child observes at an early age that some members of his family or circle of friends love Jesus, his church, and his Word, and some do not.

Eventually, such a child will be likely to say something about spiritual things to the people he suspects are not followers of Jesus.

He will probably be very direct and embarrassingly specific in his choice of words. He may not deliver them at a time you would have chosen for him to "preach." However, God has used the words of children on many occasions to accomplish his purposes.

Do not put the child up to such statements; the unsaved person may find that quite offensive. Pray, however, that God will use your child to accomplish his purposes.

Grievous Words Stir Up Anger

Visualize this scriptural principle for your child in order to help her understand her influence upon others. It may help her to respond positively when faced with true-life situations involving angry words.

Place a shallow clear glass pan of water in the microwave on high temperature. Tell your child that the calm, cool water you first poured into the pan is like a person who is not angry at all. Tell her to watch what happens as the water gets hot.

Act like you are a person saying the angry words below. Pause between each statement, showing how the water is beginning to boil until it is steaming hot—like a person getting madder and madder.

- "Hey, you look silly!" [*Pause*]
- "I don't like you!"
- "I don't want to be your friend."

Then show the opposite. To the "mad steam" (turn off the microwave) add *soft* words.

- "I'm sorry."
- "It was my fault."

- "I won't do that again."
- "Will you please forgive me?"
- "Let's be friends."

Take the pan of water out of the microwave and show your child that the steam has disappeared and the water is returning to its calm state. Remind your child that she can help people stay calm by talking to them with kind, soft words. Quote the Scripture admonition, "A gentle answer turns away wrath, but a harsh word stirs up anger" (Prov. 15:1).

Take Brother Along

Visit someone in a convalescent home or someone who cannot get out and about.

Take your child and a younger sibling or friend. Tell the older child ahead of time that you and he are going to show the younger child how to be kind. Explain to him what to expect when you arrive at the person's home and how you wish for him to behave.

Remind your child, "We must be very careful to be loving and kind because Sam will be watching us, and he will learn to act as we do."

Reflectors

"You are the light of the world" (Matt. 5:14).

Take your little one out after dark. Place a bicycle reflector on a stake in the ground or use a bicycle with a reflector on it. Shine a flashlight on the reflector.

Explain to your child that the flashlight shines on the reflector and the reflector bounces the light back to us.

Say to your child, "Jesus shines his love on us. He wants us to shine our love on other people . . . just like a reflector!"

What Happens without Light?

"Let your light shine before men" (Matt. 5:16).

Lay a small square of cardboard across a patch of grass and leave it in place for several days.

Explain to your child that grass needs light to grow healthy and green. Lift the cardboard and observe that the grass underneath is yellow and unhealthy. Leave the cardboard off, and the grass will return to normal in a few days.

Tell your child that Jesus is the light of the whole world and that when we let him be our light, he makes us grow good and wise and kind. People who do not let Jesus shine on them cannot grow strong like he wants them to.

Stress to her that she is God's little light to help shine his love on everyone!

Please Pass the Kindness

Here's a game for the whole family to play while sitting at the dinner table after a meal together. You have before you make-believe dishes of good things you want to share.

Someone starts the activity by saying, "Please pass the kindness." Someone else passes it to her, and each person takes an imaginary bite.

Other family members say, "Please pass the love [*the sharing, the helping*]."

Conclude the game by passing a loving handshake from person to person. Tell your child that Jesus really does want us to share those good things with other people.

Share the Treasure

This game is for several children. In a treasure box place construction paper hearts with pictures of Jesus on them and small New Testaments, one for each child. Sit together in a circle and pass the closed treasure box around from child to child.

After the box has been passed around several times, say, "Now share the treasure!" The child who holds the box at that moment may open it and share the treasure inside.

Say to him, "These are what we want to share with other people—God's love and God's Word, the Bible."

Pass the Love

Here are five ways your child can pass Jesus' love to friends or family:

1. *Walkie-talkies.* Make walkie-talkies from two empty tin cans. Use a nail to make a hole in the bottom of each can and put one end of a long string through each hole. Make the string as long as the distance you will be from the other person. Tie a big, strong knot on the inside of each can. Pull the string taut between the two cans as you talk with your child.

Relay to her the message that Jesus loves her! Encourage your child to tell you something about Jesus, too.

Suggest that she use her walkie-talkie to tell some other child about Jesus' love as they play together.

2. *Animal face megaphones.* An animal face megaphone can be made from a paper plate and an empty paper towel tube.

Trace around the tube on the plate where you want your animal's mouth to be. Cut out the circle to make an O-shaped mouth.

Cut four slits in the end of the tube and fold the flaps flat. Align the tube with the back of the mouth opening and tape or glue the flaps to the paper plate to make a shouting tube.

Color or paste an animal's face on the front of the paper plate and attach appropriate animal ears on the top or sides.

Let your child shout to a sister or a friend the wonderful news that Jesus loves her!

3. *Folded note.* Help your child write a short, loving message about Jesus. Fold the note and suggest that he sneak it into someone's hand or pocket during the day.

If you know your neighbors well enough to feel comfortable, include them in your game. Your child will love sending secret messages. Suggest that he leave a note on the neighbor's porch, with a rock to hold it in place.

4. *Pass the Word.* Place your child's statement about Jesus (see "Folded note") in a small cardboard tube. Cover the tube with colored construction paper if you want it to be more visible. Then hide the tube somewhere in or outside the house for another family member to find. The one who finds it then hides it.

Emphasize to your child that you are passing a message about Jesus to people you love!

5. *Magic message.* Ask your child what message about Jesus she wants to give to someone. If she needs help, suggest statements like "Jesus loves you" or "Jesus is with you!"

Write the message with invisible ink made from grapefruit, orange, lemon, or apple juice. Use a fine-tipped, clean

brush for writing. When the ink dries, it will be colorless on the paper.

Encourage your child to give the hidden message to a friend. When the paper is held close to a light bulb (or ironed with Mother's help), the secret message will be visible.

Try a magic message with your own child, just for fun!

Salt Cleans!

"You are the salt of the earth" (Matt. 5:13).

Tell your child that Jesus wants us to be like salt! Pour some salt from a shaker and allow him to taste it if he wishes to.

Talk about how salt tastes. Explain that salt makes food taste better. Tell how it makes food last longer without spoiling. Explain that salt even cleans things! Try this activity with your child to show how salt cleans:

Clean a copper-bottom pan or brass object with a cloth dipped into vinegar and pressed into salt. If you do not have a copper or brass object, a shiny pan will work well. As your child dips the cloth into the salt and wipes the pan, the mild acid of the vinegar and the abrasive edges of the salt crystals will act as a scouring powder.

Salt Lifts

Tell your child that salt performs several functions:

• It keeps food fresh.
• It cleans.
• It makes food taste good.
• It can even lift things!

Prove your last statement by floating an ice cube in a glass of water. Ask your child this question: "If you were going to pick up the ice cube with a piece of string, how would you do it?" He will soon realize that tying the string around the ice cube will not work; the ice is too slippery.

Show your child how to lift the ice cube. Dip the end of the string in the water and lay it over the top surface of the ice cube. Let your child sprinkle salt from a shaker on the string and the cube around it.

Wait for one minute as the salt causes the ice to melt slightly and the string to freeze to the ice cube. Now tell your child to pick up the cube by the string.

Explain that Jesus wants us to be like salt—to help lift up people when they fall down, when they are sad, and when they need help.

Salt Makes a Pretty Picture

Help your child to make a picture by drawing with white glue on colored construction paper.

Provide a salt shaker and instruct her to shake salt all over her glue picture. When the glue has dried, shake the surplus salt into the trash can. A picture to be proud of will be the result of your child's efforts!

Tell your little one that we are to be like salt in our world, to make it a more beautiful place in which to live.

Share a Smile with a Friend

Cut several circles from cardboard or soft model-airplane wood. Have your child draw a smiley face on each circle with a magic marker. Glue a safety pin to the backside of each circle and allow it to dry thoroughly. When the smile pins are dry, encourage your child to share a smile with friends and neighbors.

Flashlight Zoo Critters

Cut a four-inch circle from cardboard and make a hole the size of a flashlight handle in the center of it.

Ask your child to color an animal's face on the circle, letting the flashlight's head be the nose. Cut out cardboard or paper ears for your child to glue or tape on the animal's head.

Slip the handle of the flashlight into the hole and turn it on.

Explain that the Bible says we are to let our lights shine, and even the little animal is shining his light for Jesus!

Let's Be Magnets

Explain to your child that when we behave like Jesus wants us to and when we talk about him to other people, they may want to know him, too.

Tell your child that Jesus is attractive, like a magnet. He wants us to help attract our friends to him. (It will be necessary for us as adults to put aside our own inhibitions, since our child may become quite bold when she realizes that she is supposed to share Jesus with her friends and loved ones!)

Do an experiment to illustrate the principle of magnetic attraction to your child. Provide her with a magnet and several small objects that can be picked up.

A funny magnet can be made from a phonograph record and several pieces of light, puffed dry cereal. Rub the record with a wool sweater or scarf. Hold the edge of the record slightly above the dry cereal and watch the cereal jump up to the record and then hop off!

Explain that when we act like Jesus, people will often want to be with us. We will attract them like a magnet, and we will be showing God's love!

Patterns

Provide for your child a purchased stencil pattern from a craft or hardware store or make your own from poster board. Let him draw around the stencil shapes on plain paper. A five-year-old will be better able to do this.

If you prefer, let your child help you cut around a sewing pattern. Whichever activity you choose, discuss with your child the purpose of a pattern: to help us draw or to cut something exactly to match.

Talk with him briefly about how we want to be good patterns for other people to copy. Tell your child that if we act as Jesus says we should, other people may want to act that way, too.

Peekascope

Help your child make a telescope from an empty paper towel roll. Cut your child's picture to cover the round opening and tape to the end of the roll.

Make a small hole or slit at the top of the roll to let in light near your child's picture or instruct your child to look toward light as he peeks through the other end of the roll.

Remind your child that people do watch us to see how we act. When we do good like Jesus wants us to, other people will want to obey him, too.

PART THREE

Introducing Your Child to God Himself

Chapter 8

Introducing Your Child to God through Creation

For since the creation of the world God's invisible qualities-his eternal power and divine nature-have been clearly seen, being understood from what has been made.
—Romans 1:20

Time obscures from our memory the absolute amazement we once experienced as we watched a fuzzy, crawling caterpillar, touched the frosty snow, or saw a wiggling puppy for the very first time. We observe the fascination in our baby's eyes as he discovers sights, sounds, and wonders he has never known before, and our heart beats as did the psalmist's when he wrote:

O Lord, our Lord, how majestic is your name in all the earth! You have set your glory above the heavens. From the lips of children and infants you have ordained praise. (Ps. 8:1–2)

What baby has not suddenly stopped moving to watch a crib mobile come to life from a breeze through an open window or the gentle touch of mother's hand? What child has not expressed elation, and perhaps a bit of fear, as a frisky kitten playfully romps past? How can a dry leaf, a tiny bug, a round grey rock, or a blade of green grass hold such tremendous fascination for a little child?

Remarkably, the wonder of discovery does not stop with the child. Providentially, the joy of exploration is rekindled within us, too, by the example of our baby or toddler, often before she can even speak. What parent has not momentarily become a child himself as he experiences with his baby the first snow of winter, the intrigue of a campfire or cozy fireplace, the relaxing motion of a goldfish contentedly swimming in an aquarium, or the velvety feel of a lovely pink rose?

We must constantly guard against rushing through these precious days and missing the pleasure of seeing God's world through the eyes of our very young child. He wants to see and touch and listen right now, right here, and the wise and fortunate parent takes advantage of the fleeting moments as spontaneously as they occur.

A mother and her three blonde girls were enjoying a fall evening's walk together. As the children skipped along in front of their mother, one was chanting words that came to mind, including her own name. Suddenly she stopped, amazed, hearing an echo for the first time and not realizing what it was.

"Mommy, Mommy!" she said as she excitedly rushed back to tell her mother. "Jesus is calling my name!" It is natural for a child to give credit to God for the sights and sounds she experiences when introductions to the Creator have been made early in her life.

Very soon the child's passion for discovery assumes a delightful new dimension—imagination! The backyard grass, needing mowing, becomes a jungle for our ferocious preschool "tiger." The wooden swing, recently suspended from the oak tree by Grandpa's loving hands, becomes a rocket ship, blasting off to faraway places. An old tree stump becomes a rugged cliff, with our tot the mountain climber struggling to ascend.

God's created wonders are all around us every day, in each season and in every type of weather. May the Lord reveal himself to you and to your receptive little child as together you experience his marvelous world!

The Baby

Touch-See-and-Hear Nature Walk

Take your young baby on a nature walk through the wonderland of your own yard. Remember as you go that everything he feels, hears, and sees is an enchanting new sensation to him. The breeze on his face, the warm sunlight on his tender skin, and the rustling leaves of an overhead tree provide exposure to new and delightful sensory experiences.

As you walk with your baby, stop to let him feel the grass, watch the leaves moving on the trees, and pet the family dog. Talk with him about the wonders he is enjoying and about the great God who made them—and *him!*

Wonderful Water

Provide warm water in a sink or a dishpan for your baby to enjoy while you hold her. Let her experience God's wonderful water with hands touching and splashing. Or take off her shoes and let her feet get involved in the action.

Winter Solace

Bundle your baby and take him out on a winter's night to watch snowflakes falling in the light of a streetlamp, a gas light, or a flashlight. Your baby may be more interested in the light than the snowflakes, but take the opportunity to tell him about the wonders of God's winter night.

Nature Mobile

Make an interesting mobile for a young baby from nature items. On a piece of yarn or ribbon, tie pinecones, flowers, fall leaves, an apple or orange with the string running through a hole cut in the middle, a small twig with spring leaves attached, or whatever else you find that can be tied.

Suspend the mobile where baby can see God's handiwork, making sure to hang it high enough so she cannot reach it. Remove it before the items begin to wither or fall. Point to each item, and as you do, sing this song to your baby to the tune of "Mary Had a Little Lamb":

> Jesus made the pretty leaves (or other objects),
> Pretty leaves, pretty leaves.
> Jesus made the pretty leaves,
> Thank you, God, for leaves.

Baby's First Nature Book

Find enlargements of nature pictures from magazines or calendars, selecting those that show close-up views of one main object in the picture—a piece of fruit or vegetable, an animal, a rock or shell, or a pretty fall tree.

Place the enlargements in a photo album that you reserve just for baby (one that you do not mind his chewing on and that you are sure has no sharp edges to cut or pinch), or make an album by gluing two pictures on the front and back sides of a rectangle of poster board. Cover it well with clear adhesive paper and fold in half to open like a book.

A waterproof book may also be made by placing mounted pictures into large zip-seal freezer bags and sewing them together with thread or yarn at the side of their openings. Cover the sewn area with sturdy tape. Check the book frequently for tears, and replace it when it begins to show wear.

Flower Chart

Find several close-up photographs of colorful flowers from a magazine or nature calendar. Mount them on cardboard, round the corners and completely cover the pictures (front and back) with clear adhesive paper.

Place the collage in baby's playpen or crib where she can see it and reach for it. Talk about God's beautiful flowers and, if you wish, sing this song to the tune of "The Muffin Man":

Oh, do you know who made the flowers?
Who made the flowers?
Who made the flowers?
Oh, do you know who made the flowers?
The Bible tells us God did!

The Toddler

Wave Bottle

Make a miniature model of ocean waves in a clear plastic bottle or jar with a lid. The size of the container is up to you—an empty soda bottle works well, but a smaller jar may be easier for your toddler to handle and observe.

Fill the jar half full of water. If the jar's mouth is large enough, place a small plastic boat or a boat shape cut from a piece of candle or wax in it. Fill the jar as full as possible with liquid paraffin and screw the lid on tightly. (If you have a glue gun or white glue, you may wish first to put some around the edge of the bottle, and then tighten the lid.) If your child is good at opening lids, add masking tape on the outside edge of the lid for reinforcement.

Place the jar on its side, tilting it slightly as you and your child watch the realistic waves move from one end of the jar to the other. The paraffin is lighter and thicker than water and slows the water's movement.

Talk about the mighty oceans that God made, and show your child a seascape photograph if possible. Tell him that the moving water is called waves.

Quote this little rhyme to your child:

> God made the *sea*.
> God made a *tree*.
> God made a *bee* and
> God made *me!*

Ask your child to repeat it with you for fun!

The Ball Goes Down

Demonstrate the principle of gravity to your toddler through a ball or balloon game. She will not understand much about this invisible force God has created, but she can certainly see and experience that what goes up must come down! That simple concept will be a foundational truth upon which she will later build a greater understanding of God's world.

Seat your child at the top of a small flight of carpeted stairs; you sit at the bottom. Give your toddler a rubber ball and ask her to roll it *down* to you. As she does, tell her that God makes the ball come *down* to you so that you may have fun with her! Say, "Thank you, God, that the ball rolls *down!*" Repeat the game as long as your toddler seems interested.

The concept of gravity may also be exhibited by giving your toddler an inflated balloon. Show her how to throw the balloon *up* and watch it come *down*. Tell her that God makes the balloon come down (point your finger up and then move it down as you speak), and that makes playing balloon games such fun!

Water Pickup

Enhance your toddler's water play by placing the dishpan of water on a towel-covered kitchen table and providing measuring cups and a turkey baster or a clean medicine dropper for more fun. Show her how to pick up and release water by squeezing and releasing the bulb of the baster or dropper.

Attach a waterproof bib or lightweight towel around her neck with a clothespin to keep her clothes dry. Place your child on your lap or let her stand on a stool, but do *not* leave her unattended as she plays. Talk to your child about how wonderful God is to give us water to drink and to enjoy!

God's Wonderful Bubbles

Toddlers *love* bubbles! They love to watch the bubbles glide on the wind, land, and pop! An adult can always make a hit with a toddler by blowing bubbles in the yard or into his bath water for him to watch and try to capture.

Here are several bubble ideas you may wish to use to delight your child:

1. *Humongous Bubbles.* For extra-big, rainbow-striped bubbles, make this mixture in a large flat pan and use a wire clothes hanger shaped into a hoop for dipping:

1 cup water
1 tablespoon liquid dishwashing detergent
½ teaspoon sugar
1 tablespoon glycerine (available at most drugstores, it makes the bubble stronger; however, since the label contains a warning regarding ingestion, use this recipe only when *you* will be making bubbles for your child—*not* when he will be trying to blow them.)

Stir the mixture and store it in an airtight container. Pour some into the pan, dip the wire hoop into the bubble mixture, and wave it in the breeze outside. Watch the bubbles fly!

2. *Catching Bubbles.* Blow bubbles with a commercial bubble solution and wand or use the Humongous Bubbles recipe (above) and a pipe-cleaner wand.

As you blow bubbles, rub a plastic spoon, ruler, or comb against a wool sweater or blanket and show your child how to collect the bubbles on the plastic object as the static electricity attracts them.

3. *Bubble Tube.* Make an interesting bubble tube for your child to hold and observe. Securely close one end of a clear plastic tube with a cork covered with strong tape. Fill the tube with baby oil or vegetable oil, leaving room to add several drops of food coloring to form beadlike bubbles in the oil. Secure the open end of the tube in the same manner as you did the first. Supervise your child as he holds the tube and watches the food coloring beads float from end to end in the tube.

Inside Snow

On a snowy winter day when your toddler must remain inside, bring the snow inside to her in a large bowl or flat pan. Place the pan on towels on the kitchen floor and provide her with a spoon, a plastic cup, and a clean, small plastic toy that she can hide in the snow. Talk about the beautiful, cold snow God made. Make a little snow creature with raisin or candy features and place it in the freezer for a future reminder of a happy snowy day.

Snow Slushes

Let your toddler help you stir up a cool tasty drink or slush from snow. Into a cupful of clean snow, pour slightly diluted fruit-juice concentrate or fizzy soda and stir. Add less snow and more concentrate for a cool drink, more snow and less concentrate for a slush.

As your child begins to drink say, "Thank you, God, for the snow you gave us."

Watch the Sun Do It

Place an ice cube or a fruit-juice cube on a plate in direct warm sunlight. Watch with your child to see how quickly it melts. Pour the water or juice into a glass and let her drink it.

Talk with your child about God's gift to us—sunshine! Tell her that the sunshine helps the grass and flowers to grow, makes us healthier and stronger, and gives us bright, happy days to enjoy! Say, "Thank you, God, for sunshine!"

Pocketful of Acorns

Take your toddler, dressed in a shirt or jacket with several pockets, on a fall acorn walk. Wear clothing yourself that has accessible pockets, since your child may prefer putting acorns in *yours!*

Show him what acorns look like, tell him that little squirrels and chipmunks like to find them (do *not* mention eating them!), and let him fill all available pockets with the acorns he sees. Tell your child that God even makes big trees grow from tiny acorns! Say, "God is good to give us acorns. God is good to give us trees!"

God Is Good to Give Us Sand!

A plastic dishpan makes a good indoor sandbox for winter and is easy to clean up when placed on a sheet on an uncarpeted floor. The plastic dishpan allows the sand to be dampened slightly for better shaping and less mess than dry, loose sand.

Do not add so much water that the sand becomes soggy. And be sure to allow the sand to dry in the air or sunlight after each use. Covering wet sand will eventually cause it to smell unpleasant.

Provide various sizes and shapes of containers and funnels for your child's use. Show her how to pack the sand tightly in a can and then invert it to form a sand castle—complete with towers, turrets and spires—or a cake, if you wish.

For a special effect, make flags from construction-paper triangles taped to pipe cleaners and let your child stick them in the tops of the towers. Do not expect her sand castle to avoid demolition for long! The enjoyment for a toddler is in the process more than in the finished product.

Cocoons

Wrap your toddler in a blanket and instruct him to stay hidden until you say, "Pop out!" He may not immediately respond to your words or understand the game, but he will soon have fun doing as you say.

Tell him as you wrap him that God makes caterpillars wrap themselves in cocoons and then pop out as beautiful butterflies! Repeat the game occasionally during the next few years, and your child will understand that a butterfly is an interesting and marvelous work of God!

The same activity may be used to teach your child that God also created rabbits and moles that "pop out" of their warm burrows and tunnels under the ground to eat and play.

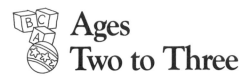

Ages Two to Three

Raisin Making

Help your child make raisins by placing green or red seedless grapes on a flat pan or tray in a dry, warm place. If it is feasible, place the tray outside to dry; the grapes should become raisins in a few days. If outdoor drying is not practical, the transition from grapes to raisins may take a few days longer in the house.

If you wish, your child may dry apple slices in the same manner. Enjoy the dried fruit together with a prayer of thanks for the fruit, the warm sunshine, and tongues to enjoy God's wonderful foods.

Bean Strata

To help your child appreciate the color and variety, as well as the good taste, of the various types of beans God has provided, help her make a paperweight from layers of dried beans.

Place several different colors and types of beans in small paper cups that can be pinched at the drinking edge to form a pouring spout. Help your child pour the different kinds of beans in layers to fill a baby-food jar, gluing and tightening the lid securely when finished. Make sure that the bean strata jar is out of the child's reach but where it can be enjoyed when you are nearby.

Cook one or more varieties of the beans for your child to taste later that day. Talk about the differences in the dried and cooked beans. Be sure to tell your child that "[God] has made everything beautiful" (Eccles. 3:11), even beans!

Want a Piece of Pie?

Allow your child to make mud pies (in a permissible area of your yard) in a large flat dishtub or an old plastic baby bathtub. Provide jar lids, cans, play dishes, or empty margarine tubs for his cooking pots. Grass, pebbles, and sand in an old salt shaker make good ingredients and spices for your child's cooking pleasure! Pies and cakes may be baked in the sun or over a heating outlet or radiator (do not use plastic containers for this!) in the winter.

When it is too cold to play outside, spread newspapers on the floor or table and let your child enjoy summer-type fun in his indoor mud tub. Remember that toddlers *are* completely washable and that they are developing positive manual and mental skills as they have a good time in the mud!

Be sure to tell your toddler that God made the dirt and that he is so good to let us have fun together. Repeat the Bible thought to him, "Work with your hands" (1 Thess. 4:11).

Sink or Float?

Provide for your child a tub or sink full of water and several heavy and light-weight objects. Explain to her that some objects float like boats on top of the water, but some sink to the bottom of the tub. Demonstrate how light-weight objects float and heavy ones sink.

Before placing each object in the water, ask your child questions such as these: "Do you think this will float?" Let her handle it to see if it is heavy or light. "Do you think it will sink to the bottom of the water?" "Do all things float?" "If you make something heavier, will it then sink?" Add a rock or block to a sponge or toy boat.

Voice your thanks for the water God gives us!

Sound Waves

Sound waves, like many of God's creations and even the great Creator himself, cannot be seen, but your child can get an introductory idea of how they move through air by observing waves in a sink or bathtub of water.

Ask your child to touch the top of the water with his finger or to drop a small rock into it and watch what happens. Small waves will circle away from the place where he touched the water. Tell your child that noise travels the same way through the air. Explain that when we make a sound, noise circles move through the air, even though we cannot see them, until our ear catches the sound and we hear it. Tell him that these sound waves are in the air all the time and that God is so kind to give us ears to hear (see Prov. 20:12).

The Great Pull

Help your young child understand that *gravity* is an invisible pull that makes things fall down to the ground. Ask her to hold a ball or toy perfectly still and then to let it go. Ask her if the ball went up (point up) or down (point down) when she let go of it.

Continue to explain to your child that something she could not see pulled the ball down—gravity! Tell her that gravity pulls her down the slide on the playground.

Do more gravity experiments with your child by making a V-shaped chute from a piece of lightweight cardboard. Place the chute on a tabletop with one end elevated on a book and the other extended slightly over the edge of the table. Roll a marble or small ball down the chute, observing the spot where it hits the floor. Place a box or a plastic bowl at that spot to catch the marble the next time it rolls down the chute.

Roll other round things down the chute—an orange, a golf ball, a walnut, a grape, or a tennis ball. All the objects will land in the box regardless of their size and weight, since gravity acts equally on all objects.

Talk with your child about our great God who makes things that we can see and things that we cannot see. Tell her that love and gravity are two things we cannot see, but that they are both real. And so is God!

Birdseed Pretzels

Ask your young child to help you put peanut butter on a large, unsalted pretzel. Provide birdseed in a cup with a pouring spout for your child to sprinkle over the pretzel. Press the seeds into the peanut butter.

Hang the bird treat by a string from a tree outside. Say, "Thank you, God, that we can help take care of your little birds."

Is the Glass Really Empty?

As your child observes, turn an empty glass upside down in a pan of water. Push the glass straight down into the water, keeping it in a vertical position. Explain to your child that no water can enter the glass because something we cannot even see is already in the glass—air!

Tip the glass slightly while it is in the water. Show your child that water has gone into the glass as air has gotten out. Remind him that God makes many things we cannot even see, like air and wind and *love!* As you hug your child, explain to him that even though we cannot see God, we *know* he is right here with us and never, ever leaves us!

God Can Change Water!

Show your child that God can change water into steam and ice! Pour a cup of water into a pan and place it on the stove to boil. Hold your child safely where she can observe the water begin to turn into steam. Ask her where the water goes, and explain that the steam disappears into the air. Use some of the steamy water for a hot drink, letting her help you add apple cider or cocoa mix to it.

Put cool water into a container or ice cube tray and let your child help you place it in the freezer. Tell her that God will make the water change into ice, and check occasionally to see if the change is taking place. Place the frozen cubes in a glass of water and thank God for the cool drink that he makes possible.

Will It Soak In?

Using a medicine dropper or a turkey baster, let your child drop water onto a dry sponge. Ask, "What happened to the water? Where did it go?" If he does not know, explain to your child that the water soaked into the sponge.

Try the same procedure on several thicknesses of paper towels, a piece of aluminum foil, waxed paper, a plastic toy or dish, a piece of wood, and the back of your hand. Explain to your child that water rolls off some things and soaks into others.

Ask your child to say aloud with you on the count of three, "Thank you, God, for water!"

Catching Rain

Place a clear plastic jar in the corner of a sandbox or in a shallow hole in the ground where it cannot tip over. Explain to your child that the jar is going to catch rain. After the next rain, bring the jar inside and measure with a ruler on the outside to see how much rainwater you have collected. Take the opportunity to explain to your child how important rain is to all God's creations. Concentrating on how much rain the jar is collecting may also help an apprehensive child to tolerate a thunderstorm better.

Rainbow Flowers

Demonstrate to your child the amazing ability of a plant to absorb water from its stem and pass it on to its leaves and flowers. Place the stems of white daisies, carnations, or wildflowers in water that has been colored with drops of red, blue, or yellow food coloring. Leave the stems in the colored water for several hours and observe occasionally that the colors are traveling to the white flower petals.

To make a lovely multicolored flower, carefully split a stem in half vertically several inches up from the end and place each half in a different color water. When the coloring process is complete, encourage your child to wrap the stems in a paper towel and give the lovely flowers to a friend. Tell the child that because God is so good to give us flowers, we want to pass his kindness on to others.

Leaf Prints

To help your child recognize and appreciate that leaves come in various interesting shapes, collect several types and make leaf prints from them.

Thumbtack the leaves to a piece of white paper placed over corkboard or Styrofoam. Show your child how to dip the end of a sponge into tempera paint that has been mixed with liquid detergent for proper painting consistency and easy cleanup.

Help her dab the paint around the edges of the leaves, leaving them in position until dry and then removing them to reveal the outlines of the leaf shapes.

If tempera paint is not available, show your child how to make leaf prints by placing white paper over the leaves and coloring on the paper with a crayon. As the prints of the leaves begin to be seen, talk about the veins and how perfectly God designed them to carry food and water to the parts of the plant or tree.

Preserved Leaves

With your child, collect bright green leaves in the spring or colored ones in the fall and preserve them in this manner:

Break paraffin in pieces and melt it in a Crock-Pot or double boiler. Dip the leaves in the melted wax and place them on a newspaper to dry. Allow your child to place the paraffin in the pan *before* it is heated, but do the dipping procedure without his help.

Make a necklace by running a thread through small leaves while they are still warm, stringing macaroni pieces between them for variety. As you work with your child, talk with him about the wonderful way God designed leaves—to bud and grow in the spring, turn beautiful colors in the fall, and drop off in the winter so new leaves can replace them in the spring. Keep your explanation simple, but let your own enthusiasm for God's wonders show!

Plant a Seed

A paper or Styrofoam cup makes an excellent container for planting seeds, and your child is sure to bring one proudly home from Sunday school sometime.

A whole flower or vegetable garden may be started in the early spring inside the protection of your house. Put potting soil or dirt in the cups and let your child punch holes around the bottom with a sharpened pencil for drainage. Set the cups in a tray or old pan to catch the runoff.

Let your child plant seeds, bulbs, or young plants in the cups and identify each with a marker on the outside of the cup or tape the seed packet picture to it.

When ready to transplant the seedlings outside, peel away the cup, leaving the tiny new roots undisturbed and ready to continue growing.

Pressed Flowers

Collect flowers with your child and let her help you place them between two sheets of white typing paper or waxed paper. Put the papers and flowers under a heavy book and wait a week or ten days before removing them.

After the flowers are pressed, they may be used by your child to decorate a gift box or homemade card. Talk with her about the beautiful way God makes the flowers grow and bloom (see Gen. 1:11).

Sand Drizzling

Provide for your child several zip-seal bags of colored sand or fill two unused salt shakers with separate colors of sand. The sand may be colored by adding a small amount of powdered tempera or one or two drops of food coloring, or by rubbing pieces of colored chalk through a cup of sand or salt.

Let your child drizzle white glue on a piece of construction paper (stay close by since he may get a bit carried away) and sprinkle colored sand over it from an open corner of the zip-seal bags or a salt shaker. Allow several hours or overnight for the glue to dry.

As your child creates a sand drizzling, talk about the immeasurable number of grains of sand on the seashore and stars in the sky and about the great God who made them. A good Bible verse to share says, "as countless as the stars of the sky and as measureless as the sand on the seashore" (Jer. 33:22).

Stone Collection

Almost any rock is a beautiful treasure to a very young child. He is fascinated by the shape, color, and texture and can soon accumulate quite an extensive collection of rocks!

Keep his lovelies in a special collection box made from an egg carton. If your child is interested, label each compartment with a small paper containing pertinent information such as where the rock was found or a description of the rock it contains. You will be encouraging your child's ability to categorize items by including descriptions such as "a round rock," "a rock with black spots," or "a small, flat rock."

Tell your child that Jesus is sometimes called our Rock because he is so strong and mighty (see 2 Sam. 22:2–3).

What Kind of Soil Works Best?

Fill paper cups with different kinds of soil (sand, potting soil, red clay, fine gravel, etc.), punch holes in the bottoms for drainage, and place the cups in a pan or on a tray. Provide grass seeds for your child to plant in each cup and a small amount of water. Water and check each plant every few days to see if the grass is growing. Help your child determine which kind of soil works best for growing grass.

Explain to her that people may plant the seeds and sometimes help by watering them, but God is the only one who can make the grass grow! Tell your child that the Bible says, "He makes grass grow" (Ps. 104:14).

Sun Tea

Fill a jar with cool water and let your child hang decaffeinated or herbal tea bags (perhaps flavored with orange, lemon, or cinnamon) over its edge and into the water. Set the jar in the sun and wait until the water turns brown.

Pour the tea into a glass of ice, add sugar or sugar substitute, and let your child enjoy it. Sip tea together and talk about how good God is to us, letting us enjoy tasty drinks that quench our thirst!

Squirmy Wormies

As you are digging in a flower bed or after a rain, place a worm or two at the bottom of a clear glass jar or drinking glass. Give your child dirt to pour on top of the worms and a small amount of water to add to the dirt. Watch with your child to see what the worms do.

After you have enjoyed observing the squirmy worms, help your child release them into a garden or flower bed. Talk about what God has equipped worms to do:
• to be food for birds
• to be bait so that fishermen can catch fish for food
• to help plants grow by making tunnels in the dirt so air can reach the roots

• to make the dirt better for vegetables and plants to grow (soil that has been occupied and enriched by earthworms contains five times more nitrogen, twice as much calcium, two and a half times more magnesium, seven times more phosphorus, and eleven times more potassium than soil without them!)

Who's Hiding There?

Your two- to three-year-old child is fascinated by every new sight he sees. He is sure to notice the tiniest bug or woolliest caterpillar that crosses his path, but all his feelings about bugs may not be positive. Some children are afraid of bugs; others delight in collecting them by hand and proudly presenting them to you at the most unsuspecting moment!

To satisfy your young child's curiosity about living things and to help allay any fears he may have about crawling things, let him dig up a shovelful of dirt and study it with you. Talk about the centipedes, roly-poly bugs, snails, worms, and grubs that the dirt may contain. Explain that birds and some animals (moles and shrews) love to eat the white grubs. Tell your child that if the grubs are not eaten, they will become beetles.

Remind him that God made even the tiniest bugs. Explain that God made some of the bugs for animals and birds to eat. Say, "Isn't God kind to take care of animals and even little bugs? Will he take care of us? Yes!"

Shadow Boxing

Encourage your child to enjoy a silly, rowdy time playing with her own shadow on a wall. Your light source can be the sun shining on an outside wall or a flashlight indoors.

Talk about the light God gives us. Tell your child that when sunlight shines on us, our shape—or shadow—shows up on a wall or the ground on the other side of us. Explain that sometimes our shadow is big and sometimes small.

Plant a Potato

Select several sweet potatoes as you grocery shop with your child. Bake one for each of you to eat for lunch and plant another one in water. Let your child help you carefully push four or more sturdy toothpicks halfway into the potato near the middle.

Place the sweet potato atop a full glass of water with the toothpicks supporting it on the edge of the glass so that the potato is resting in the water. Place the glass in a sunny place in the house and add water frequently to keep up the water level. When the potato roots have developed in the water, it may be transplanted outside.

Explain to your child how our great God causes strong roots to grow on plants so that the leaves on top can grow, too—and then fruit or vegetables will come! Mention in a very loving manner that *you* teach your child about God so that he can grow strong and good, too, like a healthy plant.

Ages Four to Five

Shadow Watching

Shadows are an interesting phenomenon to a child. Observe the ways the lengths of shadows vary as the sun moves through the sky during the day.

Early on a sunny day, go outside with your child and trace his shadow on the driveway with a piece of chalk. Repeat the process at noon and again in the late afternoon, discussing the differences in the shadows and the reasons that they are long or short.

Illustrate the same fact inside the house by using a flashlight and a small toy or houseplant. Place the object where its shadow can be easily seen on a floor or wall. Shine the light from an angle to illustrate morning sunshine, from directly overhead to illustrate noon sunshine, and from the opposite side to illustrate afternoon light. Ask your child questions such as, "Is this shadow short or long?" "Did the shadow change?" "Is this shadow longer than the toy?"

In a society that often represents shadows as sinister or spooky, your child needs to think of them as a part of God's fascinating and lovely created world!

Clear and Fuzzy Shadows

Do this fun experiment with your child. In a darkened room, shine a light toward a comb or hair pick that is held a foot away from a wall. Remark to your child that its shadow is sharp and clear like our shadows are when the sun is shining brightly.

Then give your child a piece of waxed paper to place over the end of the flashlight and secure it for her with a rubber band. Repeat the experiment with the comb and ask her if the shadow is still clear or if it is now rather fuzzy.

Explain that the waxed paper over the flashlight is like the sun shining through the clouds on a slightly cloudy or foggy day. When the weather is like that, our shadows will be fuzzy, too. If the day is *very* cloudy, we may not be able to see our shadows at all. To demonstrate this to your child, fold waxed paper into several thicknesses and place over the flashlight.

Tell your child that whether a day is bright and shiny or cloudy and gloomy, Jesus is *always* our light!

Sandwiches in a Jar

Let your child help dye sand different colors by placing some in zip-seal bags, adding one or two drops of food coloring to each bag, and shaking and gently kneading the mixture until the color mixes adequately. Undo only the corner of one bag and help your child pour the sand into a clear jar, forming a layer of colored sand.

Repeat the action with a layer of another color. Do again with more colors of sand, forming interesting stripes of color as each new layer is added. Continue to build your *sand*wich in this manner, filling the jar to the very top. Squirt on a top layer of white glue to seal and tighten the lid at the top.

Salt or grits may be used instead of sand. Fill baby food jars with salt and show your child how to rub sticks of colored chalk through the salt to color it. Layer the colored salt into a clear jar and pretend the layers are desert, ocean, and rock formations. Allow the layers to be uneven rather than perfectly level. Seal the finished product with glue and a tightly closed lid.

Talk with your child about the tiny grains of sand and the Scripture that tells of his importance to God: "How precious to me are your thoughts, O God! . . . Were I to count them, they would outnumber the grains of sand" (Ps. 139:17–18).

Swinging Spoon

Attach a spoon handle to the middle of a yard-long piece of string. Hold the ends of the string to your child's ears as she bumps the spoon against the floor or tabletop.

Your child will notice an interesting vibration as the sound travels through the string to her ears. Explain to her that sounds move through the air or along the string until they reach our ears. Our outside ears are like little cups that catch the sounds and bring them into our inside ears and then to our brain.

Teach your child the Bible verse, "Ears that hear and eyes that see—the Lord has made them both" (Prov. 20:12). Tell her how thankful you are for ears to hear, and explain that people who cannot hear still pay close attention to the vibrations they feel to help them be aware of the world around them.

Don't Spill the Bucket!

Here is a rather active game that demonstrates a principle God has built into his created world. Your child will enjoy the game, but you must supervise the activity carefully and set rules regarding when and where it may be repeated.

Try this experiment outside where there is plenty of room! Fill a plastic bucket half full of water and whirl it in a circular motion over your head and down again. The water will stay in the upside-down bucket as long as you move it quickly. This involves the same principle used in the safe operation of a circular roller coaster at a carnival. God's gravity pulls down on the water and bucket, but another power, *centrifugal force*, pushes the water into the bucket.

Tell your child that God's secrets are often invisible but very real—like his love, his care, and his nearness to us.

Thermometer Changes

Purchase two inexpensive thermometers and hang them outside your house on nails, one in the sun and the other in the shade. Talk about how thermometers work, comparing the sunny and shady temperatures for several days. Call attention, too, to the temperature changes that take place from early morning to noon and evening.

Tell your child that God is good to make the temperature change from cold to warm to hot to cool to warm again, making our world a more pleasant place to live!

There's Water in the Air

Talk with your child about the water God has placed in the air we breathe. Tell her that we can sometimes see the water drops, or dew, on flowers and grass in the mornings. Do this experiment to demonstrate:

Place several ice cubes in a tin can from which the label has been removed. Fill the can to the top with water and set it on the edge of a sink that contains warm water. In a short time, water that is in the air will form drops on the cold can and run down its sides. You may wish to call the water drops God's water jewels and to voice your gratitude for the hidden secret of water in the air, which helps both plants and people.

Rolling Water Drops

Place a small saucepan or a metal cup containing pieces of wax candles or paraffin in a larger pan of boiling water. Continue to boil the water until the wax is melted, trying not to get water in the wax. Pour the melted wax onto a saucer to cool.

When the wax has cooled and hardened, ask your child to drop a small spoonful of water on it. Notice with him how the water beads up. Explain to him that the waxy surface will not let the water soak in.

Tell your child that God has given ducks and swans oil in their feathers that acts like the wax in keeping out water and preventing the feathers from becoming too wet and heavy. Remind your child, too, that God, who knows everything, also told Noah to put tar (pitch) on the ark in order that the floodwater could not soak or leak in to sink the boat! Tell the whole story of Noah and the big boat to your child.

Water Travels Up!

Talk with your child about how perfectly God designed trees and plants to soak up water from the ground and move it to their very top leaves through tiny little tubes called *capillaries*. Explain that the water traveling *up* is remarkable because it defies gravity.

Demonstrate this process to your child with two stalks of celery with leaves still attached and two containers of water, one with red food coloring and the other with blue food coloring.

Place the cut end of each celery stalk in a container of colored water and wait about forty-five minutes. As your child observes, slice a thin outside layer from one stalk of celery in a vertical direction, exposing the capillaries that now contain color. Next, cut across the same celery horizontally to make the capillaries even more obvious to your child.

Leave the second stalk of celery in the food coloring for several hours or overnight. If you wish, split the cut edge of the celery vertically and place one half in each color. Later, observe that the leaves have turned both red and blue! It is perfectly safe to let your child eat the colored celery. Or you may slice a fresh stalk for her eating and crunching pleasure. Say, "Thank you, God, for the wonderful way you take care of even the vegetables we eat!"

Sink or Float

Explain to your child that in God's perfectly designed world, he has planned for heavy things to sink and light things to float on water. Ask your child to tell you if these items would sink or float: a rock, a feather, a toy boat, and a brick.

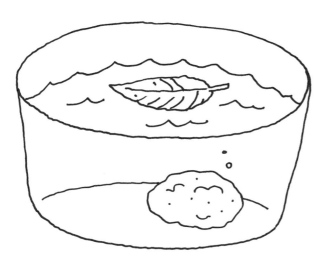

Make God's Lovely Leaves Last!

To preserve fall leaves, dip them in melted paraffin (canning wax, available at supermarkets) and place on newspaper to dry, or press them between pieces of waxed paper in the pages of a heavy book for several days. Mount them for your child's enjoyment in the pages of a photo album.

Snow Shapes

Enjoy your child's creative imagination—and your own—as you create snow shapes together. The shapes can be anything that will delight your small child, but do not get so carried away with your snow sculptures that you forget to make an ordinary snowman now and then. As you have fun with your child, refer often to God who makes the beautiful white snow.

Here are a few fun snow shapes to try—but be sure to design your own!

- *Snowbots.* Make snow robots by using a square or rectangular box to form the basic shape. Pack the container with snow, and slowly roll it over until it is upside down. Carefully remove the box, with your child's help. Make the snowbot's buttons and keys from rocks or sewing buttons.
- *Funny face.* Scoop or push the snow into a small hill. On top of the hill, place strips of paper, yarn, or grass

for hair and top it with a stocking cap, old cowboy hat, bowl, or flowerpot for a hat. If you use a clay flowerpot, stick an artificial flower into the drainage hole. Make a face from fruit or vegetable slices, gumdrops, mints, or licorice strips, rocks, and broken sticks. Make the outline of the funny face from a ribbon or piece of yarn, tied in a bow at the chin.

- *No-bake cake.* Shape a round mountain of snow and flatten the top with your hands or the back of a snow shovel. Let your child decorate the cake with ribbon or lace and top it with candles of any size. When night comes, bundle up with your child and go outside to light the candles! This candle-lighting fun could easily become a tradition to be enjoyed for Jesus' birthday at Christmas, or for your child's own birthday.
- *Snowpoke.* Turn an ordinary snowman into a cowpoke by adding your child's toy holster and guns, cowboy hat, and bandanna. Place your child's small cowboy boots in front of the snowpoke to complete the look. If your child wants the boots attached in some way, place one end of a stick in each boot and the other into the body of the snowpoke.

Captured Snowflakes

Take the glass from a picture frame and cool it in the refrigerator for several hours. Let your child watch as you carry it outside by the corners and capture snowflakes on its surface. Immediately place the glass where your child can observe the snowflakes with a magnifying glass or microscope. As she does, remark to her that God makes all snowflakes with six sides and that no two are ever alike. Marvel with your child about the almighty Creator who makes snowflakes and little children so special. Give your special little child a big, sincere hug and kiss!

Capture a Web

To capture a spiderweb, you will need a can of white spray paint, a sheet of black construction paper, a pair of scissors, and an observant eye.

When you or your child locates an interesting web, hold the can of spray paint at arm's length, aim from the same direction the wind is blowing, and cover the web with a fine coat of paint. Quickly place a black piece of paper against the wet web, pressing the paper first in the center of the web and then carefully against the side sections. Allow the web to dry against the paper, and snip the supporting threads with your scissors.

As you and your child observe the amazing symmetry of the spider web, talk about how God gave the spider the know-how to create such a marvelous resting place and that no one had to teach the spider how to do it. If you have an insect book or encyclopedia, learn more about spiders with your child.

Jar Garden

Place a widemouthed jar on its side. Remove the lid and ask your child to spoon into the jar a layer of pebbles, then sand mixed with potting soil, and on top of these, a layer of dirt from your yard. Keep these layers shallow, extending no higher than the mouth of the jar.

Give your child small seedlings to plant, ones that will not grow very tall and that will grow well in a warm, moist environment. The seedlings may be purchased from a nearby nursery or transplanted from your own backyard. Even a weed garden can be interesting!

Desert Garden

A desert garden may be planted in an upright jar by placing sand in the bottom and adding some pretty rocks, a few sprinkles of water, and one or two small cactus plants. If your child wishes, she may add a small toy turtle or miniature plastic animal. Talk with her about the creation of the world as recorded in Genesis 1 and about the interesting types of plants that God made for our enjoyment.

Nutshell Fleets

Provide a hammer and several walnuts and let your child carefully crack them on a piece of newspaper. (Let him eat the nuts if he desires.) Help him crack some nuts so that several half-shells may be left intact and uncracked when the nut meats are removed. From those half-shells let him make a fleet of tiny boats to float in the sink or bathtub.

In each shell, place a bit of clay or Play-Doh and a toothpick or used matchstick to which a tiny white paper sail has been pasted. Thank God for the tasty nuts and their shells he provides.

Treasure Rocks

Let your child paint selected rocks with nontoxic gold or silver paint. When the rocks are dry, place them in a treasure chest and play a hide-and-seek game with her.

Hide the gold pieces in a sandbox and let your child discover the hidden treasure! Or do the same with smaller gold pebbles in lumps of clay or Play-Doh.

Ask her if she knows who is more valuable than all the gold in the world. If she answers, "I am," agree with her! Then tell her that the greatest treasure we all have is *Jesus!*

Design a Den

Talk with your child about the underground nests and tunnels that shrews, moles, gophers, mice, chipmunks, skunks, porcupines, woodchucks, and groundhogs all construct and inhabit. Look together at books or encyclopedias that picture authentic or imaginative cutout views of animals' burrows.

Encourage your child to use her imagination and draw her own ideas of what an animal's burrow is like. Her drawing may be realistic or drawn the way she would want it to look if she were the animal—with rooms, furniture, and all the modern conveniences!

Teach this little rhyme to your child:

If I were an animal
Living in a den,
I'd think of God who made me
And praise him *right then!*

But since I am a child
With a house in which to live,
I'll thank my God for making *me,*
My praise to him I'll give.

Detective Prints

If you find the opening to an animal den, ask your child to help you make a ring of mud around it. Leave the mud ring intact for several nights, rewetting it and smoothing it as necessary. With patience, you may capture some sets of the resident's footprints. Compare them with pictures of animal prints in an encyclopedia or animal book, and try to identify the animal who occupies the den.

Talk about how great God is to make animals with paws or feet that are perfectly suited for the way they live. You may want to thank God for all animals.

Crystal Creations

Let your child observe the formation of delicate needlelike crystals on the glass from an unused picture frame.

Instruct him to place two table-spoons of water in a pan. Then you, par-ent, bring the water to nearly boiling (use a glass pan, if possible, allowing him to observe from a safe vantage point). Lower the heat and gradually add five tablespoons of Epsom salts. Keep adding spoonfuls of Epsom salts until no more will dissolve. Remove the solution from the heat, cool it slightly, and let your child add two drops of clear, soluble liquid glue, stirring until it dissolves. Let your child paint the cooling liquid on the glass with a paint brush or cotton ball and watch the crystals begin to form.

If he enjoys this activity, instruct your child to color a picture on paper with crayons and paint over it with the liquid to give his drawing a frosty or foggy appearance. Study the crystals carefully with a magnifying glass and talk about our great God who makes huge moons and stars and beautiful tiny crystals.

Plants Help the Soil

Explain to your child that when rain falls, leaves and flowers help to break the fall of the raindrops. If there are no plants in a certain area, the rain hits the soil so hard that it washes away the topsoil, which is the very best kind of soil.

To help your child better understand the benefit that plants are to soil, let her place a pencil through a small square piece of paper (about three by four inches) and put the pencil in a flowerpot containing soil only. Place another pencil and paper in a flowerpot containing a plant. Set both pots out-side a window where they can be ob-served the next time it rains. Notice how much mud is splashed on each pa-per; the pot with the plant loses less dirt when the rain falls.

Talk in a simple manner with your child about the interdependency of plants and soil. Compare this rela-tionship of nature to our dependency upon God and each other.

Make a Sundial

On a sheet of white paper draw a large circle for your child to cut out. Stick a sharpened pencil through the middle of the paper and into the ground to hold it in place. Make sure that you place the paper in a sunny spot in the yard.

At a designated time (perhaps eight or nine o'clock in the morning), make a pencil line to the edge of the paper at the point where the shadow falls. Write the time of day beside it. Do the same at each hour of the day, noticing that the shadow lines are longer in the morning and afternoon than they are at noon. If the weather permits, leave the sundial out for several days and refer to it with your child for the time of day. Tell him that the Bible says "he . . . appoints the sun to shine by day [and] decrees the moon and stars to shine by night" (Jer. 31:35).

Please Save the Soil

Explain to your child that erosion is good soil being washed away by the rain. Tell him that grass or plants that grow on a hillside help to keep the dirt in place. Mention that farmers in some countries make stairs from the hillsides and plant their seeds on the tops of the stairs to keep the seeds from washing away when it rains.

Demonstrate erosion as you and your child do this activity together. Use two identical pans, one containing dirt only and one with dirt in which grass is growing. Hold the pans at an angle and play "rain man" with a watering can. Empty one can full of water over the pan of dirt and another can full of water over the other pan. Ask your child to check which pan retained the most dirt.

Tell your child that one of the reasons God causes plants, grass, and wild flowers to grow is to protect the important dirt under them. Teach him the Bible verse thought, "[God] makes the grass grow" (Ps. 104:14).

Light or Dark?

Tell your child that heat soaks into dark colors and bounces off light ones. Explain that wearing white or light-colored clothing on hot summer days will keep us cooler than wearing dark colors.

To illustrate this principle, take your child outside on a hot day and place a white handkerchief over the back of her outstretched hand. Cover her other hand with a black cloth, making sure that the sun is shining directly on both hands. Tell her to remain in this position until she feels the sun's heat. Ask her to tell you which hand feels hotter. If you wish, your child may also paint one rock black and one white; leave both in the sunlight and later check to see which feels hotter.

Pretty Wall Designs

Ask your child to make a design on a piece of paper, preferably one with small parts that can be cut out, like petals on a flower. If he wishes, he may do the cutting or you may do it for him.

Hold his picture to a window where the sunlight can shine on it and cast a shadow on a nearby wall. Your child will be delighted with the pretty design that he has made. Tell him that the Bible says to "work with your hands" (1 Thess. 4:11), and that he has done a great job with *his!*

Static Electricity

Perform these interesting experiments with your child as you introduce her to static electricity.

- *Make my hair stand on end.* Rub a balloon or comb against a wool rug or sweater and hold it near your child's head for a hair-raising effect!
- *Darkroom electricity.* Try the make-my-hair-stand-on-end experiment in the dark, during dry winter weather, and watch the sparks fly!
- *Pepper trick.* Shake a pile of salt onto the tabletop, flatten it with your hand, and top with some black pepper. Ask your child if she thinks you can now take the pepper *out* of the salt.

To remove the pepper grains, run a comb through your hair several times or rub it against a wool sweater, and then hold the comb about one inch above the salt. The pepper grains, which are surprisingly lighter than salt, will jump up onto the comb.

I-Love-You-More-Than Song

This spontaneous musical activity may become a simple family tradition and will definitely increase your child's sense of self-worth each time you play it together.

As you are riding with your child in the car, sing a little love song to him using a made-up tune and scenes from nature. Begin each line with "I love you more than . . ." and end with something like "a beautiful sunset," "a lovely flower," "a bright sunny day," or "a shiny diamond."

The tune (or lack of it) doesn't matter; the words will carry the message that God's creations are wonderful, but of them all, your child is the dearest to you. Encourage him to sing a love song back to you, using word pictures of things from the natural world that he most enjoys.

Just for fun, sing the phrase "I love you more than . . ." using silly objects from nature, such as a lizard's tail, a tumbleweed, a cactus, or a cat's whiskers. Laugh and be silly together, but end your fun with an affirmation to your precious child that you value him greatly.

Chapter 9

Introducing Your Child to God through the Church

Christ is the head of the church, his body,
of which he is the Savior.
—Ephesians 5:23

The Bible places much emphasis upon local congregations of believers. We are commanded in Scripture to meet together in collective worship, fellowship, instruction, and mutual encouragement. As we include our young children in a churchgoing life-style, they benefit greatly! They are taught early in life that God is real, Jesus is love, his people care and share, and the Christian life is a truly worthy one.

In a recent survey of eighty Christian families whose children grew up to serve the Lord Jesus and his church, an important common denominator was evident: in nearly every home surveyed, faithful, joyful church attendance was an integral part of the lives of its members. Identification with a local congregation was considered to be a privilege and a responsibility. Each family made a deliberate and sincere practice of emphasizing the many positive aspects of the Christian life and the church. One family had a picnic on their future church site, allowing time for their children to run and play on the property where they would one day worship. Other parents and children picked up rocks and mowed weeds together to prepare the way for the place of worship that would be their second home in the years ahead.

The words we speak and the subtle attitudes we portray about church (Is it a bore or a joy to get up early Sunday morning and go to church?) will most certainly be observed and absorbed by our young child. If our church occupies its rightful place in our hearts and home, it will be our supportive friend to help meet the spiritual, emotional, and social needs of our child throughout his preschool, childhood, teenage, and adult years. He will be much more likely to find personal fulfillment through church involvement, and our parenting job will be infinitely easier.

A tiny two-year-old made this statement one Sunday morning as her family arrived at the parking lot of their local church: "I go to church to learn about Jeezees!" The pronunciation was not yet correct, but the concept of the church and the anticipation of learning about the Savior were already rooted in her impressionable mind.

As you endeavor to instill in your child a love for God through the church of the Lord Jesus Christ, may some of these ideas and activities prove helpful.

 # The Baby

God's Special Day

On Sunday morning, greet your waking baby with happy words about church, such as, "Lindsey, do you know what today is? It's church day! It's God's very special day!"

Sing this song to your baby to the tune of "Three Blind Mice":

> Today is the day.
> Today is the day.
> We will go to church.
> We will go to church.
> It is Sunday morning.
> It is Sunday morning.
> Thank you, God.
> Thank you, God.

Don't Sabotage Sunday

Make careful preparations on Saturday for Sunday morning church attendance. Pack the diaper bag and lay out clothes for baby and yourself. Make sure that breakfast is planned, that socks and shoes are located, and that the car has enough gas. Let the nonessentials at home slide for this morning!

Keep your own preparations as simple as possible, and plan to be interrupted as you get ready for church.

Have an alternate outfit in mind for every family member in case of last-minute disasters.

Ask God to eliminate all obstacles Satan throws in your way. Let Sunday bring glory to God and be a wonderful memory in your child's mind. (Some adults remember their childhood Sundays as days of temper, fussing, and unhappy looks!)

Expect some accidents, spills, and complications, but don't let them throw you! Remember the big picture—you are instilling in your child the lifelong habit of giving God his day in worship and praise. Picture your child as an adult, loving and serving God. It will be worth every effort you make to establish the churchgoing habit in your little child's life.

If I Cry, Feed Me

Be sure to pack *extra* bottles of milk, water, or juice for Sunday nursery stays. Babies, like adults, do not always get hungry at the same time nor do they always eat the same amount. Eating a good breakfast does not insure that your baby will not feel hungry again soon, and babies can't wait! The service may last longer than expected, and a full tummy is a crucial factor in a baby's contentment wherever she is. And it will make the ride home much more pleasant for the family, too!

If you are a nursing mother, let the nursery workers or coordinator know where you will be seated during the service or Sunday school class.

Entertain a Nursery Worker

If your baby seems to have a hard time adjusting to the nursery at your church, invite the nursery worker to your home for a brief visit. Try to arrange it at a time when your baby is ordinarily content and comfortable. You might offer the worker lunch as a way of expressing appreciation for the care of your child. (Many good nursery attendants receive more complaints than compliments!)

Allow time for your baby and her teacher to get better acquainted on the baby's home turf with you nearby for reassurance. Give your guest a new or loved toy to use with your baby, but let baby come to you when she wishes to get acquainted with the worker from a distance!

Security Pillow

Take a small pillow to church with your new baby's other belongings. Ask the nursery attendant to place the pillow *behind* the baby's back as she lies on her side or to place a rolled-up receiving blanket on each side of your new baby to make her feel more secure in a full-sized crib, especially if she sleeps in a smaller bed at home.

Dress Me Comfortably

It is difficult to know how warmly to dress your baby for the nursery, especially if he spends part of his time on the floor and part of it in a bed. Some nurseries are kept a little too warm; others seem cool for babies to play on tile or linoleum floors.

Take some extra articles of clothing that can be put on or taken off to keep your baby comfortable. Make a quick evaluation of the room temperature as you bring him in, and suggest to the attendant any changes to what your baby is wearing.

Make sure you provide an entire additional change of clothing, including socks, in case your baby has an accident.

A Photo Friend

Make an inexpensive enlargement of a close-up photograph of a parent, a family pet, or a sight that is familiar to your baby. Or you can use a picture of each parent side by side, if you wish.

Round the corners of the photo(s), mount on lightweight cardboard, and cover with clear adhesive paper.

Ask the nursery attendant to place the picture in baby's crib on its side, so that it will be upright as she views it.

Saturday Rehearsal

Place in your baby's crib on Saturday the same items you will take with him to church the next morning: diaper bag, blanket, and picture or familiar toy. Place the items in the same places in baby's bed as you will request that the worker place them on Sunday.

Use only one or two items and keep your instructions simple; the nursery attendant will be *busy* when Sunday morning church time arrives!

Music Box

Purchase a small music box for your brand-new baby, selecting a melody that you enjoy. Play it frequently at home to your baby. If you wish, you may use a cassette player with a Christian lullaby tape instead.

On Sundays, bring the music box or tape player to church with you and ask the attendant if you can place the music player near or in your baby's bed. The music, played softly, will provide a familiar sound for your baby, and the other children will enjoy it, too.

 # The Toddler

Church Every Week

Church is more than a place to take your child for an occasional Bible lesson, even if you supplement his spiritual education with a daily Bible story. Church attendance can become so natural that *not going* doesn't seem right. If your young child develops a commitment to the church, your parenting responsibilities will be infinitely easier at every stage of his future development. The friends he makes and the experiences he has at church will become a central part of his life. He will grow in spiritual knowledge and grace. In addition, any objections he expresses in going into his classroom will generally be less frequent, less intense, and shorter-lived than if his attendance is sporadic. You are being more kind to your child by consistent attendance than by there-one-week, home-one-week church habits.

My Church

Take a photograph of your church building, enlarge it if you desire, mount it on a paper heart, and place it on the refrigerator door at your toddler's eye level so she can see and enjoy it. Hold the picture in place with a magnet and let her carry it around and then put it back on the door as often as she wishes!

There's the Church

Take a photograph of your church building, round the edges of the picture, mount it on heavy cardboard, and cover the entire picture with clear adhesive paper.

Let the baby see the picture and tell her that it is a picture of Michelle's church. Then hide it under a blanket or cloth diaper as the baby watches you.

Say, "Where's Michelle's church? Where's Michelle's church?" If the baby does not attempt to find the picture, pull the covering off and say, "There it is! We love Michelle's church!" Repeat the game several times if your baby seems interested.

When you approach the church the next Sunday, say the words, "There's Michelle's big church! We love Michelle's church!"

Trial Run

Ask permission to bring your baby or toddler for a tour of his nursery classroom on a weekday when it is empty. Walk around the room with him, talking cheerfully about what you see there. Put him in a bed to play if he will do so contentedly, sit with him on your lap, or place him beside you on the floor.

Tell your toddler, "This is your very own room at church. We'll bring you back again soon to play." Leave with him while he is still happily playing, even if he wants to stay longer. You may wish to arrange your tour with two or three other parents and babies in order to familiarize your child with them.

Put a Friend in My Bag

Choose a sturdy security bear for your child to take with her to church each Sunday. If your child objects to going to church one morning, say something like this:

"But Bongo really wants to go to your class! [*Make the toy jump up and down.*] He loves to play with the boys and girls [*name some specifically, if possible*], with the [*name a particular nursery toy*], to have a snack, and especially to hear about Jesus! How will he get there if you don't take him?" Get the bear ready for church, too. This approach may not change your reluctant churchgoer into a willing one, but it is worth a try!

Let Me Pack My Bag

On Saturday evening right before bed, let your toddler help pack his own diaper bag for church the next morning.

Call your child's attention to his name that you have taped or written on the diaper bag. Talk about his own special room at church, the toys he will play with, and the teachers there who love him. Tell him that when he wakes in the morning, you will all get dressed and go to church!

Pick Me Up First

In order for a toddler to feel secure about your returning to get her after church, try to be one of the very first parents to return to the nursery each Sunday. She will not mind the temporary separation from you as much if she does not have to watch all the other children leave for home with their parents when hers are nowhere in sight!

That's My Church!

Make a special point of driving by your church often without stopping or stopping only long enough to take your toddler in with you to pick up literature or to do some other short errand. Letting your child occasionally be at church without leaving him there will help associate feelings of security and familiarity with the place he goes on Sundays.

When you drive by the church or leave the parking lot, say, "That's Bryan's church!" Clap your hands, and he will soon join in your enthusiasm.

I-Love-My-Church Album

Use an inexpensive photo album for this activity, or make one by sewing together several felt squares down the center. Place in the album photographs of familiar places in your church building, taken from a child's eye level.

You may wish to photograph the door where your child enters the building, the view from the parking lot, a toy cabinet with a teacher nearby, or a stained-glass window that she often sees.

Sit and look at the album with your child during the week.

Happy-Church-Time Album

Bring a camera to church one Sunday morning and ask your child's teacher if you can take a few pictures of the children at play. Some suggested moments for picture-taking would be when the toddlers are playing with toys and friends, when they are having a snack or listening to Bible stories, or when a teacher is holding or hugging your child. It is better to get someone else to take the pictures if your toddler doesn't react well with you in his classroom.

Put the photos in a happy-church-time album that your child can handle and look at whenever he wishes. Talk with him about the happy times he has at church.

Make the photographs available to other parents and to nursery coordinators. They may want to use them when visiting prospective families for the church or when recruiting preschool workers.

A Friendly Voice

Tape record a brief greeting from your child's nursery teachers inviting your baby to church and telling her what she will get to do in her class when she comes.

Play the tape for your toddler during the week and especially the day before she goes to church.

Picture My Teachers

Take a photograph of your child's nursery teachers. If he has several teachers, take a separate close-up photo of each and place them in a book made of construction paper covered with clear adhesive paper for durability.

Talk with your toddler about the people who take care of him and love him. Say "Thank you, God" for his teachers at church.

That Good Sunday Feeling

Even when we do our best to make Sunday morning with a toddler a less-than-frantic time, it often turns out that way. We can compensate to a degree and make Sunday the loving day it should be by reserving some quality time for our child when we get home from church.

After hungry mouths are fed, sit down with your child in your arms, play a while, and gently talk about what a wonderful day Sunday is. Tell her how great it is that you can go to church to learn about God and how precious it is now to be with her!

Ages Two to Three

I Like Church Because . . .

While riding in the car, waiting for an appointment, or tucking your child in bed, play this simple game.

Begin the game by saying, "I like church because . . ." and then finish the sentence. Your child will then repeat the same phrase and end it himself. To make the game more fun, be quite detailed in your responses. Instead of simply saying, "I like Mrs. Taylor," say, "I like Mrs. Taylor's smile" or "I like how Mr. Taylor looks in his blue suit." Another possible response might be, "I like how the pastor bends down to say hi."

Sunday Drive

Sit down on the sofa or a chair beside your child. Tell her that you are going to pretend to drive your car to church and that you want her to go with you!

Pretend to turn the steering wheel, push the accelerator and brakes, and talk about all the places or things you pass on the way to church. You may want to talk about the people that you will see as you and your child drive to church each week.

If you want to make this game even more fun, use a box that is large enough to hold both of you as a car, or link several boxes together with string to form a train.

Cut holes in the bottom of the box for your child's legs to go through, calling them the car's wheels. Cut out a rectangular hole on each box side for handles to hold as your child "drives" to church. Add as many other details to your vehicles as you wish.

My New-Town Book

If your family has recently moved to a new town, help your child adjust to his new surroundings by making a photo book of people and places you will frequently see. Include a picture of your own house, the grocery store, the doctor's office, the library, and especially your new church.

On the church page of your child's book include a picture or two of people your child has met and liked at church, if you have already visited there.

The photo book may be made of heart-shaped construction paper to show the love you have for the new home and church God has given your family.

We Love You, Pastor

Express your love often for your church staff and teachers to your child. As a result of hearing your positive statements, he will very likely develop a deep admiration for church leaders and a respect for their positions of leadership.

It is not necessary to make them appear too good to be true. Explain that the people in your church love and help each other and want to please God, but the only person who has ever been perfect is the Lord Jesus himself.

Relate to your children incidents when church people have helped each other. Be sure to include those examples of times when Christian brothers and sisters have helped your own family. You may be helping your child develop an early openness to God's work, so that if God chooses to call him into vocational Christian service someday, he will willingly respond.

Invite Me to Church

Purchase two inexpensive toy telephones to use for conversation games with your child. In your conversation, tell your child to please invite you to come to church. When she does, ask questions to encourage conversation such as, "How will we get there?" or "What will we do there?"

Let's Get Ready for Church

Playing church has been a favorite activity of children for generations. Children in Bible days may have played temple, too.

Provide a few props for your child such as a box pulpit, a Bible, a songbook, chairs in a row or circle, and perhaps a piano or a keyboard you have

Fellowship Time

Include your child in the fun as you entertain other families from church in your home or go out occasionally to eat ice cream or pizza with them. Tell your child that these are "our friends from church." Enjoying fellowship together is an important part of church life, even for a very young child! (See 1 John 1:3.)

Church in the Winter

On a flat piece of white Styrofoam, let your child make a winter church scene. If she plays with it carefully, it can be reused numerous times.

Purchase an inexpensive church bank from a Christian bookstore or make one from a small box by drawing doors and stained-glass windows and attaching a cardboard steeple or cross on top. Place the church building on the Styrofoam and let your child stick in artificial greenery or sticks to represent trees in winter, with bits of cotton added or dropped on the scene for snow.

Use small toy people for the churchgoers, riding on toy cars or walking to church because they do not want to miss the service! Lift the church building to let them go inside where it is warm.

drawn on paper and placed on the sofa to provide music as it is "played."

Younger children may not have been in an actual worship service to know what goes on there, but they will be great imitators as you show them how a worship service is conducted. Also, you will be preparing them to one day sit with you in church.

Box Church

Make a play church out of a large empty box. Paint, color, or paste pictures on it to make it look more like a church building. Tape two end flaps together to form the pointed roof and attach a cardboard cross to the top. Make a parking lot from a piece of black paper marked with chalk, and let your child park toy cars there.

Or you may cover a table with an old sheet or cloth and pretend that it is a church building. (Let your child color stained-glass windows on the sheet before covering the table.)

Accompany your child inside and pretend you are in church. Sing church songs and listen to a Bible story tape you have prerecorded.

Build a Church!

Make blocks with your child by filling paper grocery sacks with loosely crumpled newspaper and taping them shut. Or provide several sizes of square, flat, and cylindrical boxes for her use along with paper-towel rolls for pillars. Let her stack them up to make a church building like King Solomon did in Bible days. The blocks and boxes may be glued together or just stacked and reused.

This Is the Way

To the tune of "Mulberry Bush," act out the song "This is the way I get ready for church." Include phrases such as "This is the way I brush my hair [*pray to God, wear a big smile, carry my Bible, etc.*]," ending each verse with "every Sunday morning."

My Church Art

Keep a scrapbook of the earliest examples of the artwork your child has created in Sunday school or nursery. As he becomes old enough to attend the worship service, include the art work he sketches as he sits in the pew. Some of his most inspired artistic creations may arise from moments such as these and will one day be treasures!

If you wish his scrapbook to be more of a spiritual log, include notable quotes, experiences, and observations you make as he grows in his spiritual awareness.

First Time at Church

Pretend that it is the first time your child's doll has gone to church. Ask your child to explain to the doll what to expect at church—what she will learn and do, how she should act and listen, and what she will especially enjoy. Tell her to be sure to tell her friend (the doll) that going to church pleases God.

Dressing for Church

In a suitcase or box, place several articles of clothing: coats, hats, mittens, and shoes or boots. Try to include clothes with a variety of kinds of fasteners. Let your child dress up in the clothes and pretend to get ready for church. As he plays, talk with him about what activities he enjoys most at church.

Church Chants and Songs

> We love to sing!
> We love to pray!
> We'll go to church
> On this special day!
>
> Church is great!
> Church is good!
> We will go there
> 'Cause we *should!*

To the tune of "Are You Sleeping?":

> Are you ready?
> Are you ready
> To go to church?
> To go to church?
> It's a special morning!
> It's a special morning!
> Thank you, God.
> Thank you, God.

A Note to Say Thanks

Make paper cutouts of flowers, snow-flakes, hearts, or leaves—whichever is appropriate for the season of the year. Let your child glue the shapes on a strip of white shelf paper or butcher's paper.

In the center of each shape, glue an appropriate Bible verse, such as "We always thank God, the Father of our Lord Jesus Christ, when we pray for you" (Col. 1:3), or a sentence, such as "I thank God for all the nice things you do."

Roll up the paper and let your child give it to the pastor, the music minister, or her teacher the next Sunday at church.

Little Boy Jesus at Church

Tell your child the story of Jesus going to the temple with his mother and Joseph. Explain that Jesus' own family took him to worship because their going pleased God just as our going to church pleases him. Emphasize to your child that Jesus loves the church (see Eph. 5:25). Mention Jesus' conversation with the teachers at the temple and their surprise at all that Jesus knew at such a young age.

Act out the story with your child as little boy Jesus. Use a bathrobe or a large shirt and a rolled handkerchief or bandanna headband for a simple costume. Roll up a piece of paper for a scroll Bible, and make simple sandals from cardboard footprint cutouts and twine, if you wish. Pretend to walk to the temple or ride on a donkey.

Bring the Church a Gift

Call your church office and ask what gift you and your child may give that would be of benefit to your church. Suggest a price range and perhaps some ideas you may have, such as a nursery toy, a new stapler or paper punch, a box of pencils, or a plant for someone's office. Do not donate a plaque or picture that must be displayed on a wall; this type of gift may present a dilemma for the person who must try to find a place to hang it.

Wrap the gift with your child's help and let her deliver it as the representative of your family. Make sure that she knows you are giving a gift to your church because you love and appreciate being a part of it.

Refrigerator Reminders

On your refrigerator door, place one or both of these I-love-my-church visual reminders:

- A picture of the thought in Ephesians 5:25, "Christ loved the church." On a rectangular piece of paper, let your child paste a picture of Jesus on the left-hand side. Then help him to draw a heart, write the word *the,* and end the visual sentence with a drawing or cutout of a church. Make sure your child understands that the Bible says, "Christ loved the church."
- A picture collage your child has made by pasting paper cutout pictures of churches, including a picture of your own church from a church bulletin or photograph. As your child pastes, talk with him about your church and why you love going there.

I Was Glad

Teach Psalm 122:1 to your child, and as you do, give her a piece of paper and a pencil. Ask her to fill up the whole paper by making a child's face, instructing her step by step if necessary. A young child's drawing will be less than perfect, but resist the urge to correct it too much. Let it remain as she is satisfied with it, knowing her drawings of people will improve greatly in the next few years.

Tell her to put a *big* smile on the face—the biggest and happiest she can make. Say, "Do you know why she's so happy? She's going to church!" Repeat the Bible verse with your child.

Things I See at Church

Name three things your child can see at church. Ask him to repeat them to you in the same order. Some ideas might be a pretty window, a door, a piano.

Let him tell you two or three other items to repeat back to him, adding more if repeating three becomes easy. This is an excellent listening exercise as well as a subtle reminder that church is very much a part of our life.

Church Cleanup Day

If your church is sponsoring a volunteer cleanup day, let your child join you in this labor of love.

Work together to clean an area of the building or church property, picking up trash, washing walls, pulling weeds, raking, and planting flowers. As you work, tell her the story of King Josiah and God's people who cleaned their church (2 Kings 22–23) or the story of Samuel helping Eli at church (1 Sam. 2:11, 18–19).

A Pop-up Church Friend

Make a pop-up puppet from a paper cup with a hole in the bottom for a drinking straw. On one end of the straw paste a small face you or your child has drawn on a circle of paper. The face may be a grown-up or a child.

Slide the plain end of the straw down through the right-side-up cup until the face is hidden inside it. As your child watches, make the face pop up and play this guessing game with him:

"Hi! I'm the one who preaches from the Bible at church. Who am I?"

"I'm the one who tells you a Bible story at church. Who am I?"

Let the puppet's final words be, "Don't forget to go to church!"

There's My Teacher

Sit down with your child and show him your church's pictorial directory. Take special notice of the pictures of people your child knows well, especially the pastor, your child's teacher, and other church staff individuals. Say, "Thank you, God, for our friends at church."

Ages Four to Five

Days of the Week

Act out this rhyme with your child:

Monday's my day for clapping! [*clap twice*]
and Tuesday's my day to walk. [*walk in place*]
Wednesday's my day for hopping, [*hop twice*]
and Thursday's the day to talk! [*say yakety yak*]
Friday comes with laughter, [*say ha, ha!*]
and Saturday's full of joy! [*clap hands*]
But Sunday's the very best day of all, 'cause we go to church! *Oh, boy!* [*jump up*]

Tent Church

Explain that before we had church buildings, long ago God's people had a tent called a *tabernacle*, and they carried it with them as they traveled from place to place (see Exodus). Talk about how glad you are to have a church right in your own town!

Make a tent church for your child by draping a sheet over a table or between the backs of chairs.

A Church That Shared

Involve your child in a church sharing project such as food baskets, food showers, and collections for benevolence needs in your community. Take advantage of missionary offering opportunities to let your child have a special experience in the joy of giving! In connection with her own sharing, briefly tell her in your own words the story from Acts 11:26–30 of a Bible church that shared:

For a whole year Barnabas and Saul met with the church and taught great numbers of people. The disciples were called Christians first at Antioch.

During this time some prophets came down from Jerusalem to Antioch. One of them, named Agabus, stood up and through the Spirit predicted that a severe famine would spread over the entire Roman world. . . . The disciples, each according to his ability, decided to provide help for the brothers living in Judea. This they did, sending their gift to the elders by Barnabas and Saul.

Love Pocket

Make a large heart from construction paper and glue a paper pocket on the front of it. (A doily glued in place with the top portion left open works well for a pocket, or you may glue on an envelope instead.) When the pocket is dry, place inside it small pictures of family, toys, pets, and places your child enjoys. Make sure the last picture in the pocket is of your church. Ask your child to take one picture at a time from the pocket to see what and whom he loves.

A Church Is People!

Draw a simple outline of a church on paper or let your child draw one. Help him cut out faces from a catalog and glue them inside the church sketch, placing them side by side to make a crowd! If you have actual photographs of people from your church, that would be even better.

On the front row of faces, ask your child to draw bodies and arms, feet, and legs. Talk about the fact that your church is much more than a pretty building—it's loving, caring *people!*

I Can Give Too!

Help your child think of a job to earn money for church or for a special mission offering. For young children, the time between earning the money and giving it should not be long.

As an alternate or additional money-for-Jesus game, place a shallow dish of water on a low table or stool and let your child drop coins into the dish. Give him a quarter to drop first and then provide pennies or dimes for him to drop into the dish to try to cover up the quarter. Make sure the dish is on a towel to catch splashes.

Your child may want to repeat the game several times, but when he is through playing, keep the money in a special box or an envelope until the day it is to be given at church. Tell him the Bible story of the widow who gave all her money because she loved God.

How Sweet It Is to Go to Church!

Let your child make a small church building by gluing sugar cubes together using a squeeze bag of icing, or let your child sparingly spoon on chocolate fudge sauce for the "cement" between the cubes.

Another sweet idea for making an edible church is to glue graham crackers or cookies to the sides of a small box with frosting or peanut butter. A roof may be made from round cookies cut in half and overlapped. The steeple may be a small inverted funnel with a paper cross inserted in the narrow end.

While you and your child are constructing the edible building is a good time to talk positively about your real-life church.

Church Packet

Make a church packet to take with you to the worship service, especially while your child is adjusting to sitting quietly and listening.

Let the packet be a cloth bag or box of some kind that will hold a coloring book, small books to look at, a quiet toy, a small tablet, and blank envelopes on which to draw peek-a-boo pictures (you will save your church money by not using the offering envelopes in the pews for art work), something to write and color with, and a surprise now and then of a packet of stickers or some mints.

I'm Thinking of . . .

Play this thinking and guessing game with your child: I'm thinking of . . .
- something in our church we can sit on.
- something in our church that makes music.
- something in our church that is very beautiful.
- someone *extra* wonderful we learn about at church.
- someone who comes to our church, is small and wonderful, and who loves Jesus!

Find Your Way to Church

Blindfold your child and let him find his way through the house or yard to a spot designated the church. After he has completed his walk, talk with him about how easy it is for your family to get to the real church on Sundays.

Tell him that people in other lands sometimes have a hard time getting to church. In Russia and China, whole families often have to walk miles in all kinds of weather to reach their churches. Remind him that church is a very important place to go when people love God.

Find Those Church Shoes

Place a pair of shoes and socks for every member of the family in a pile in the center of the room. Then sit with your family several feet away on the floor.

Play a tape or record of church music. When you stop the music, all the players must hurry to the pile and get their own shoes and socks, putting them on if they are able. When each child is dressed or has her shoes in hand, she yells, "I'm ready for church!" Repeat the game if the child is interested.

Ring the Church Bell

Hang a bell from a sturdy light fixture inside the house or a tree limb outside. Tell your child that you are going to pretend that the bell is in the tower of a church and that you must ring it to tell everyone it is time for church.

Try to hit the bell with a rubber ball or sock rolled up into a ball shape. Tell your child you really want to invite people to your real church, too. Think of a couple of people to invite to your church, and make sure you follow through and really do invite them when your child is around to help or observe.

Build a Church

Let your child make a picture of a church building from one or more of the following craft items:

- Toothpicks—Draw the outline of a church on paper and glue toothpicks or craft sticks on the outside lines.
- Sticks—Draw the outline of a church and fill it in with sticks you and your child have collected and broken to the appropriate size. Suggest that your child glue them side by side horizontally on the paper to make a log church.

• Popcorn, beans, or pebbles—Draw the outline of a church and fill it in with glue. Then press popped popcorn or small pebbles or beans into the glue for a rock church.

Stained-glass windows may be made in any of the following ways:

• *Colored popcorn* which has been dipped in food coloring and water, then quickly removed and dried on paper towels.
• *Tissue paper pieces* glued on paper.
• *Colored grits, salt, or sand* poured over white glue. Color them by stirring in drops of food coloring and spreading them out in a pan to dry.
• *Crayon shavings* sprinkled between two sheets of waxed paper and ironed on a low heat setting.
• *A crayon drawing* on white paper, crumpled and straightened out, then painted with a thin layer of blue tempera paint.

The stained-glass papers may be taped or glued to the back of a church picture with the window spaces cut out so that the stained-glass effect will show.

As your child enjoys these activities, talk with her about different kinds of church buildings, emphasize to her that regardless of whether a church building is big or small, fancy or plain, people still love their church and go to worship God there.

I'm Important to My Church

Talk with your child about how people in a church love and help each other. Think of someone in your church who needs a visit, a card, a phone call, some help around the house, or a prayer. Include your little child in specifically meeting that need.

Afterward, reminisce about the smile on the man's face, the hugs, the thanks, or just the good feeling inside yourself because you have pleased God.

How Is It Used at Church?

In the center of the room, place several objects that are used at church: a Bible, a hymnal, crayons, an offering envelope (or basket for an offering plate), a toy musical instrument, a printed bulletin, and a microphone (if your church uses one). Sit on the floor in an opposite corner of the room from your child. At the verbal signal *Go!* you and your child must dash to the center of the room, pick up an object, and return to your place. In turn, you each must demonstrate or explain how your object is used at church. Repeat the game until all the objects have been picked up.

Church Songs

To the tune of "The Farmer in the Dell":

> We're going to church today;
> We're brushing teeth and hair;
> We'll go to that most special place,
> To learn of Jesus there.

To the tune of "London Bridge":

> We will go to church today.
> We will sing; we will pray.
> We will read God's precious Word,
> Greatest story every heard!

Church Rhyme Game

You say the verse, your child provides the missing rhyming word.

> I come to church.
> I rhyme with *toy*.
> Who am I?
> I'm a (boy).

> I come to church.
> I rhyme with *pearl*.
> Who am I?
> I'm a (girl).

> I speak at church.
> I rhyme with *teacher*.
> Who am I?
> I'm the (preacher).

Doorkeepers in the House of God

Give special appreciation to the maintenance people who serve so well in our churches. Their role is vital, and they deserve to be recognized for their service.

Encourage your child always to greet the maintenance men and women at church. In addition, let her make a drawing of a person sweeping, cleaning, or vacuuming. Roll it up with a colorful ribbon and attach it to a new package of sponges or window cleaner. Ask your child to present it to your maintenance person for a job well done!

Boy Jesus at Church

Tell your child the story of Jesus' visit to the temple in Jerusalem when he was a boy. Remark that Mary and Joseph took Jesus to church just as you take your child.

Prepare a box with a hole in the lid the size of your child's fist. Inside the box place several objects he might see or use at church: a small Bible, a pencil, a coin, scissors, an offering envelope, or a toy. Ask your child to feel in the box, identify the object without looking, and tell how it is used at church. Open the Bible and read to your child a paraphrase of Luke 4:16

about Jesus going to church. Tell him that if going to church was important to Jesus, it is important to you, too.

Church Means Love!

Make church days special times with an extra portion of demonstrative love, attention, and affection for your children. Take time to give free smiles, hugs, and praise for the slightest good behavior. Try, with God's help, to make as little mention as possible of spills, accidents, and crankiness.

Especially if your child is adjusting to attending big church, make it a place of holding, stroking, smiling, and love!

Some adults have many unpleasant church memories of frowns, scowls, wait-till-you-get-home looks, and snapping fingers! Others have good memories of warmth, acceptance, and family closeness that were conveyed to them on Sundays. The unspoken message that *my family loves me and is glad we're at church together* is an invaluable memory etched in a child's mind.

Puppet Show

Entertain your child with a short puppet show from behind a box or chair. Use stick or sock puppets or stuffed animals as the characters.

Make the puppets talk about something important they must do today. (One puppet knows where they are going, and the other does not.) The puppet "in the know" begins the dialogue:

First puppet: We're going somewhere important today.

Second puppet: Is it the day to go to the doctor for a checkup?

First: No, it's even more important than that!

Second: Is it the day to go to a birthday party?

First: No, it's even more special than that.

Second: Is it a shopping day?

First: No, it's something much better!

Second: *I* know! It's a day to go to *church!* Let's go! (The two march off together.)

Body Life

Explain to your child that the Bible says your church is like a person's body, with all the parts like eyes, ears, hands, and toes (the people) working together, and each part (or person) is very special and important.

Keep your explanation simple and illustrate it by tracing around your child on a large strip of butcher paper or opened paper grocery bags taped together. As she stretches out on her back on the paper, make sure you include her fingers and toes in the tracing. Let her color in the facial features and clothes. As she does, tell her that she is a very important part of your church body.

Let's Ride the Bus

Make a shoebox bus with yellow paper glued to its sides, circular shapes glued in place as wheels, and a sign bearing your church's name or simply Church Bus.

Let your child do the gluing and ask him to draw windows and doors to finish the bus. Leave a rectangular opening in the top of the box. Cut out catalog pictures of people and lay them out on the floor. Instruct your child to drive by and pick up the passengers to bring to church.

Take a Friend to Church

Help your child develop the habit of inviting and taking a friend to Sunday school and church. To do so will mean extra effort for you, but it will be worthwhile in teaching your child to reach out to others for Jesus' sake.

Help him to make invitations on three-by-five-inch cards or folded papers. Write a message such as:

I go to church on Sundays.
If you don't already go to church, would you go with me next Sunday? Please let me know.
My phone number is _____,
and I live at _____.

Thank you!
Kevin James

Distribute the cards in your neighborhood to families with children or to any homes you wish.

I'm Praying for You

Talk with your child about how important it is that we pray for other people. Mention to her the name of someone at church that you especially appreciate or who needs her prayers. Talk first about what she might want to pray for this person, but do not give too much guidance or your child's prayer will not be very spontaneous. Tell her to use her own ideas and words as she prays to God for the person.

I'm Going to Church and I'm Going to . . .

Play this game with your child on the way to church. Begin the game by saying, "I'm going to church, and I'm going to . . ." and end the sentence with an activity your child might perform. Take turns with your child at making up sentences. Here are some possible endings:

- eat breakfast
- brush my teeth
- take my Bible
- wear a big smile
- say hi to my teacher

- share with my friends
- walk down the hall
- hear pretty music
- see smiling faces
- learn about Jesus

Pick a Church Friend

In a hat, place names or titles of church friends: pastor, teachers, minister of music, preschool director, bus driver, custodians, and so forth. Ask your child to pick a name and tell you what that person does to help you at church. Your child may select one name each night before bed or one after another as a game.

After all the names have been drawn from the hat, return them and choose one each night to pray for at bedtime.

Chapter 10

Introducing Your Child to God through Prayer and Praise

I will tell of the kindnesses of the Lord,
the deeds for which he is to be praised.
—Isaiah 63:7

Parents of very young children have two basic responsibilities regarding prayer—to pray *for* their child and to pray *with* their child. There is no more powerful learning experience for a child than hearing and saying prayers at the side of a loving parent! Keep your prayers very simple, brief, personal, and sincere, like a pleasant conversation with someone very dear to you. Fervency is an important element in our own personal prayers to God, but too much display of emotion or the use of flowery words may bewilder children.

Much of our prayer time with a very young child should center on praise and thanksgiving, which come as easily to children today as they did at the time of Jesus' triumphal entry into Jerusalem! Any additional time spent in prayer may include voicing simple requests that are of personal interest to our child.

Little else will strengthen our own faith as much as praying daily with our children. They will ask us to pray for lost toys, sick birds, and bumped knees. Expect to hear questions such as "Why didn't God send Daisy's puppies *to-night?*" and "Why didn't Grandpa get better when I prayed for him?" Our child's own walk of faith has begun, and ours will constantly be challenged.

How much better to meet questions head-on when our child is young and her faith is *gigantic!* Answers that are both biblical and simple will usually suffice: "God knows better than we do," "God hurts when we hurt," "God turns *all* things that seem bad into good when we trust him," "God sometimes says no," or "God sometimes says wait." The fundamental faith of our child will be built upon these earliest experiences with prayer. If we do not address such questions when our child is small, they may create disillusionment in later years.

God will enable us to meet every challenge, giving promised wisdom when we ask him! May God motivate and empower you as you pray for and with your tiny child.

The Baby

Bathtime, Prayertime

As you bathe your baby, talk about each part of her tiny body with a prayer of thanks: "Thank you, Lord, for Rachel's precious face. Thank you for her sparkling little eyes that can see, her tiny fingers that grip so tightly right now, her feet that will soon be able to walk, her round little tummy," and so on.

Mothers and daddies can have a very personal time of worship as they simultaneously meet baby's physical needs and offer their thanks to the heavenly Father.

Prayer for Your Sleeping Angel

When you tiptoe in to check on your sleeping baby, slip to your knees beside the crib to pray for him. Make these times of sincere prayer frequent during your baby's preschool years.

Praise God for the gift of this child. Pray for his safety, his health, and his emotional and spiritual development. Pray for his childhood to be guarded and protected from trauma and for his future to be one of surrender to the Lord. Give your child back to God each time you pray for him, acknowledging that this priceless little treasure has been entrusted to you by the one to whom he rightfully belongs.

Write a Prayer

At special times such as your child's first step, first word, or first day of school, write a prayer for your child. Or you may choose days of special accomplishments, birthdays, or holidays. Include his present needs and your future dreams for him in the wording. Write your prayers in his baby book or purchase a small notebook to use as a prayer book. Continue to write prayers for him and to pray them sincerely throughout his childhood and teenage years.

Bless this Trip

From the time your child is a baby, make a tradition of praying together as a family before you leave home on a trip or vacation.

Pray for Me, Mommy

When your baby is sick or hurt, pray aloud for her as you comfort her. Let her hear your gentle voice talking to the heavenly Father even before she can understand your words.

I Will Bless My Child

Begin when your baby is born to bless his life with prayer. When putting him in bed at night, pray a blessing as you hold or touch him. Pray for his comfort, safety, and peace. The phrase *good night* itself comes from an ancient medieval blessing.

As we deliver our child to the church nursery or kindergarten door, we may pray the simple blessing, "May Andy feel you very near him today, Lord."

The blessing of prayer for your child should be accompanied as often as possible by your physical touch to help assure him of his value within our human family as well as his infinite value to God.

Thank You, God, for Warm Milk

Make prayer before meals a part of baby's life from her earliest days. As you nurse her or provide her a warm bottle, gently say, "Thank you, God, for the warm milk you give to my baby."

Thank You for My Head-Knocker

Play this funny little game with your baby.

Thank you, God, for my:
Head-knocker [*gently knock on baby's head*]
Eye-looker [*gently touch his eyes*]
Nose-sniffer [*tap on his nose*]
Mouth-muncher [*touch his mouth*]
Chin-chopper [*touch his chin*]
Tummy-tickler
Gitchee, gitchee, goo! [*tickle very gently and briefly*]

Sing a Prayer

Instead of speaking your prayer to God in baby's presence, put it to music. The tune need not be recognizable—babies usually respond positively to any soft, gentle music. Throughout history, lullabies have been used to soothe and quiet babies because the effect has been positive. Our baby's sense of security and acceptance is enhanced as we hold him close and sing our prayer for him.

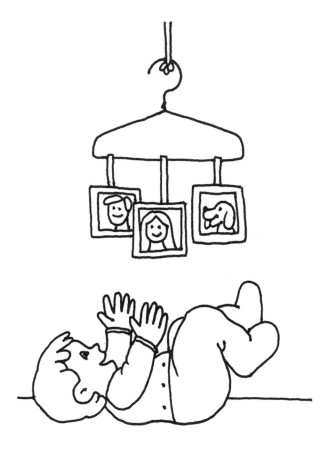

Thank-You Mobile

Hang pictures of familiar people, animals, or toys for which you are thankful within your baby's view. They may be attached vertically to a ribbon and hung from a coat hanger (make sure that baby cannot reach them) and then suspended from a ceiling light fixture, nail, or doorknob.

Your young baby will enjoy the movement of the pictures on the strings if the mobile is hung where it turns freely. Occasionally, take your baby close enough to get a good look at each picture, and as he does, say a simple prayer of thanks for each or a blessing on each person pictured.

The Toddler

Tape a Prayer

Ask family members and close friends (whose voices are familiar to your child) to record a brief prayer or blessing for your child on a cassette recorder that you provide. Remind each person to allow for a brief pause following the preceding message before recording his or her own prayer.

Let their choice of blessings be entirely spontaneous. Play one prayer each day for your child at a quiet time or before he goes to sleep at night.

Choose a Prayer

Decorate a shoe box with wrapping paper and large pictures of animals or children, or let your toddler color its sides with crayon marks. Leave the top off or make a hole in it large enough for your child's hand to slip through.

Each day, place in the box a specific prayer that your toddler will understand and may attempt to say as she begins to imitate your words and phrases. If feasible, attach the prayer to an appropriate picture to help your child better understand what the words mean. Let her reach into the box and remove the paper, handing it to you to say as a prayer. Use this activity before she eats for mealtime prayers or at any time of day you choose.

Prayer Gallery

Make a prayer gallery, or display, of pictures on your child's bedroom door or wall, or on your refrigerator door. Put up several pictures of people for whom you wish to pray—family members, friends, community helpers, or your church pastor and staff, if they are familiar to your child. Or you may let your child make the selection.

You can find pictures of community helpers in teachers' supply stores. Even better, ask your child's doctor, Sunday school teacher, pastor, or friends if you may have their pictures, explaining the reason for your request. Very few people will refuse an offer that includes someone's prayers on their behalf. In addition, your simple request may be a positive witness for the Lord in someone's life.

Prayer at the Doctor's Office

Say a prayer with your child in the doctor's office during the time you are waiting to see him. If your child is not apprehensive, pray a simple prayer of thanksgiving for the doctor and request a good report for your child. If your child is upset, pray for him to feel calm and safe and to realize that Jesus is right there with him. Make the prayer brief. As long as he hears and sees enough to know that you are praying for him, an important impression will be made on his mind.

If the doctor's treatment is going to be difficult for your child, ask the doctor if you may offer a brief prayer, or whisper one in your child's ear. Asking God's blessing upon your child is important enough to risk your doctor's opinion that you may be a bit fanatical! If you are calm, brief, and confident in the Lord as you pray, the doctor and staff will probably appreciate your parental concern. Do not word your prayer in such a way that your child will anticipate that something dreadful is about to happen. Keep it centered on God's presence and help.

Snatch a Prayer

At moments when your toddler has just found a pretty rock, tasted a yummy bite of something, noticed a lightning bug's flash, or seen a pink sky at sundown, snatch the moment for a sentence prayer of thanks. "Thank You, God, for John's good eyes. He saw the beautiful sky you made!"

Make prayer a very spontaneous, integral part of your life with your child, and it will probably continue to be so as he grows older.

My Hands Can Praise

Say to your child, "Let's see some ways our hands can praise God!"

Clap and say this rhyme:

> Clapping, clapping!
> This is *one* way
> I can praise God
> With my hands today.

Wave and say this rhyme:

> Wave and say this rhyme:
> Waving, waving,
> Waving at you!
> Waving means I see you
> Praising God, too!

This Is the Way

Sing this prayer in the morning, either before or after breakfast.

To the tune of "Mulberry Bush":

> This is the way I say my prayers,
> Say my prayers,
> Say my prayers.
> This is the way I say my prayers
> Every single morning.

Prayer Chain

Toddlers especially like being included with a family group for prayer. Even if there are only you and your toddler, you can hold both her hands as you pray for her. Keep your prayer very simple and brief!

Praise Package

When you shop for new shoes or clothes, help your child to recognize that God is our true source of everything beneficial. It is not necessary for your child to repeat your words. He will absorb your attitude of gratitude, and before long, his own response will be one of praise and thanksgiving to God and to those who are kind and generous to him.

Praise God with Instruments

Turn on recorded praise music, sing a praise song with no accompaniment, or play and sing with a piano. Provide homemade band instruments for your child, such as pan lids for cymbals, a paper tube for a trumpet, two paper plates stapled together with bells tied around the edges for a tamborine, two spoons to bang on a pan for drums, or a few dried beans inside an empty potato chip cylinder. (Do not let your child play with instruments containing dried beans without your supervision.) Encourage her to praise God with her instrument and to march around as you play the more melodious praise music for her.

Ages
Two to Three

Let's Pray for Friends

Sit cross-legged on the floor facing your child, or in a circle if several children are present. Say, "Let's pray today for some friends. I'll start and then you pray, if you would like a turn."

Pray one sentence such as, "Thank you, God, for David." Your child should then pray for another friend, alternating prayers from one of you to the next until you run out of friends' names. End the prayer chain with this prayer: "Thank you most of all for our very *best* friend, Jesus! Amen!"

Prayer Clock

On the face of a **clock** next to the hour that you select, let your child tape a small cutout letter *p*, a small picture of a child praying, or whatever symbol you choose as a reminder that it is time to pray.

Encourage your child to look at the clock occasionally and to let you know when the little hand points to the specified hour. When the time arrives, be sure to stop whatever you are doing and pay with him!

Loud and Soft Praise

Play a record or cassette of praise songs for your child's listening pleasure. A wonderful selection of praise music is available at most Christian bookstores. As she enjoys the music, ask your child to listen for loud and soft moments in the music. When the music becomes loud or fast, ask her to clap her hands; when it is soft or very slow, instruct her to place her finger to her lips and say, "Shhh!"

Your child will begin to recognize that musical praise may be fast or slow, loud or soft.

Eyes Open, Eyes Closed

Play this simple game with your child. Ask him to open his eyes wide, look around, and tell you what he sees. Then instruct him to close his eyes and ask him, "Now what do you see?"

Tell your child that we normally close our eyes when we pray to make it easier to think about God and to talk to him. Explain that when we look around, we cannot help thinking about what we see. And when we pray at home or at church, we will usually close our eyes, but sometimes we do pray with our eyes wide open and name all the things for which we thank God!

Prayer Chants, Rhymes, and Songs

Teach your child this action rhyme:

A little child can walk, [*walk around the room*]
A little child can talk, [*pantomine talking*]
A little child can hop, [*do so*]
A little child can stop! [*do so*]
A little child can pray [*fold hands, close eyes*]
And talk to God each day! [*say a very brief prayer if the moment seems right*]

To the tune of "Are You Sleeping?":

> Are you praying?
> Are you praying?
> I am too.
> I am too.
> God will surely hear us.
> God will surely hear us.
> Thank you, God.
> Thank you, God.

To the tune of "Oh, Be Careful":

> When I don't know what to do,
> I will pray!
> When I don't know what to do,
> I will pray!
> Though I'm very, very small
> He will hear me when I call.
> When I don't know what to do,
> I will pray!

Prayer Cloth

On a clean white sheet or inexpensive tablecloth, trace around your child's hands with his palms together and fingers straight, as if they were placed together in prayer. Make outlines of his hands all over the sheet with a waterproof marker. On each outline of your child's hands, write the name of someone for whom to pray, or draw a simple picture of that person with the name underneath.

Thank-you Chain

Help your child make a paper chain to hang over a doorway in your home. Make the chain from colored strips of construction paper on which have been written things for which your child expresses thanks and ask her for specific ideas. Glue or staple (children *love* to staple) the links together to form a colorful thank-you chain.

Prayer Glove

On each finger of a small gardening or child's glove, write the name of a person for whom you wish to pray. Or label each finger with one of the following categories of people: family members, your church, neighbors, sick people, missionaries. Ask your child to hold up a finger and pray with him for that person.

Prayer after Discipline

After your child has been disciplined for misbehavior, hold her on your lap or by your side as you lovingly explain the reason for the disciplinary action and verbalize your deep love for her. Pray briefly for your child to feel the Lord's forgiveness and for God's strength to help her to do right. Pray that she will know how very much Jesus loves her and that you do, too!

End the prayer time with a hug, a kiss, and a smile. Spend a few minutes playing with your child as if the wrong had never been done, silently assuring her by your actions that she is completely forgiven.

Prayer Garden

Plant flowers with your child in an area of your yard you have designated as your prayer garden. Even in a very small yard with no digging space, you may plant a few flowers in pots and arrange them to add beauty to a deck or small porch. Keep your prayer garden small and easy to care for and let your child help you tend the plants.

Arrange logs for seats or take along a blanket to sit on when you and your child go there to pray.

Thanksgiving Basket

In a basket, place acorn, leaf, snowflake, or flower shapes made from paper. On each shape write those things, people, or events for which your child can be thankful. Ask her to select a paper each day, say a short prayer of thanks in her own words and then stick the paper to the refrigerator or a door in the house as a reminder to be thankful.

This basket of thanks may be used at Thanksgiving season or at any time of the year!

May the Words of My Mouth

Teach prayer Scriptures to your child by using them at the table for the blessing before meals. Let members of the family take turns (yes—parents, too) quoting verses at the table before a meal and congratulate each other on the good job of memorizing!

Here are a few suggested verses:

Psalm 136:1—Give thanks to the Lord, for he is good.
Psalm 147:1—How good it is to sing praises to our God.
Mark 11:22—Have faith in God.
Colossians 1:3—We always thank God . . . when we pray for you.

Everything That Has Breath, Praise!

When a bird is singing or chirping, a dog is barking for no apparent reason, or squirrels are chattering outside, tell your child that they may be praising God for his goodness! Say, "The bird may be singing, 'This is a beautiful, sunshiny day. Thank you, God!'" or "The squirrel may be chattering his praise and thanks to God for acorns!"

Encourage your child to think of ways to praise God and suggest that together you sing or say some of the praise songs or rhymes suggested in this chapter.

Puppet Praise

Use hand puppets or stuffed animals to sing along with a praise tape or a song that you and your child sing together. Let your child hold up the puppet and make it sing along as you praise God.

Clap Your Hands!

Call attention to one of God's magnificent creations—a lovely sunset, a full shining moon, sparkling dew on a leaf, or the silky petals of a flower—and lead your child to say, "Thank You, God. That's so beautiful!" Clap your praise and applaud for the Lord's marvelous handiwork!

Prayer-Go-Round

Praying together at meals may include a time when each family member asks God for only one request or thanks him for one blessing that he has graciously provided. Including your child in this circle of prayer will help her recognize that she belongs in your family and that her prayers are of equal importance to yours.

Prayer Puzzles

Enlarge several photos of family members, friends, close neighbors, and your pastor and mount them on cardboard. Cut the pictures into simple puzzles of three or four pieces each, being careful to cut around facial features.

Put each puzzle in a separate envelope and let your child choose one each day to take out and put together. When the picture is complete, say a prayer with your child for the person whose face you see.

Sing While I Swing

Encourage your child to sing praise to God as you push him on the swing set at home or at a playground. Talk about the sky, clouds, trees, warm sunshine, or gentle breeze and how good God is to give them to you to enjoy.

You may need to show him how to sing his praise by getting into a swing near him and delighting him with your own rendition of a familiar song of praise or one that you compose as you swing. Your willingness to share your faith through song may take some Christian boldness!

We Thank God For . . .

Every child loves to see her parent draw a picture! Enjoy the sensation of being an artist in your child's eyes and help her learn to be thankful for God's goodness in one easy activity!

Let her watch as you draw things for which you and she are thankful to God. Some pictures you may wish to include are pets, toys, shoes, ears, eyes, hands, and smiles.

Ages Four to Five

A Conversation with God

As your child matures, you can have a very special conversation with him about prayer. You might start by saying that although God is holy and mighty, we are able to talk to him as we would our very best friend. Say, "Jesus told us that God knows what you need before you ask him [see Matt. 6:8], but we still should ask him. I'll tell God something and then you may have a turn, if you wish."

Start statements like this: "Dear God, you gave us a beautiful, sunny day. Thank you! It was so much fun to watch that fuzzy caterpillar crawl across the sidewalk."

Then ask your child if he has thought of something he wants to tell God. Continue back and forth until you feel that your child is finished praying. After saying amen, give Jimmy a big hug, a kiss, and say, "I love you!"

Kneel before the King

Explain to your child that our *real* king is Jesus and when we talk to him, it is very proper to bow down. Describe a few of his characteristics to your child—his kind face, his royal scepter of gold, his crown of beautiful jewels. Ask your boy or girl to kneel down with you before King Jesus, imagining that he is in your home's best chair.

Briefly pray, "Lord God, *you* are our real king, and we bow before you to show you that we love and worship you. In the name of Jesus we pray. Amen." When you kneel to pray at another time, remind your child that you are bowing before your king!

I Can Pray Anywhere!

To demonstrate to your child that prayer can take place at any time or place, play this guessing game with him.

Say, "I'm thinking of a place I can pray when I am lying down at night. Where is that place?"

After he guesses successfully, ask other questions such as these:

"I'm thinking of a place I can lie down and pray while I am looking up at the clouds. Where is that place?"

"I'm thinking of a place I can pray when I'm hungry and getting ready to eat. Where is that place?"

To end the game, say a brief prayer of thanks that you can pray anywhere, even where you are right now.

Daniel Prayed

Tell your child the story of Daniel and the lions' den from Daniel 6. Act out the story with puppets you and your child make by gluing faces on tongue depressors or Popsicle sticks. Make lion puppets from paper sacks on which you glue yarn or fringed paper manes. Talk about how important it was to Daniel to pray and how very important it is to us, too!

Prayer Chants and Songs

Jesus helps me when I'm sick.
Jesus helps me when I'm sad.
Jesus helps me when I pray.
He's the best friend I've *ever* had!

To the tune of "The Farmer in the Dell":

I say my prayer to you.
You hear the words I say.
You answer what is best for me,
So I will pray today.

[*Conclude the song with the following spoken prayer*]
I'll talk to God in the morning,
I'll talk to God at noon.
I'll talk to God before I sleep.
I'll talk to God real soon!

Prayer before Play

Make a pleasant routine of saying a short prayer before a friend arrives to play with your child. Or pray after she arrives, as a blessing upon their play, if excitement permits. (If neither of these times seems appropriate, pray with the children a thanks-for-a-good-time prayer as your guest prepares to go home.)

Thank God for your child's friend and his family and pray that they may please God as they have fun together!

The Lord's Prayer

Tell your child that Jesus' friends wanted to know how to pray and Jesus taught them the prayer found in Luke 11:2–4. Briefly explain its meaning in your own words.

Teach the Lord's Prayer to your child simply by repeating it in its entirety once or twice daily. Each time you say the verses ask your child to say as many words as she can with you. You will be amazed how quickly she picks up the verses. If your child resists, do not insist that she learn it right then. She *will* in time. If you want to reward her memorization with an appropriate reward for effort, do so.

Prayer Hike

Make a backpack from a paper grocery sack, attaching yarn rings through reinforced holes on the sides for your child's arms to fit through. In the backpack, place an old bed sheet, a paper on which prayer requests have been written, and a Bible or Bible storybook.

Take a "hike" into your backyard, a nearby park, or some other selected spot. Spread out the sheet and have a quiet Bible story and prayer time together.

Emergency Prayer

When you and your child hear a siren or see an emergency vehicle, be sure to say, "Somebody needs help. We don't know what the person needs, but God does. Let's pray for him right now." With your eyes open, offer a simple prayer of intercession for the unknown person in need.

Birthday Prayers

Include prayer as a part of your child's birthday celebration in one or more of the following ways:

1. Pray for your child the night before his party, thanking God that he is part of your family.

2. Pray a thanksgiving prayer before eating birthday cake and ice cream.

3. Pray a prayer of blessing upon all the children before they leave the party for home.

4. Pray as a family in a circle of love, with the birthday child in the center as the object of your special love and prayers.

5. Write a special birthday prayer for your child to save among his meaningful keepsakes.

Praise Party

Have a celebration party—just because God is worthy of our praise! Blow up colored balloons and let your child help you decorate a cake with the name of Jesus on it. Or cut out a picture of Jesus from a Sunday school leaflet, lay it on the plain frosted cake, and decorate around it. Encourage your child to do her very best work on the cake "because it is an offering of praise to the God we love." This idea is especially suitable for use at Christmastime.

Prayer Tree for the Family

Make a tree from construction paper and glue it on another sheet of paper. Provide round photographs, which are about the same size, of the faces of family members for your child to glue to the tree branches. Include pictures of your child and of his pets, if you wish.

Each day, ask your child, "Who would you like to pray for today?" Make his chosen person the object of your prayers at each meal and bedtime that day. Leave the "family tree" on the refrigerator for a while as a reminder to be thankful for the great family God gave you!

Sing a Prayer

At mealtime or before tucking your child into bed at night, sing a prayer song from a hymnal, a children's songbook, a familiar tape—or make up your own!

Do not be concerned about the tune or making the phrases rhyme. Neither will matter to your child or to God.

Praying for the Sick

Ask your child to draw a picture of a hospital on a piece of white paper, making a red cross on the front wall to emphasize the service provided there. You may wish to explain that the red cross means medical help and kindness take place there, just as the cross of Jesus stands for his mercy and love.

Ask your child to include several windows and a door in his drawing. Then cut along three sides of each and fold them back to look like an open door and open windows. Glue the hospital picture to a piece of construction paper for reinforcement. Ask your child to tape behind each window and door the name of someone in your neighborhood, family, church, or community who is sick. If your child is not acquainted with some of the people, briefly describe their needs to him.

Open the windows and doors of the hospital picture one at a time and pray with your child, mentioning the needs of that individual.

Prayer Bouquet

Place several cut flowers of various colors in a vase or glass of water. Let each color of flower represent a prayer request for someone whom your child knows or for specific needs that someone has.

For example, one color of flower may represent a prayer that your loved one will have a safe trip, another flower that she will have a wonderful time while she is gone, and a third flower that she will stay well while she is away.

As you pray with your child for the person, you will be turning a very general be-with-Aunt-Mary type of prayer request into one that will be much more specific and meaningful. After you have prayed, tie a ribbon around the flower bouquet and give it to the person for whom you prayed with an explanation of its meaning.

Recipe for Prayer

When you and your child are making cookies or mixing a cake, say to him, "Mixing these ingredients reminds me of what we do when we pray! When we say a prayer we add a little bit of thanking [*put flour in your bowl*], some praising [*add sugar*], a bit of telling [*add some liquid*], some asking [*add another ingredient*], and end with lots of obeying [*add the final ingredient*]! That's how we make a prayer!"

Prayer Cards

Against a background of blue or black construction paper folded in half, place your child's hands, palms together, as though praying. Ask your child to hold them very still (not easy to do!) as you spray around them with a nonaerosol spray bottle containing white tempera paint diluted with water. Let the outline dry and trace around the handprints with magic marker, providing enough detail to make the silhouette look like folded hands.

Inside the card write this message on white paper and glue it in place: "These are my hands. They are folded to pray for *you*." Ask your child to sign the card and then deliver it to someone who is in need of prayer. Be sure to pray with your child for the person.

Angel Choir of Praise

"Praise him, all his angels, praise him, all his heavenly hosts" (Ps. 148:2).

Make an angel choir from paper cones that have been taped or glued into shape. Be sure to leave a hole at the small end. For each cone, cut out a small paper circle and ask your child to draw the face of an angel with an open mouth. To the back of each face, tape or glue a craft stick and insert the opposite end of each stick into the opening at the small end of a cone. Tape paper wings to the backs of the angels and set them side by side on a shelf as a reminder that angels praise God.

Praise List

Let your child help you compile a praise list and keep it in a prominent place such as on the refrigerator door or taped to the headboard of his bed. Refer to the lists when you have a prayer time with your child. Your praise list may be the answers to requests you have made to God, or it may be a separate list of reasons to praise God, such as:

- He is love.
- He is great and mighty.
- He knows what we need even before we ask him.
- He died for us.
- He forgives us when we do wrong.

Enter His Courts with Praise

Draw a picture of a gate to represent this passage from Psalm 100:4: "Enter his gates with thanksgiving, and his courts with praise." Ask your child to make an arched gate in the lower center of her building and cut it out, leaving the left side attached as a hinge so the gate will open and shut.

Paste the drawing on another piece of paper and ask your child to draw a picture of himself behind the open gate. Tell her to draw her mouth in the shape of an O, as if she were singing praises to God. Inform your child that the Bible says we come close to God as we offer praise and thanksgiving.

Help her to memorize all of Psalm 100 by reading or quoting it to her once each day, perhaps at bedtime, and asking her to join you in saying as many of the words as she can after hearing the psalm once or twice.

You will be amazed at how quickly she is able to memorize the entire passage. Give her much praise for her success, but do not insist that she learn the psalm if she resists. Make sure that your child understands that this Scripture is all about praising and thanking God for his goodness!

A
Parent's
Prayer

O Lord, You have graciously given me a tiny
child to teach and to lead to a personal
knowledge of You. I first give my own life to
You as my source of forgiveness, salvation,
security, and strength. I am not sufficient for
this task, but *you* are . . . through me. Use me,
enable me, guide my steps, and graciously
provide the godly wisdom and power that I
will need daily. Keep me consistent in word
and example, and please compensate for my
inevitable errors. I am totally dependent upon
You to introduce Your Infinite Self to my child,
O Lord, my strength and my redeemer.
Amen